NOT
by
Bread
ALONE

NOT by Bread ALONE

GREG HINNANT

CREATION HOUSE

NOT BY BREAD ALONE: DAILY DEVOTIONS FOR DISCIPLES
By Greg Hinnant
Published by Creation House
Charisma House Book Group/Charisma Media
600 Rinehart Road
Lake Mary, FL 32746

Scripture quotations marked YLT are from *Young's Literal Translation*. Public domain.

Design Director: Bill Johnson
Cover design by Terry Clifton

AUTHOR'S NOTE: Some Scripture quotations have specific words and/or phrases that I am emphasizing. I have added italics to these verses to show that emphasis. Also, in some of the Scripture quotations, with the exception of the Amplified Bible, I have inserted in brackets explanatory text to help with the understanding of certain words and phrases.

Visit the author's website at www.greghinnantministries.org

Library of Congress Control Number: 2011936193
International Standard Book Number: 978-1-61638-688-7
E-International Standard Book Number: 978-1-61638-689-4

While the author has made every effort to provide accurate Internet addresses at the time of publication, neither the publisher nor the author assumes any responsibility for errors or for changes that occur after publication.

First Edition

11 12 13 14 15 — 987654321
Printed in Canada

DEDICATION

To my coworkers and friends at Greg Hinnant Ministries. Your wonderfully faithful prayers, support, and assistance have made this book possible.

CONTENTS

Preface

*E*XCELLENT NUTRITION ALONE sustains most once-born people, but not spiritually reborn Christians. We need more.

We need bread for not only the stomach but also the soul—and that "finest of the wheat" (Ps. 81:16) is God's delicious, spiritually nutritious Word, correctly understood and accurately applied to our heart and life needs. Jesus declared God's Word is vital: "Man shall not live by bread alone, but by every word of God" (Luke 4:4).

Moses agreed. Centuries earlier the lawgiver said this was the main lesson God tried to teach the Israelites in the desert: "That he might make thee know that man doth not live by bread only, but by every word that proceedeth out of the mouth of the LORD" (Deut. 8:3). Sadly, they never learned how desperately they needed to feed on the Immortal's utterances daily. Therefore, malnourished and weak in spirit, they failed.

By God's grace I began learning this lesson early in my Christian walk. The foundation of my spiritual education has come from biblical devotional literature. Oswald Chambers' *My Utmost for His Highest* was my first devotional manna. My mother gave it to me on entering college, and I've feasted on its pages countless times since. I still read occasionally from my well-worn original copy. I also love Mrs. Charles E. Cowman's devotional classic *Streams in the Desert*. Convinced I need "bread time" daily, I always take or make time for devotional nutrition—and God always shows me something I need to know or do. Invariably I rise nourished, stronger, and more fit for life and work. So now let me offer you some "Word-bread."

Not by Bread Alone is the first book in a devotional trilogy that, together with its subsequent companion works *Sweeter Than Honey* and *Water From the Rock*, will provide a full year of daily readings. As you feed on these devotionals—morning, evening, midday, or whenever hungry—may they nourish and inspire you. May God speak to you every time you read them.

—GREG HINNANT

Chapter 1

THE WONDER OF RIGHTEOUS EXHILARATION!

O F KING JEHOSHAPHAT the sacred historian wrote, "His heart was lifted up in the ways of the LORD" (2 Chron. 17:6), or "his heart took delight in the ways of the LORD" (NKJV). Put simply, the king of Judah experienced righteous exhilaration.

It was a wonder. God poured out more of His Spirit on His servant and filled him with a distinctly new and holy energy. Jehoshaphat received a potent dose of what Jesus called "life…more abundantly" (John 10:10), or "life in all its fullness" (NCV). Divinely supercharged, Jehoshaphat was freshly inspired to walk more devotedly, diligently, and delightedly in God's ways of living. He was elated, spurred on, and carried forward with a surprising burst of enthusiasm from above. This wonder made him and his reign a wonder—one we still marvel at today. But why?

Why did Jehoshaphat receive this arousing impartation of heavenly vitality and joy at this time? Why did God grant him this personal revival when other Judean kings—Rehoboam, Joram, Amaziah, Ahaz, and Zedekiah, to name a few—did not receive it? Was his heart "lifted up" solely by God's sovereign grace? Or did Jehoshaphat also do something to put himself in a position to receive such a powerful influx of new life? Let's examine the record.

In 2 Chronicles 17, we find Jehoshaphat making some hard choices and key changes early in his kingship.

Wisely, he chose to live a separated life, not fraternizing with the wayward, idol-worshiping Israelites of the northern kingdom: "Jehoshaphat…strengthened himself against Israel" (2 Chron. 17:1), or "strengthened his position against Israel" (GNT). He chose not a worldly but a righteous role model for his life, King David: "He walked in the first ways of his father, David" (v. 3).[1] He chose to walk in God's "ways," or daily spiritual life habits and work methods, not the more popular idolatrous lifestyle of typical ancient Middle Eastern monarchs: "He walked in the…ways [of God]…[and] sought not Balaam" (v. 3). Not content to renounce idols, he went on to commit himself to privately seek and worship Yahweh daily: "But [he] sought the LORD God of his father" (v. 4). He chose to carefully examine himself and implement, not ignore, God's biblical commands in his daily living: "...and walked in his commandments" (v. 4). Furthermore, he chose to honor and spread God's Word by sending Levites to teach it throughout his land: "He sent Levites...and they taught in Judah...the book of the law of the LORD" (vv. 8–9). And he chose to continue living in these "ways of the LORD" all his life (v. 6), even after "the LORD established the kingdom in his hand" and lavished upon him "riches and honor in abundance" (v. 5). It was during this time that "his heart was lifted up" with delight in God.

So strong was this holy elation that it moved him to make further reforms. He "took away the high places" (v. 6), thus removing the last vestiges of idolatry in Judah, a deep purging few Judean monarchs accomplished. Was the timing of his inspiration a coincidence? Was it by chance?

Not by chance but by choice! It was God's rich spiritual reward for his key choices and changes. Yes, God's sovereign grace was at work, because strictly speaking no soul deserves revival, but Jehoshaphat was also reaping what he had sowed. He planted righteousness in his life and harvested revival in his heart. His reward is our call. The God of Jehoshaphat is trying to say something to us through the inspired chronicler's pen.

Here's His message: If you're tired of the sadness and sullenness of sinfulness, or the dullness and deadness of worldliness, you can be free of it. The pure wonder of righteous exhilaration awaits, if only you will ponder and practice Jehoshaphat's choices: separate from practicing sinners, abandon your heart idols, seek the Lord every morning, follow godly role models, study and share God's Word and obey it, carefully examine yourself, and walk in God's "ways" always, in prosperity and adversity. If you commit to these changes, you'll receive a fresh burst of abundant life from above. How can I be sure?

God, who cannot lie or change, has declared repeatedly that He is "no respecter of persons" (Acts 10:34). So what He did for Jehoshaphat He will do for you, if you follow his example. You can exchange your woeful dryness for a wonderful refilling of God's living water. Today take the first step toward your revival. Test the Promiser! "Test me now...if I will not open for you the windows of heaven, and pour out for you a blessing" (Mal. 3:10).

Discover the wonder of righteous exhilaration!

Chapter 2

AT CRESCENDO POINT

*I*N MUSIC, A "crescendo" is a gradual increase of volume that climaxes just before a quieter passage or the end of a musical composition. As the crescendo builds, so does the excitement.

More and more orchestral players enter the growing wave of consonant and dissonant sounds, each gradually playing louder. The strings sing out, the woodwinds too, the brass blares, the percussion roars, and the conductor, electric with the powerful current of sound, closes his eyes with ecstasy, shakes his hair, and flails his baton wildly. Then, with a dramatic and decisive, "Ta-dah…dah…daaaah," the soaring sounds suddenly stop, serene peace refills the tribulated concert hall, and players and patrons alike rest and prepare for the next piece.

Just like the crescendo, so goes the testing of our faith and patience. Long biblical study, life observation, and personal experience have taught me that often a crescendo of trouble occurs just before God intervenes to perform His promises, fulfill His plans, or answer our prayers for help.

In Mark 4:35–41, Jesus quietly informed His disciples they were going to the "other side" of Galilee for ministry, and they promptly launched their vessel. Immediately their crescendo of stress began.

Out of nowhere a "great storm" arose (Mark 4:37), and the tremors of trouble began building. The waves started buffeting the exterior of the boat. Then they invaded it, "beat[ing] into the boat" (v. 37). The distressing on-board waters gradually rose until, at "crescendo point," the boat was "now full" (v. 37) of perilous difficulties from which the disciples could see no escape. And they saw correctly, because there was no way out without Jesus' help. Panicky, they called on Him with rude accusations of negligence and indifference: "Master, carest thou not that we perish?" (v. 38). Yet, graciously, He arose to save them, "and there was a great calm" (v. 39). So their roaring tribulation ended—and our spiritual education began. Why did the disciples fail at their "crescendo point"?

They believed two lies: (1) they were about to die, and (2) Jesus, who was sleeping, didn't care. Thus deceived, they prayed with offense and panic rather than trust and peace. Theirs is a pattern *not* to follow.

When waves of trouble begin crashing into our circumstantial "boats"—one surge at home, one swell at work, another wave at church, another breaker in our neighborhood—and no solutions are in sight, we're exactly where the disciples were. Our boat is "full" of trouble. How can we hold firm while this crescendo of chaos is rising? Here's some biblical guidance.

First, remember Jesus is with you in your "boat." Twice Mark affirms that, as wild and watery as things were, "he was in the boat" (Mark 4:36, 38). Second, never be offended with Jesus, who's always faithful to His promises and kind to His pupils. Jesus taught, "Blessed is he who does not take offense at Me" (Luke 7:23, NAS). Third, watch your thoughts diligently and reject the fearful imaginations that caused the disciples' rebellion and panic—that you'll fail or die and Jesus doesn't care about you! Paul commanded, "Casting down imaginations [reasonings], and every high thing that exalteth itself against the knowledge of God, and bringing into captivity every thought to the obedience of Christ" (2 Cor. 10:5). Fourth, meditate on the biblical truths that counter these fears.

For instance:

> In everything give thanks; for this is the will of God in Christ Jesus concerning you.
>
> —1 THESSALONIANS 5:18

> Count it all joy when ye fall into various trials, knowing this, that the testing of your faith worketh patience. But let patience have her perfect work, that ye may be perfect and entire, lacking nothing.
>
> —JAMES 1:2–4

> Trust in the LORD with all thine heart, and lean not unto thine own understanding. In all thy ways acknowledge him, and he shall direct thy paths.
>
> —PROVERBS 3:5–6

> God is faithful, who will not permit you to be tempted above that ye are able, but will, with the temptation, also make the way to escape, that ye may be able to bear it.
>
> —1 CORINTHIANS 10:13

> We know that God causes all things to work together for good to those who love God...who are called according to His purpose.
>
> —ROMANS 8:28, NAS

Believe, memorize, and faithfully practice these truths until they're written on your heart! Your life will change forever.

The next time you experience a nerve-racking crescendo of stress, your nerves won't snap or prayers become panicky. Despite your "full boat," you'll continue confidently praying, worshiping, and working until Jesus arises to change your "great storm" into a "great calm" (Mark 4:39).

And thereafter you'll be consistently calm, cool, and collected at every "crescendo point"!

Chapter 3

PREPARED PEOPLE, PREPARED PLACES

THROUGHOUT HISTORY GOD has simultaneously prepared people and places for the performance of His predestined purposes. The Old Testament reveals His work.

While God was preparing Moses to lead the Israelites, He was also preparing the Israelites to be led by Moses. As Moses became a wiser and stronger deliverer, they became thirstier and hungrier for deliverance. And at the right moment—"when forty years were expired" (Acts 7:30)—God brought them together and began fulfilling His purpose of delivering the chosen people from their long, bitter oppression. The New Testament unfolds this revelation further.

While God was preparing Paul to lead a mighty awakening among the Gentiles, He was also preparing the hearts of Gentiles all over the Mediterranean world to turn from idols to Christ. As Paul grew more knowledgeable in God's Word and ways, they grew more dissatisfied with Greco-Roman gods and philosophies. And at the right moment—after the outpouring of the Spirit at Cornelius' house and the founding of the largely Gentile church in Antioch—God brought His prepared man, Paul, to His prepared place, Antioch, to begin performing His predestined purpose: "Separate me Barnabas and Saul for the work unto which I have called them" (Acts 13:2). Specifically, that "work" was to launch apostolic missions for the founding and maturity of primarily Gentile Christians and churches all over the Roman world. The Lord has continued this pattern throughout the Church Age.

While Luther searched the Scriptures for spiritual light, hungry medieval European Christians, languishing in spiritual darkness, prayed for new light to refill and reform their dead churches and corrupt clergy. And at the right moment—October 31, 1517—in Wittenberg, Germany, God launched the epic protest that brought the chief Protestant and his protesters together. These providential preparations persisted in the post-Reformation church.

The Master of transition, God prepared John Wesley for England and the English for Wesley; Francis Asbury for America and the Americans for Asbury; William Booth for England's poor and England's poor for Booth;

George Mueller for England's orphans and England's orphans for Mueller; William Carey for India and the Indian people for Carey; Charles Spurgeon for metropolitan London and London's thousands for Spurgeon; Wang Ming-Dao and other brave Chinese leaders for China's oppressed millions and China's millions for them; Billy Graham for the world and the world for Billy Graham. And we could go on.

The Master is still performing perfect preparations today. He wants to prepare each of us for our predestined places and works in the body of Christ, whether as tithes-paying congregants, helpers, pastors, administrators, intercessors, foreign or home missionaries, editors, scholars, evangelists, prophets, teachers, elders, deacons, mentors, and so forth. Why? Every born-again believer is "created in Christ Jesus unto good works, which God hath before ordained that we should walk in them" (Eph. 2:10). We prepare ourselves for these "good works" by fully cooperating with the Master of transition. Do we understand how He works?

Our preparation is gradual, not sudden; occurring over time, not in a single religious experience however real and powerful. It is humble, not heady; occurring in private obedience, not public show. It is arduous, not easy; involving self-discipline, self-examination, and frequent sacrifices of self-will—though His grace is always sufficient! To be divinely prepared souls ready for divinely prepared places of service, we must steadily and gladly seek the Lord in prayer, Bible study, and worship; receive instruction from Spirit-taught Bible teachers; receive correction as needed from pastors and mentors; faithfully discharge small duties; accept humble circumstances; deny temptations; endure long adversities; and fellowship with other trainees.

While preparing for our places in God's service, we may take comfort in knowing that God is preparing the places He has chosen for us: "I go to *prepare a place for you*" (John 14:2). He's also preparing the people— Aarons, Barnabases, Silases—with whom, in those prepared places, we will work, pray, minister, suffer, and rejoice—until we're all prepared for Jesus' appearing.

So however rigorously God is training you, keep patiently paying the price of preparation. Continue working steadily. Keep enduring distress. Go on trusting the Master of transition. Maintain your hope in His vision. Persevere in praising Him, who, as you read this, is arranging a setting and duty tailor-made for you, your gifts, and your calling—so you can serve Him, His people, and His kingdom! His angel will lead you there.

He first preached this good news to Moses: "Behold, I send an angel before thee, to keep thee...and to bring thee into the place which I have prepared" (Exod. 23:20). Believe Him and His gospel of prepared people, prepared places.

Chapter 4

READY FOR SPIRITUAL CONSTRUCTION TESTING?

SING A SIMPLE story about two houses facing a severe storm, Jesus ended His greatest teaching, the Sermon on the Mount, with a sober warning. It reads:

Therefore, whosoever heareth these sayings of mine, and doeth them, I will liken him unto a wise man, who built his house upon a rock. And the rain descended, and the floods came, and the winds blew and beat upon that house, and it fell not; for it was founded upon a rock.

And every one that heareth these sayings of mine, and doeth them not, shall be likened unto a foolish man, who built his house upon the sand. And the rain descended, and the floods came, and the winds blew and beat upon that house, and it fell; and great was the fall of it.

—MATTHEW 7:24–27

Briefly, His admonition is this: "Eventually God will thoroughly test the spiritual construction of every Christian, wise and foolish." Why?

He wants to know what kind of Christians we are. Are we possessors or mere professors of the faith? Doers of His Word or hearers only? Disciples indeed or hypocrites? Spiritual or carnal Christians? Fervent followers or apostates? Overcomers or succumbers? So Matthew puts us on notice.

Later, Matthew's Gospel records Jesus' prophetic parable of the Ten Virgins (Matt. 25:1–13). This prophecy reveals that in the church's last days an unflatteringly large number of Christians will be "foolish." "Five of them [the virgins] were wise, and five were foolish" (v. 2). Generally, "foolish" means without the fear of God and biblical wisdom; in this context, it means thoughtlessly unprepared for Jesus' appearing. If meant to be statistically accurate, this parable's implications are shocking: approximately 50 percent of Christians today are foolishly unprepared for Jesus' appearing! These aren't the ramblings of a suspect prophet; they're the final, authoritative words of our all-knowing Master concerning these times. Though humiliating, they accurately depict the current body of Christians, particularly in America. (Jesus' further prophetic description of this "Laodicean" era[1] confirms this, in Revelation 3:15–17.) When combined with His earlier warning in the Sermon on the Mount, this one sounds an ear-splitting alarm.

Merged and paraphrased, Jesus' alerts read:

> Your spiritual construction—the foundation of the "house" of character you're building daily—will be rigorously tested in the last days. Many Christians will be foolishly unprepared for these trials…and My subsequent appearing!

Indeed, in these last days God will permit powerful storms of adversity to "beat upon" our "houses," and "vehemently" (Luke 6:48–49). Specifically, what will "beat" upon us?

Jesus described these trying assaults. The "rains" are seasons of trouble and hindrance, which temporarily block the sunshine of our peace, progress, and prosperity. The "floods" are sudden, overwhelming losses or defeats, or rebellious uprisings against us. The "winds" speak of the "prince of the power of the air" (Eph. 2:2), Satan, and his wicked spirits, "the rulers of the darkness of this world" (Eph. 6:12), who create various pressures intended to bring down those who seek to know, obey, and share the Light of the world and the light of His Word. These diabolical forces combine to "blow" and "beat" upon us by causing fresh downpours, waves, or gusts of resistant wind to strike the "house" of our mind, body, family, possessions, churches, or ministries. Is our spiritual foundation ready for this "beating"?

Are we preparing Christian character? Or procrastinating? Intrepid, fearlessly building our spiritual foundations? Or incredulous, disbelieving and ignoring Jesus' prophetic warning? Carefully practicing Jesus' teachings? Or just casually professing them? Seeking, studying, interceding, worshiping, giving, loving, suffering, forgiving, and thanking God in all circumstances? Or avoiding the secret place, ignoring Bible study, praying as little as possible, neglecting worship, withholding tithes or offerings, harboring grudges, compromising to avoid rejection, and complaining in every situation?

If the former is true, we're standing on solid rock—consistent obedience to the unfailing Word of our unfailing God. Our spiritual foundation is firmly in place. We're ready for any storm any time anywhere.

If the latter is true, no matter how long we've been saved and how much we've been churched, we're building on the shifting sands of biblical disobedience. And we have a serious foundation—and storm preparedness—problem. Yet it's better to know this now than later.

In 2005, New Orleans' infrastructure wasn't ready for a direct hit from a major hurricane, and Katrina proved it. It was too late to repair its canal walls and levees once the storm hit. But there's still time for us to finish securing our spiritual foundations.

So be wise! Be building consistent Christian character! Be ready for your spiritual construction testing and Jesus' appearing!

Chapter 5

SWIFT AS EAGLES!

AGLES FLY AND attack prey swiftly. Very swiftly! This hasn't gone unnoticed by the Creator or His creatures.

The Creator's Word repeatedly attests to eagles' swiftness in flight. Moses warned if Israel turned from God, it would suffer invasion from "a nation...as swift as the eagle flieth" (Deut. 28:49). Jeremiah lamented that, indeed, the Babylonians were just that: "Our persecutors are swifter than the eagles" (Lam. 4:19). David eulogized Saul and Jonathan for being "swifter than eagles" in combating the Philistines (2 Sam. 1:23). The apostle John used "two wings of a great eagle" to symbolize the swiftness of the believing Jewish remnant's flight to refuge in the Great Tribulation (Rev. 12:14). The Creator's findings haven't been lost on His chief creature.

Mankind has rediscovered and reveled in the wonders of eagles. Ornithologists concur that the golden eagle can indeed fly very rapidly, at approximately thirty to thirty-five miles an hour in level flight (and even faster when chasing prey) and eighty to one hundred miles an hour in a dive.[1] Thus, like other predators, the eagle moves fastest when pursuing prey.

In complete agreement, God's Word asserts eagles are speedy hunters. Job draws a parallel between his swiftly passing days and "the eagle that hasteneth to the prey" (Job 9:26). A herdsman, Job may have often seen eagles "hastening" to clutch unsuspecting rabbits, fish, or other birds. Whether disciples or Darwinists, naturalists observing eagles on the hunt will "amen" Job's observation. Eagles' typical method of pursuing prey is worthy of note.

Flying high over a field or body of water, an eagle first spots his prey, often from as far as a mile away. Then, without warning, it suddenly dives and seizes it, often killing smaller prey instantly by piercing its heart with his sharp talons. A *raptor*, or "one who seizes by force,"[2] an eagle is specially created to seek, see, seize, carry, kill, and devour prey. In addition to its exceptional size, speed, and eyesight, it is made with a large hooked beak, two large feet, and four very strong toes capped with sharp hooked claws or "talons." So when the eagle pursues its prey, it's just doing what the Creator made it to do. It's doing God's will. And swiftly—as overcoming Christians do.

Eagles symbolize overcoming Christians. In His messages to the churches of Asia Minor, Jesus challenges born-again believers, who are already basic overcomers (1 John 5:4–5), to become master overcomers. To incentivize us, He repeatedly offers special rewards and honors if we respond: "To him that overcometh will I give to eat of the tree of life" (Rev. 2:7; see also Rev. 2:11, 17, 26–28; 3:5, 12, 21). As eagles fly and hunt swiftly, so eagle Christians, or master "overcomers," do God's will swiftly.

They are quick to see His plans. Once atop Mount Moriah, Abraham speedily discerned that the "ram caught in a thicket" was a divinely provided substitute for Isaac (Gen. 22:13). They are swift to follow God's guidance. Once the apostle Paul realized God wanted him to go to Macedonia, he "immediately" endeavored to do so (Acts 16:10). They are quick to speak for God. When the Spirit urged Philip to "go near" the Ethiopian eunuch, Philip promptly approached his chariot and "preached unto him Jesus" (Acts 8:29, 35). They are quick to give to the needy. The Antioch Christians promptly "determined to send relief" to the poor Judean saints after Agabus foretold an approaching great famine (Acts 11:29).

Furthermore, master overcomers are quick to feed on the "prey," or spiritual food, God provides—biblical sermons, teachings, books, magazines, CDs, DVDs, website postings, and so forth. As "the eagle that hasteneth to eat" (Hab. 1:8), the Bereans swiftly fed on Paul's teachings, confirming their veracity "with all readiness of mind" by their own Bible studies (Acts 17:11). They are quick to receive instruction. When Aquila and Priscilla "expounded" to Apollos "the way of God more perfectly," the learned but humble theologian promptly received their inspired teaching (Acts 18:26). They are quick to correct themselves. When Paul realized that, even though the high priest had mistreated him, he himself had disobeyed God's Word by responding disrespectfully, Paul quickly repented (Acts 23:1–5). They also are swift to forgive penitent offenders. Joseph immediately received and comforted his brothers once he saw they were truly changed men. These spiritual eagles are swift to discern and do God's will.

Where are you now? Flying swift and high with other spiritually minded, overcoming eagle Christians? Or earthbound and slow as crow Christians, sitting idly on the telephone lines of life? To the sky—spiritual thinking and living! To the prey—God's will! And quickly—swift as eagles!

Chapter 6

THE PRAYER OF THE HOUR

*M*OST CHRISTIANS RECOGNIZE Daniel as a man of outstanding godliness and prophetic insight. And that he was.

Many, however, fail to see he was also an outstanding prayer warrior. As few before or since, this man knew how to speak words that moved God to help nations. Humility was his greatest secret and tool.

Though it wasn't yet written, Daniel realized, "God resisteth the proud, but giveth grace unto the humble" (James 4:6). We know this because, when praying for his nation's restoration, he approached God not with self-justifying pride but with God-justifying humility. Daniel 9:3–19 records his amazingly honest, humble, and effective talk with God.

After discovering God's seventy-year limit on the Babylonian captivity (Dan. 9:2) and realizing sixty-seven years had already passed, Daniel began praying for Jerusalem's restoration with fervor and fasting. He repeatedly declared God had been totally fair in bringing His terrible judgments upon His people, who had been utterly foolish. They had rebelled against God's Word and rejected His prophets' loving warnings. Even after God's shocking judgments they remained asleep with indifference, despite their "confusion [shame] of face." Even so, Daniel reasoned, God might still show Judah mercy for His great name's sake, which was so publicly at stake in its history. The frankness and meekness of his prayer is unmatched in the Bible. To Daniel, national restoration wasn't just a matter of faith. It was also one of humble truthfulness. Therefore he was brutally frank before God. Was his petition answered?

It was not only answered, but swiftly! "Yea, while I was speaking in prayer...Gabriel...being caused to fly swiftly, touched me...and talked with me" (Dan. 9:21–22). And specially! Gabriel gave Daniel a key revelation of Israel's future (vv. 20–27). And powerfully! Daniel's humble words moved his all-powerful God to move earth's most powerful king, Cyrus the Persian, to issue a decree that very year (538 B.C.) permitting Jews to return to Jerusalem and rebuild their temple, worship, and way of life. Thus a nation long held in hopeless captivity to sin was suddenly reborn. So we see Daniel's prayer of truth prompted a swift, special, and powerful response from the God of truth. What a timely word!

America isn't Israel and never will be, yet Israel's restoration reveals how God deals with all nations. Listen well!

Long ago God declared, "Righteousness exalteth a nation, but sin is a reproach to any people" (Prov. 14:34). Years of increasing sinfulness in America—immorality, abortion, greed, idolatry, pride, and so forth—have forced a holy God to disfavor this nation. The shocking events of September 11, 2001, were an ominous token of His growing wrath. The respite following was a grace period, God's silent call to turn from sin to the Savior. Since that time, however, America has gone the way of Judah: "confusion of face" is upon us. The financial collapse of September 15, 2008—seven years after the twin towers fell—only confirmed and increased our "confusion." Why? Our nation is impenitent. But far more importantly, most *Christians* are still impenitent. Like Daniel's Judean compatriots, even after seeing judgment, we're still oblivious to its cause and too proud to face, much less confess, the truth that we too have sinned against God's Word, ways, and warnings. Lukewarm, many of us have fallen back into the old sleep of church as usual. Rather than smiting their breasts in prayer, some Christians are smiting their political rivals with sole blame for the national demise. Daily this self-righteous sleep and smiting goes on. But don't despair.

Two giant hopes stand before Christians in this and every nation: a promise and a prayer.

The promise is God's. He vowed to heal any "land" if His redeemed people there will only meet His conditions: "If my people...called by my name, shall humble themselves, and pray, and seek my face, and turn from their wicked ways, then will I hear from heaven...forgive their sin...heal their land" (2 Chron. 7:14). For decades we've done everything with this promise but obey it. Yet it's still valid—if *we*, not liberals, atheists, Darwinists, or Muslims, will only "humble ourselves," "turn," "seek," and "pray."

The prayer is Daniel's. Our prayers will be just as effective as his if we plead with not only his faith but also his humble truthfulness. It's time for truth.

And the truth is America's worst darkness, and its church's midnight hour, has come. It's time we re-pray Daniel's petition. Will we humble ourselves, repent, seek God, and pray it? A confused nation and lost world are watching to see if we have the humility and love to pray the prayer of the hour.

Chapter 7

THE KING'S COLLEGE

PON OPENING DANIEL'S scroll, we read that, once crowned, King Nebuchadnezzar decided to employ the best and brightest of his conquered Judean subjects to help govern his vast and growing empire (Dan. 1:1–7). But before employing them, he had to educate and examine them.

So Judah's most promising youths were placed in a three-year educational institution, comparable to a prestigious college or university in today's world. Among these young nobles and royals "of the king's seed" (Dan. 1:3) were the "faithful four," or four principle characters of Daniel's story: Daniel, Hananiah, Mishael, and Azariah. Their curriculum of higher learning was a thinly veiled attempt to "Babylonianize" them. The king's plan was simple: they would enter his college as loyal, orthodox Jews and three years later, after being intellectually transformed, culturally redressed, and religiously converted, exit as wise and worldly Babylonians. In the king's school, the most learned sages and scholars of Babylonia rigorously taught them all the subjects they needed to master to subsequently serve as the king's courtiers and administrators—mathematics, agriculture, architecture, language, literature, art, astronomy, history, and so forth. But before serving, they had to pass a final test, a thorough oral examination administered by King Nebuchadnezzar himself (v. 18).

Pause and realize there's more than history here. Daniel's inspired record contains subtle symbolism that every Christian should see and study. So let's go to school.

Paradoxically, Nebuchadnezzar's actions here foreshadow those of another King. Like the king of Babylon, Jesus, the "King of kings" (Rev. 19:16), needs able leaders to help administrate His coming millennial kingdom. He can't entrust and employ believers based solely upon their spiritual potential, however great. They must be educated and tested so their potential may be developed and used to its maximum capability. So just as Nebuchadnezzar recruited Judah's best and brightest for his school, King Jesus is now enrolling the church's best—His true disciples, born of spiritually royal heritage with the "King's seed," or divine nature and

Word, in them—in His "college," or spiritual training institution. There we study different essential "courses," or vital subjects, in various "classrooms," or divinely arranged circumstances, in which He personally "examines" our progress. This curriculum is designed to "kingdomize" us, or transform our characters so we'll be ready to live and labor forever in Christ's kingdom.

His plan, like Nebuchadnezzar's, is simple: His disciples enter His "college" as saved but worldly minded Christians and, after sufficient teaching, training, and testing, emerge as His deeply changed, spiritually minded servants. The chief Sage and Professor in Christ's college is the Holy Spirit: "He shall teach you all things" (John 14:26). He teaches and trains us as we study the Bible and receive biblical teaching, counsel, and correction from pastors, teachers, and elders. Simultaneously, He arranges daily tests, or "courses," for us. These challenging situations are opportunities to show the King that our spiritual potential—of being "fit for the master's use, and prepared unto every good work" (2 Tim. 2:21)—is indeed being realized. What "courses" are you presently enrolled in?

Yours may be a course on devotion, in which you must learn to seek the Lord early, pray, and study your Bible daily to show yourself "approved unto God" (2 Tim. 2:15). Or you may be studying humility and grace, and daily must learn to think spiritually and react graciously to proud, unspiritual, ungracious people. You may be in a class on patience, where you must wait a season to have what you need or desire. Or you may be taking a course on faithfulness, in which you must do unnoticed work willingly, diligently, and thoroughly "as to the Lord" (Col. 3:23), for little or no pay, and even less recognition. You may be doing an internship on suffering and must learn to be misunderstood, misrepresented, maligned, and even hated for Christ's sake. Or you may be in a class on submission, in which you must learn to heartily obey the human authorities God has placed over you in the home, school, workplace, or church. Whatever or wherever your "courses," the more biblical verses, principles, and methods you consistently obey, the more complete will be your character transformation. Once you're sufficiently "kingdomized," the King will personally approve you for higher service in His church now and kingdom later: "Friend, go up higher" (Luke 14:10).

He's taking applications now, so enroll and pursue your spiritual education. Study your "courses" well, obey your Professor joyfully, pass your "exams" thoroughly, and receive your kingdom degree—a distinguished "*man [or woman] of God...complete, thoroughly equipped for every good work*" (2 Tim. 3:17, NKJV).

Honorable service awaits all graduates of the King's college.

Chapter 8

DO YOU HAVE THIS COMPASSION?

*O*F ALL JESUS' wondrous and winsome qualities—gentleness, truthfulness, boldness, wisdom, fairness, patience—the most endearing was His compassion. The Gospels make much of it.

Expertly informed, the Gospel writers describe Christ's compassion drawing men to faith in Him, love for Him, and a loyalty so strong they willingly suffered and died for the Son of Compassion. They unanimously assert that Jesus' compassion drove every phase of His ministry.

Mark says it moved Jesus to touch and heal a hopelessly afflicted leper, to release a wild, psychotic man from thousands of demons, and to deliver a young man (and his distraught father) from a powerful demon that had bound him from childhood. Matthew says it moved Jesus to urge His disciples to ask His Father to send out faithful spiritual laborers to help His confused, unshepherded people—and He then sent them out to do the same. Compassion also moved Him to heal the multitudes of sick people who constantly thronged Him, to feed the bodies of those who fed on His teachings, and to give precious sight to two blind men who begged for the mercy of seeing eyes. Luke describes how Jesus had compassion on a brokenhearted widow in Nain by raising her only son (and provider) from death. Without using the word *compassion*, John nevertheless described it moving Jesus to defend Mary against Judas' criticism, wash His disciples' feet, pray for their future needs, and on the cross provide for His mother. Thus the compassionate One continuously helped helpless people by teaching, healing, delivering, reviving, praying, and providing for them. How active His sympathy was!

Do we understand the difference between Christlike compassion and mere human pity? The latter is an inactive sympathetic feeling toward sufferers, while the former is sympathy plus a determination to help in a practical way. The original language bears this out.

The Greek word used most in the Gospels to describe Jesus' compassion is *splanchnizomai*. It means, "to be moved as to [or in] one's inwards; to be moved with compassion; to yearn with compassion."[1] Five times in the King James Version it's rendered "moved with compassion." For instance:

Many love statistics and trust more in polls, studies, and cutting-edge theories than in the inspired declarations of the Bible. Others go for nationalistic messages, which usually put one's own nation as the head (and all others as the tail!) and tend to overstate its righteousness and overlook its sinfulness. Politics, with all its passion, policy, punditry, and putrid scandal, is another topic sure to gain the ear and titillate the curiosity of many. Condemning the sins of our unredeemed society is another sure way to satisfy those who prefer to focus on sinners' sins to evade examining their own. And there's more.

Sentimentality is a proven method of coddling babes in Christ, as sad-story-telling preachers wring rivers of tears from their eyes three Sunday mornings out of four, yet leave their hearers' hearts dry and empty. Constant comedy will get the congregation rolling with laughter but leave them without the biblical nutrients they need to walk in love, truth, and holiness come Monday morning. Fine literature, classic philosophy, and beautiful poetry may impress and stir more intellectual congregations yet leave their spirits unfed and dangerously unprepared to face this harshly unpoetic world. Liturgical readings and rituals may move us with religious enchantment, but they don't release the reviving river of life from above. These are some of the more tasty entrees appearing on the ecclesiastical menu today. It's a shame they're so unhealthy.

It's time our churches get healthy. For that, the Great Physician recommends that, like our devotional feeding, our congregational diet always include the spiritually wholesome, nutrient-rich, whole-grain, no additive, high-fiber Bread of Life—and the more the better! He taught us to measure our spiritual vitality "by every Word" we receive from Him. "Man shall not live by bread alone, but by every word that proceedeth out of the mouth of God" (Matt. 4:4). No matter how large and multifaceted our church ministries, we can't afford to stray from "the simplicity that is in Christ" (2 Cor. 11:3). We must hold tightly to the simple, pure, life-giving Word. Then the sermon-meals we feed on will be like those Jesus served. And we'll understand that Mark's comment on Jesus' early meeting in Capernaum wasn't incidental.

It was illuminating. May God help us walk in the light of it. In this spiritually demanding and draining world, poor spiritual nutrition is not an option. Like growing children, developing disciples of Christ must have a steady supply of the solid spiritual nourishment that comes only from sound, Spirit-illuminated, Spirit-led Bible exposition. Disciples should demand it and pastors deliver it. Why?

It was Jesus' way. It still is. Let's be sure our way is like His: "He preached the word."

Chapter 11

CAN HE WRITE HIS NAME ON YOU?

*J*ESUS PROMISED TO honor the overcoming Christians in Philadelphia for their outstanding trust, obedience, and loyalty. John recalled His pledge.

Jesus vowed to write His name on the Philadelphians in the kingdom: "Him that overcometh...I will write upon him my new name" (Rev. 3:12). He further guaranteed to inscribe on them the names of His Father and His eternal city, New Jerusalem: "I will write upon him the name of my God, and...the city of my God, the new Jerusalem" (v. 12). What do these distinctions signify?

In the Bible, name is often associated with character. So changed names usually signify changed characters. "Jacob" the trickster becomes the princely "Israel." "Saul" the abusive Jewish Pharisee becomes "Paul" the loving Christian apostle. This explains Jesus' promise to the Philadelphians.

Primarily, writing His name on them reveals that *the divine character is now fully integrated into their characters* (as He prayed in John 17:26). It is the Holy Spirit's trademark, or logo, being placed upon His finished product! It is also the distinctive monogram or coat of arms of the family of God. Whatever its appearance, this distinctive inscription signifies that, by Christ's redemption, grace, and power, those marked consistently manifest the same character traits as the Father, Son, and inhabitants of New Jerusalem. The long process of conforming them to the image of the Son in their minds, values, goals, and ways of living and working is finally complete. They are now ready to live, labor, and lead in God's kingdom...forever!

Furthermore, this Messianic monogram declares its recipients are: (1) God's true children and members of the most honorable social unit, the family of God; (2) His personal "reward" (Ps. 127:3) and "rich and glorious inheritance" (Eph. 1:18, NLT); and (3) full citizens of New Jerusalem, their eternal home. This, Christ's "mark," also sheds light on the beast's "mark."

Driven by envy to imitate the divine One, Satan will prompt his "son," the man of sin, to inscribe his monogram or family symbol on his followers during the Great Tribulation: "He causeth all...to receive a mark in their right hand, or...foreheads...the mark, or the name of the beast"

(Rev. 13:16–17). This "mark" indicates that Antichrist's devotees have also been thoroughly transformed—but in a horribly different way. The terrible work of sin, with its demand to have one's way in defiance of God, has run its awful course and produced legions of Antichrist-like, mutant souls, whose dark characters are now like that of sin's originator, Lucifer. Thus they wear his trademark or logo.

The beast's monogram declares that Satan's character traits (pride, lying, lust, greed, malice, and so forth) are now fully integrated into their characters. Also, it says they are: (1) Satan's true children; (2) his demons' finished work; and (4) headed for his eternal home, the lake of fire. There hell's "trinity"—Satan, the Antichrist, and the false prophet—and children will share chaotic torment…forever. These facts are as true as they are sad.

But here is a fact that's as glad as it is true: if we bear Jesus' name now, we'll wear His name later! We "bear" His name by "carrying" and displaying His character in our daily living. How do we do this? We follow His footsteps.

We obey the Father, as Jesus did, joyfully! "I delight to do thy will, O my God" (Ps. 40:8). We love mercy, as Jesus did: "He was moved with compassion on them" (Matt. 9:36). We speak truth, as Jesus did: "Speaking the truth in love" (Eph. 4:15). We minister freely, as Jesus did, without preferencc or prejudice. We suffer willingly, as Jesus did, without complaining and with thanksgiving and perseverance in duty. And in every situation and season of life, we seek Christ's presence, feed on His Word, obey His wisdom, and walk in His ways. The more we do so, the more the Spirit conforms our characters to Christ's image, and the more we "bear" His name now in this life—and prepare to wear it in the next.

Are you bearing Jesus' name? Are you carrying and displaying His character traits, the "fruit of the Spirit" (Gal. 5:22–23)? Sometimes? Increasingly? Consistently? By God's grace and His Spirit's help, keep bearing Jesus' name, so you can wear it. By inscribing His marvelous monogram on you, the Messiah will proclaim: "I've finished making this man (or woman) a bearer of My divine character. He is a true, taught, trained, transformed child of God—and treasured, a jewel in My Father's glorious inheritance, a citizen of our eternal city."

He will grant the Philadelphians this distinction. Can He write His name on you?

Chapter 12

ARE YOU SLEEPING?

ATURAL SLEEP MAY be a blessing or a curse. Good and bad things happen while we slumber.

While sleeping nightly, our bodies are restored, our emotions released, and our minds cleared, thus refitting us for the demands of life and work. Yet, while sleeping, thieves may also quietly break in and stealthily take everything we own!

Besides describing slumber, the Bible uses sleep to symbolize both right and wrong spiritual conditions. Let's examine its illuminating and instructive examples.

Jesus, Peter, and Daniel show us the sleep of faith. Jesus was so confident in His Father's perfect care that He slept soundly in a small boat being tossed by a huge storm. While others screamed in terror, He rested in trust, "in the stern of the boat, asleep on a pillow" (Mark 4:38). In Herod's prison, Peter was so sure Jesus would give him the longevity He promised and answer the church's prayers for his release that, though scheduled for execution at daybreak, "the same night Peter was sleeping [deeply] between two soldiers, bound with two chains" (Acts 12:6). Daniel was so convinced the God he served "continually" would deliver him that he slept peacefully among hungry lions—while they paced anxiously with insomnia. This sleep of trusting hearts is the sleep God blesses, "for He gives [blessings] to His beloved in sleep" (Ps. 127:2, AMP). Those who wholly lean on God's loving, faithful character and unchanging, unfailing Word receive sweet, serene restoration every time they recline: "Thou shalt lie down, and thy sleep shall be sweet" (Prov. 3:24). We admire this sleep, but there are other kinds we must avoid.

Deep in the hold of a ship headed west to Tarshish, the prophet Jonah slept the sleep of rebellion. "Jonah was gone down into the sides of the ship; and...was fast asleep" (Jonah 1:5). Try as he may to use unconsciousness to escape the consciousness of his disobedience, he failed. Every time he awoke he heard a still, small voice urging, "Go east...to Nineveh! Now!"

Samson succumbed to the sleep of immorality, first in a harlot's house and later in Delilah's lap: "She made him sleep upon her knees" (Judg.

16:19). Every hour he continued not judging his senseless sin, he made himself more senseless—and vulnerable to his enemies. Finally "he awoke out of his sleep" (v. 20), but it was too late. His strength and ministry were gone.

In Gethsemane, the apostles slept the sleep of sorrow. Jesus' announcement of His imminent betrayal and death puzzled them. The thought of one of their own turning on Jesus was numbing. This smashing of their hope—that Jesus' kingdom would immediately begin—and the strangeness of God's plan deeply disappointed them, and "he found them sleeping for sorrow" (Luke 22:45).

King Solomon described the sleep of laziness, warning, "Slothfulness casteth into a deep sleep" (Prov. 19:15). Wisely, he knew too much sleep turns the prosperity of the diligent into the poverty of the indolent: "Love not sleep, lest thou come to poverty" (Prov. 20:13).

Though called to be watchful shepherds, some Christian leaders fall into the sleep of misleadership. Isaiah says, "His watchmen are blind…sleeping, lying down, loving to slumber" (Isa. 56:10). God depends upon pastors and elders to protect His flocks and fields from wolves and workers of iniquity. But while they sleep on duty, demons work dutifully: "While men slept, his enemy came and sowed tares among the wheat" (Matt. 13:25).

Jesus told of ten virgins who fell into the sleep of unbelief. When their bridegroom delayed his coming, they slowly slid from active expectation into disappointment, doubt, and disbelief—and from their prayerful watchtowers to their beds! "While the bridegroom tarried, they all slumbered and slept" (Matt. 25:5). These kinds of "sleep" are adverse, not admirable.

They reflect indifference to our spiritual condition or circumstances. Every time we fail to examine ourselves, unconfessed sin dulls our spiritual senses and hinders our awareness of and communication with God, leaving us "asleep" to Him and His will, and to our times, blessings, and dangers. Are you slumbering?

If yours is the sweet sleep of trust in God, sleep on! If it's any other kind, may God kindly disturb and awaken you—to full alertness, fellowship with God, confidence in Him, communication from Him, fruitfulness in His service, and stimulating hope in His appearing. Still need nudging?

If you "awake," Christ promises you "light," the fullest possible awareness of Him and knowledge of His Word, plan, and guidance: "Awake thou that sleepest…and Christ shall give thee light" (Eph. 5:14). His "light" will keep you alert till He comes.

So I ask, are you sleeping?

Chapter 13

COMFORTED OR CHAFED BY HIS ROD?

*I*N HIS MOST famous psalm Israel's most famous shepherd wrote, "Thy rod and thy staff they comfort me" (Ps. 23:4). David knew well what a shepherd's rod symbolizes.

It speaks of defending, examining, and disciplining his sheep. A watchful shepherd will use his "rod"—usually a short wooden club—to defend his sheep, as if it were an extension of his right arm. He will strike nearby predators with it, throw it at those farther away, and beat the bushes to warn snakes and other foes to stay away from his wooly, four-legged followers. The sight of their shepherd with club in hand is an enormous source of security to otherwise defenseless sheep, especially while traversing the deadly, dark "valley of the shadow" (Ps. 23:4). It's an equally strong intimidation to their would-be attackers. Sheep are further relieved by knowing they will pass under their shepherd's rod nightly.

To "pass under the rod" refers to a shepherd counting his sheep as they enter the door to their sheep pen every evening. As they enter, the shepherd not only numbers but also carefully examines them with his eyes and hands for signs of injury, disease, scabs, nose flies, or other parasites.[1] Without this close vetting, their hidden ills would remain undetected beneath their thick coats of wool, leaving them weak, sick, and vulnerable to predators. This intimate, unerring care warms the hearts of the sheep. They are confident that if they should fail to detect any harmful condition, their shepherd will discover and remedy it when they "pass under the rod."

Conversely, the shepherd's rod is further used, when necessary, to discipline his sheep. When sheep stray from the safety of their shepherd's side and flock's fellowship and come near predators, poisonous weeds or flowers, or other dangers, the shepherd may fling his rod in their direction to alert them to return to safety. If they stubbornly continue in their own way, he may strike them with it! Ouch! But the temporary discomfort inflicted is motivated by the tenderest love—to spare them needless, painful wounds or tragic, premature death at the hands of their ever-waiting, ever-watching, ever-malicious enemies. A shepherd from his youth, David wisely pondered these benefits of the "rod" he used while nurturing Jesse's flocks.

Consequently, in his most trying "valleys," he was deeply reassured and relieved every time he remembered that, however chaotic and cruel his circumstances, he was still "under the rod" of the Lord, the heavenly Shepherd: "Thy rod…comfort[s] me." And it obviously soothed his oft-troubled soul whenever he saw the Lord using His "rod" on his enemies, humbling, confounding, or turning back those who proudly pursued or plotted against him, such as Saul, Nabal, and Shimei. But David's insight went further.

The more he let God humble him, the more David also learned to be comforted rather than chafed when the Lord used His rod on him. Every time the Lord's searching examination, precise conviction, or stinging discipline overtook him, though initially distressed, he always found consolation. How? He recognized the soul and life correction as a sign of the holy love of his Shepherd, who centuries later said, "As many as I love, I rebuke and chasten" (Rev. 3:19). He also wisely reasoned that the rod's agitation was better than its alternative—remaining uncorrected, self-deceived, troubled by sin, and vulnerable to his persistent, pitiless enemies. Inspired by these insights, David meekly vowed to love the rod of reproof, even if wielded by his peers! "Let the righteous smite me; it shall be a kindness. And let him reprove me; it shall be an excellent ["perfumed," NCV] oil, which shall not break my head" (Ps. 141:5). His quick, quiet, and humble acceptance of the "perfumed oil" of correction applied by Abigail, Nathan, and Joab at crucial moments proved he meant what he vowed.

Are we as humble as David or still harboring foolish pride? Do we rejoice when God's "rod" stops our enemies, yet chafe when He pokes us by peering under our wooly pride and self-defense to convict us of wrong motives, attitudes, words, actions, or reactions, or when He smites us with adversity for persisting in sin or self-will? It's time we despise the pride that hates correction and delight in the Spirit who convicts us, the Abigails who counsel us, the Joabs who warn us, and the Nathans who face us with our secret hypocrisies. These "rods" are proofs of the Shepherd's love—and we're far better off with than without them. Don't just contemplate the famous words of Israel's famous psalm.

Live them. Be comforted, not chafed, by the Good Shepherd's rod.

Chapter 15

THE FORGE OF EXTRAORDINARY LEADERS

*O*UR WAY OF making extraordinary Christian leaders is very different from God's.

We take a young Christian and educate him (or her), ordain him, and set him on the commonly accepted path to religious elevation—associate ministry, pastoral or evangelistic work, missions, denominational service, and so forth—until he rises to the enviable high ground of ministerial success and acclaim. There, ideally, he influences many believers, churches, cities, and perhaps nations. This relatively pain- and humility-free way of preparation is widely accepted as God's own. But it isn't.

God's way of making powerful leaders is not just academic and ecclesiastical but also experiential. He not only educates the mind and polishes the manners but also molds the character. For this deeper work, God puts ministerial trainees into His forge. A forge is a place where, by the wise handiwork of a master smith, repetitive exposure to burning heat, cruel blows, and shocking cold transforms otherwise useless iron into useful instruments. The way of God's forge is seen in Joseph's exceptional training.

Knowing His people would experience great difficulty in Egypt, God prepared Joseph to lead them through that dark hour: "He sent a man before them, even Joseph" (Ps. 105:17). Psalm 105 reveals how drastically God's training differs from ours.

We would have given Joseph a pleasant trip to Egypt and, immediately upon arrival, wide favor and loyal support. But God ordained that he first be shocked and "sold" for a few pieces of silver—and by his own brothers! "Joseph, who was sold" (v. 17). We would have quickly given Joseph a position of authority. But God stripped away all authority and sense of honor and made him a lowly "servant"—to learn to serve a master, submissively, faithfully, and diligently: "Sold for a servant" (v. 17). We would have sent messengers to comfort and reassure him in his emotional trauma. But God ordained that, again, he be "hurt"—wounded now by fetters as well as family—and forced to suffer unrelieved loneliness in a dark, cold prison. "Whose feet they hurt with fetters" (v. 18). We would have released him to travel, expecting him to grow in ministry by going in ministry. But God ordered him "laid in iron"—bound by an iron collar by night and hard, rigorous duties by day. "He was laid in iron" (v. 18), or "they put…an iron ring around his neck" (NCV). If we dared to thus hold back our minister-in-training, we would at least make his captivity brief. But God made Joseph's wait long—thirteen years of slavery and imprisonment—until his faith in God's "word" (dream of honorable service) and his patient endurance were fully tested, proven, and established. "Until the time…the word of the LORD tested him" (v. 19, NAS). Though strange to us, these hot fires, cruel blows, and cold shocks made Joseph a well-formed piece of work.

When "the king sent and loosed him" (Ps. 105:20), Joseph emerged an extraordinary leader ready to guide God's people through extraordinary hardship. God's way of making his character strong wasn't fun, but it was faithful; he accomplished God's will! God's forge was also fruitful. Very fruitful! Joseph's ministries were marvelous—and many.

He commanded, ruling everyone and everything in Pharaoh's "house" (palace and kingdom): "He made him lord of his house" (Ps. 105:21), or "Joseph was put in charge of all the king's household" (NLT). He controlled, managing Pharaoh's possessions and increasing the nation's wealth by selling its grain: "He made him…ruler of all his substance" (v. 21). He judged, arresting and freeing Egypt's nobles, citizens, slaves, and visitors at his discretion: "To bind his princes at his pleasure" (v. 22). He taught, instructing Pharaoh's courtiers and priests in the words and ways of divine wisdom: "And teach[ing] his elders wisdom" (v. 22). He healed, mollifying the deep, self-inflicted wounds that tormented his brothers' consciences by being generous and kind to them (Gen. 50:21). This sweet end eclipsed all the bitterness of Joseph's forge. He said, "*Manasseh* [forgetting[1]]: 'For…God has made me forget all my hardship'" (Gen. 41:51, ESV).

Like Joseph, have you received a vision of honorable service for God? Yet has your pleasant path of ministerial studies and service suddenly become filled with very unpleasant experiences—betrayals, failures, injustices, rejections, and low, hidden duties? God is using these fires, blows, and shocks to mold you in His forge. So follow Joseph's example. Give the heavenly Smith extraordinary submission, trust, and obedience, and one day He'll bring you forth an extraordinary "instrument for his work" (Isa. 54:16).

In that sweet day you too will say, "Manasseh!"—and praise God for the forge of extraordinary leaders.

Chapter 16

WITH WHOM ARE YOU WALKING?

ITH WHOM ARE you walking through life? Faithful souls or fools? Worshipers or mockers of God? Spiritual or carnal Christians? Your answer is more important than you think.

Proverbs, the Bible's chief source of wisdom, declares confidently, "He that walketh with wise men shall be wise, but a companion of fools shall be destroyed" (Prov. 13:20). This emphasizes the sure consequences of the close friends and leaders we choose. Note the contrasting associations—"with wise men" or "fools"—and the drastically different ends—"be wise" or "destroyed."

Paraphrased, this adage says:

> If we respect, stay close to, and obey the counsel of God-fearing, virtuous friends and leaders, we'll gradually become like them. But if we befriend and spend time with those who neither know nor respect the Lord, we'll eventually take on their ways—and judgment!
>
> —PROVERBS 13:20, AUTHOR'S PARAPHRASE

Why this heavy warning about our close companions?

We are more impressionable than we think. As we rub shoulders regularly with our friends, their opinions, values, and habits rub off on us. Consciously or subconsciously we assess their behavior in various situations. Because we like them, we're inclined to approve most of their words and ways. As a result, when we experience similar situations, we catch ourselves thinking, speaking, or reacting as they have. Thus the importance of the close friends, confidants, and leaders we choose: they are influencers.

Daily our friends form us, mentors mold us, and teachers transform us—into the image of their values, beliefs, opinions, practices, and, yes, prejudices! Of course, we can freely choose to not imitate them, and often do. Nevertheless the underlying impulse to imitate is subtly present and stronger than we think. We may fancy ourselves as pure, unaffected originals, but the truth is there's a lot of "copy" in us too. This "formed by friendship" principle is universal.

We can take anyone, anywhere, anytime and link some part of their present condition to a friend's influence. The committed Christian disciple is such because he (or she) befriended another devout Christian years earlier. The stingy man was introduced to greed by an ungenerous Scrooge he once worked for. The generous Christian, conversely, learned liberality from a philanthropist in his church. The crack addict learned how to get high from a neighborhood friend. The scholar remembers the thoughtful teacher who inspired him to read, think, and write. The chronic complainer learned grumbling from his murmuring mother. And we could go on.

Recognizing this impressionable bent, Jehovah ordered the Israelites to live separately from the sinful Canaanites—and their noncompliance led straight to observation, imitation, judgment, and exile.

Continuing this call to godly separation, the New Testament orders us, "Be ye not unequally yoked together with unbelievers" (2 Cor. 6:14), and, "Have no fellowship with the unfruitful works of darkness" (Eph. 5:11). Repeatedly it asserts the contagiousness of sin: "Do not be misled: 'Bad company corrupts good character'" (1 Cor. 15:33, NIV). Dare we think we can circumvent this divine warning? It's time we realize that "chilling" with sinners will cool our devotion, not warm their cold hearts.

With equal earnestness God's Book calls us to seek the blessings and benefits of fellowship with good Christians. John urges his readers, "That ye also may have fellowship with us" (1 John 1:3). The Book of Hebrews calls us to increased association and conversation with spiritually minded believers: "Let us consider one another to provoke unto love and unto good works, not forsaking the assembling of ourselves together...but exhorting one another, and so much the more, as ye see the day approaching" (Heb. 10:24–25). Luke cited fellowship as one of the pillars of the early church: "They continued steadfastly in the apostle's doctrine and fellowship" (Acts 2:42). Jesus called the Twelve to "be with him" (Mark 3:14) in continuous friendship as well as study. He sent His disciples out "two by two" and later directed younger disciples like Timothy to accompany elders such as Paul so they could learn their "ways which are in Christ" (1 Cor. 4:17). Shouldn't we too "walk with" wise Christians until their ways are ours?

So choose your influencers well. Whatever your close friends and leaders are like—thoughtful or thoughtless, true or treacherous, committed or compromised—their "spirit" is increasingly resting on, infiltrating, and manifesting in you. Because Elisha accompanied, assisted, and humbly learned from Elijah, one day he became just like the great prophet. And the young ministers said of him, "The spirit of Elijah doth rest on Elisha" (2 Kings 2:15). Whose spirit is increasingly resting on you?

The answer is being determined daily by your response to this question: With whom are you walking?

Chapter 17

ARE YOU JUST "FOLLOWING JESUS"?

HEN JESUS CALLED Matthew, He said simply, "Follow me" (Matt. 9:9). That was all.

There was no enticing promise attached, no lofty revelation given, no grand prophecy uttered. Jesus just said, "Follow Me." He issued Philip the same quiet, unspectacular summons: "Jesus...findeth Philip, and saith...Follow me" (John 1:43).

By contrast, when Jesus called Peter, Andrew, James, and John, He attached a specific promise to motivate them: "Follow me, and I will make you fishers of men." So as they began their long trek to glory, they expected at some point to become "fishers of men." When Jesus called the rich young ruler, He promised him "treasure in heaven," though the young entrepreneur declined the offer. When Jesus called Saul of Tarsus, He set before him the hope of a great ministry: "I have appeared unto thee for this purpose, to make thee a minister and a witness...to open their [the Gentiles'] eyes, and to turn them from darkness to light" (Acts 26:16–18). Ananias surely added what Jesus told him, that Saul was a "chosen [divinely selected] vessel" to bear Christ's name before "kings" (Acts 9:15). Becoming fishers of men, rich men in heaven, enlighteners of Gentiles, emissaries to kings—my, those are compelling reasons to follow Jesus! But strangely, inexplicably, Matthew and Philip were promised nothing—nothing but Jesus! "Follow Me." "Follow" was Christ's command; "Me" was the sole object and reward of the following. Why this simple invitation?

No reason is given. Yet this is clearly the purest call Jesus issued. Paraphrasing, He said to Matthew:

> Matthew, just follow Me. From now on, I'll be what you seek. I'll be your focal point. I'll be the prime authority you respect, learn from, and obey. And, in the end, I'll be what you get—your richest eternal inheritance and greatest reward.
>
> —AUTHOR'S PARAPHRASE

39

That was enough for Matthew. He immediately "arose" (Matt. 9:9) and left his tax booth, lucrative income, comfortable home, rich friends, and familiar city. And he followed Jesus. And he did His will. And he hung on His words. And he believed and obeyed those words. And he inscribed them in his Gospel for us to ponder, practice, praise, and proliferate. This points to something else.

In a time when few could write, Matthew did so, and well! But becoming a renowned author, an inscriber of the inspired good news, wasn't part of the "deal" Jesus offered Matthew. That privilege and ministry came later and by Jesus' initiative, not Matthew's ambition. Initially Matthew was content to simply "follow Me."

Here's our challenge: Is Matthew's call enough for us? Are we "following" to have *Jesus* or something, anything else, even His clearly promised benefits, gifts, and blessings? Do we have any end in mind—financial prosperity, professional achievements, ministry success, fame, marriage, political office, and so forth—besides finding, following, and enjoying Jesus? It's very easy to serve Jesus with mixed motives. Frankly, we all do until God deals with us. The question then is, how are we responding to His dealings? With denial and resistance—and inward agitation? Or with honest confession and surrender of our secret selfishness—and fresh flowing inner peace and joy? Hannah faced this.

For years she followed her Savior to conceive her sons...and fretted when she couldn't! We do well to remember Elkanah's words to her: "Why is thy heart grieved?...Am not I better to thee than ten sons?" (1 Sam. 1:8). Envision Jesus asking, "Why are you restless and vexed, My disciple? Am I not enough to satisfy you? Must you have more? Won't you choose to be content—satisfied enough—with Me?" Hannah responded, delighting herself in her Savior (v. 18). And, delighted by her preference for Him, her Savior gave her not one but four sons, and among them a mighty prophet!

"Delight thyself also in the LORD, and he will give thee the desires of thine heart" (Ps. 37:4). Are you delighted or dutiful? Do you dutifully recite, "In thy presence is fullness of joy," yet live far from your profession? Or are you delighting in Jesus' fellowship so consistently that, whether He delivers or defers your heart's desires, you're joyful and at rest? It's "Hannah time"—time to learn (or relearn) to be content with *Jesus*, to find satisfaction in exploring His wondrous personality, enjoying the permeating peace of His presence, and enthusiastically pursuing your work with Him daily! That's the rich life: "Godliness with contentment is great gain" (1 Tim. 6:6). All others are "wretched, and miserable, and poor" (Rev. 3:17). It's also the purest life. Hannah, Matthew, and Philip found it. Have you?

Are you just following Jesus?

Chapter 18

THE SIMILITUDES ARE SPEAKING TO US

*I*N THE SIMILITUDES, Jesus used two great symbols to describe Christians and churches. Individually and corporately, we are the "salt of the earth" (Matt. 5:13) and the "light of the world" (v. 14). But not automatically.

To be spiritual salt and light in this corrupt and dark world, we must live right. With the Similitudes Jesus gave us two great commands. First, He charged us to maintain our "savor," or spiritual strength and purity (v. 13). We do so by staying spiritually edified daily and avoiding the corruptions of sin. Second, He told us to not repress but rather release His light: "Let your light so shine before men, that they may see your good works, and glorify your Father" (v. 16). We do this by walking in the light of God's Word (1 John 1:7), relating rightly and lovingly to others, and sharing the light of the Savior and His Word from every "lampstand," or ministry opportunity, God gives us.

If we do so, our presence and witness in this world, like salt, is an antiseptic. As bacteria cannot grow on salted meat, so wickedness cannot pervade a society when abiding, believing, obedient Christians are present. Also, like light, our presence and witness penetrate and dispel spiritual darkness, preventing heresies, false religions, and secularism from taking complete and unchallenged control. How is this?

Christ in us is the key. He is the essential and enduring Salt of the earth. Because His spiritually antiseptic life, grace, and truth are in us, we too are the salt of the earth. Also, He is the essential and enduring "light of the world" (John 8:12) and the bright, life-giving "Sun of righteousness" (Mal. 4:2), whose glorious dawn and rising open the Gospels. First, Matthew records the quiet dawning of the Sun: "Now the birth of Jesus Christ was in this way" (Matt. 1:18). Three chapters later he describes the full rising of His ministry with its healing light beams: "Leaving Nazareth, he [Jesus] came and dwelt in Capernaum…that it might be fulfilled which was spoken by Isaiah…the people who sat in darkness saw great light, and to them who sat in the region and shadow of death, light is sprung up" (Matt. 4:13–16).

It's only because the Son-light of Christ's Word, righteousness, and love are in us that we are the "light of the world." The body of Christ is therefore a temporary substitute for Christ in this sin-darkened world. While here bodily, He was the Salt that held sin in check and the Light that dispelled its darkness: "As long as I am in the world, I am the light of the world" (John 9:5). Since His ascension, His Spirit-filled body, the true or remnant church, has taken His place. There is no other salt and light. Prophetically, these facts are hugely significant.

They prove the Rapture of the true (or bride) church will, it must, occur *before* the Tribulation. Why? Daniel and Revelation concur that that seven-year period, especially its latter half, is one of total spiritual corruption and spiritual darkness—the world uniting to reject God's Son and persecute His remaining witnesses, while worshiping Satan's son (Antichrist) and believing his witness (false prophet)! And despite an awesome outpouring of divine punishment, the vast majority will persist in every conceivable sin and vice. John describes this: "The rest of the men who were not killed by these plagues yet repented not of the works of their hands, that they should not worship demons, and idols.... Neither repented they of their murders, nor of their sorceries, nor of their fornication, nor of their thefts" (Rev. 9:20–21). Such universal spiritual corruption cannot occur until the "salt of the earth" is removed. Such total darkness cannot pervade the world until its "light" is taken away. Therefore, the Similitudes are speaking to us. And loudly!

They are shouting from the housetops this encouraging report: "Let every truly Spirit-filled believer and church be reassured and comforted! As this world's salt and light, you must be removed before Antichrist's kingdom and sin's fullness can take over." Or, in Paul's words:

> And now ye know what restraineth that he [Antichrist] might be revealed in his time. For the mystery of iniquity [spirit of Antichrist] doth already work; only he who now hindereth [the Holy Spirit in the true church] will continue to hinder until he [and those he indwells] be taken out of the way [at the Rapture]. And then [with the Spirit and church gone] shall that wicked one [Antichrist] be revealed [released to rise and rule].
>
> —2 Thessalonians 2:6–8

Indeed, the Similitudes are speaking to us. Are you listening? Believing? Reassured?

Chapter 19

For What Do You "Hunger"?

ATTHEW 12 DISCLOSES a stunning fact. One Sabbath day while Jesus and His disciples were traveling to their next ministry stop, "his disciples were hungry" (Matt. 12:1).

Yes, driven by physical hunger, the Twelve "began to pluck the ears [heads] of grain" and, after rubbing them to separate kernels and chaff, proceeded "to eat" (v. 1). What a shock! Jesus actually let His disciples—yes, His very handpicked apostles—go hungry one day! (If they had food, why did they resort to eating raw wheat?)

But their privation didn't last long. In His unfailing faithfulness, the Good Shepherd graciously provided His sheep with this high-fiber, "whole-grain" snack to keep them until they could recline at the table for a more nourishing meal—though for even this kindness His enemies accused Him of Sabbath-breaking! (v. 2). But the question remains: Why did the heavenly Father permit His Son and His followers to temporarily hunger?

It enabled Jesus, who by baptism had already identified with mankind's sinfulness, to also identify in a very personal way with our most basic and universal form of suffering: hunger! He and His students didn't just study or witness hunger pangs; they *experienced* them, albeit briefly. Afterward Jesus manifested acute compassion for Earth's malnourished masses: "I have compassion on the multitude, because they continue with me now three days, and have nothing to eat" (Matt. 15:32). Thus, this incident helped move Him to feed the poor more earnestly, and twice miraculously. It also moved His followers to commit themselves to "feed" His sheep—spiritually and literally. Why? They remembered the pangs they felt when "his disciples were hungry." We're His disciples too. For what do we hunger?

Figuratively, "hunger" speaks of *unsatisfied desire*. Human and earthy, we naturally hunger for many worldly things. Many believers hunger for vocational or professional success, income, possessions, property, pleasures, friends, spouses, or children. Many churches hunger for more members, buildings, programs, funding, political influence, or community respect. Many ministers hunger for visible church growth, educational distinctions, or ecclesiastical recognition. These human hungers are perfectly understandable, but if we only crave these temporal, worldly things, and not the eternal things of God's kingdom, we are shortsighted, or spiritually "blind" (Rev. 3:17). In His wondrously wide goodness, our Father often satisfies our human hungers: "Thou openest thine hand, and satisfiest the desire of every living thing" (Ps. 145:16). But He hopes we'll identify with His hunger. Jesus did.

One morning as Jesus left Bethany, "he was hungry" (Mark 11:12)—not only for figs but also for fulfillment; not just to fill His stomach but also to satisfy His Father's heart. A consummately hungry man, Jesus was starving to end His Father's hunger, or unsatisfied will: "My food [the satisfaction of my hunger] is to do the will of him that sent me, and to finish his work" (John 4:34). He still shares the Father's unsatisfied desires, such as redeeming the lost, raising up the redeemed, receiving their true worship, relieving the oppressed, revealing His glory, spreading His Word, releasing more of His Spirit, transforming and translating His church, and, later, establishing His eternal kingdom in this world. For these things Jesus hungers—and searches.

He's looking for Christians who will identify with His hunger as He identified with His Father's. True disciples will embrace and labor for heaven's unsatisfied desires: "Blessed are they who do hunger and thirst after righteousness..." (Matt. 5:6). One day they'll be deeply satisfied: "...for they shall be filled."

But today, they hunger. By their devotion, prayers, studies, sermons, counsels, labors, donations, helps, and other works, they crave and pursue the yearnings of God's own heart.

For instance, to:

- Let the Spirit develop Christ's graces and character in them
- Fulfill their calling
- See people from all nations, races, and cultures come to Christ
- Participate in a revival that doesn't turn aside or stop short of God's goals
- See demonstrations of Christlike faith, love, and power
- Observe churches learning and living all God's truth rightly divided

- Witness the fulfillment of Jesus' high priestly prayer (John 17), and Paul's descriptions of the church as a purified bride (Eph. 5:25–27), a mature man (Eph. 4:14–16), and a God-indwelt corporate human temple (Eph. 2:19–22)

- See the Bridegroom appear and catch away His people

In His presence, and forever "with the Lord" (1 Thess. 4:17), we shall "hunger no more" (Rev. 7:16).

But in this world we hunger—and hope, knowing if we'll crave not our desires but God's, one day He'll deeply comfort us: "Blessed are ye that hunger now, for ye shall be filled" (Luke 6:21).

For what do you hunger?

Chapter 20

WHAT'S IT ALL ABOUT, JESUS?

*I*N ALL OUR earnest Christian endeavors—praying, fasting, sacrificing, studying, working, testifying, giving, planning, teaching, counseling, worshiping, missionary work—we rarely stop to ask, "What's it all about, Jesus?"

Fast and furious, the merry-go-round of church or ministry activities is hard to stop long enough to clear our heads. It's time we shut down the religious carnival, at least temporarily, to get our spiritual bearings and compare our present course with that set in the New Testament. Here's your "sextant," or, if you prefer, your GPS receiver: Ask yourself: Why are we here? What's the highest, truest goal we should aim for as Christians and churches? The apostle Paul knew and focused on this divinely set "mark." "I press toward the mark [goal] for the prize of the high calling of God in Christ Jesus" (Phil. 3:14). To have his focus, we must first know what is *not* our goal in this Church Age.

From Pentecost to the Rapture, it's not about moneymaking, image-building, materialism, fame, or worldly achievements. We may safely write off all these things as the distracting desires of our natural hearts. Gaining or losing them has nothing to do with Christian success.

It's not about political power. For centuries the Roman church chased this mirage only to discover after many futile wars, inquisitions, and crusades it wasn't God's will. Today many earnest evangelicals are consumed with politics. We must wake up and realize our primary calling is prophetic, not political: "Blessed are ye, when men shall revile you, and persecute you...for so persecuted they the prophets who were before you" (Matt. 5:11–12).

Nor is it about constructing a theocratic kingdom for Jesus in America or any other nation. Jesus never attempted or ordered nation building in these "times of the Gentiles" (Luke 21:24). To the contrary He plainly said, "The [political] kingdom of God cometh *not* with [outward] observation [now]" (Luke 17:20); and "My kingdom is *not* of this [present] world [order]...now is my kingdom *not* from here" (John 18:36). What part of "not" do we fail to comprehend? He further taught that the worldwide body of Christians, not any nation or empire, is His present "kingdom" (sphere of

Besides these emphatic declarations, Jesus' endless deeds of service to His Father prove that sonship and servantship are not mutually exclusive. They may and should coexist in us as they did in Jesus, the first and greatest servant-son of this Christian Age. Jesus gave us another example.

In His parable of the prodigal son (Luke 15:11–32), Jesus described two classes of servants serving on a family estate, "hired" (v. 17) and family servants. The latter is represented by the "elder son" who, though a son, is found working "in the field" (v. 25) and tells his father, "Lo, these many years do I serve thee" (v. 29). (This implies the younger son was also a family servant before leaving.) Once humbled, the formerly wayward younger son offered to exchange his status as a family servant for the lower position of "hired servant" (v. 19) if only his father would receive him back. So both sons, who represent Christians, were also servants. Do we know the characteristics of God's servants?

A servant of God is sent by God, not himself, and serves not his but his Lord's initiatives. Completely dedicated to his calling, he avoids all distractions and hindrances. He follows not the peoples' voices but the Spirit's voice. He seeks only the approval of his Lord, not men, and accepts patiently the latter's periodic rejections. No hireling, he does God's will heartily, whether highly or hardly paid. Not self-indulgent, he's prepared to suffer inconvenience, discomfort, or pain, if necessary, to fulfill his mission. He ministers the whole counsel of God's Word, not just popular truths. Aware his orders may change, he waits in his Lord's presence daily for renewed or new instructions. Attuned by this immersion in God's presence, he detects His voice distinctly. Alert, he responds promptly. Adaptable, he easily abandons his plans and embraces God's. These are the distinctive traits of God's servants. And their benefits?

God reserves His best blessings for His servant-sons. He chooses them for special service: "He chose David his servant...to feed...his people" (Ps. 78:70–71). He gives them exceptional understanding and wisdom: "Give...thy servant an understanding heart....Lo, I have given thee a wise and an understanding heart" (1 Kings 3:9, 12). He gives them special insight into His Word and character: "Speak, for thy servant [Samuel] heareth....The LORD revealed himself to Samuel...by the word of the LORD" (1 Sam. 3:10, 21). He anoints them heavily with His Spirit: "Behold my servant...I have put my Spirit upon him" (Isa. 42:1). He delights in them with a special love: "Behold my servant...in whom my soul delighteth" (v. 1). He defends them before their critics: "Wherefore...were ye not afraid to speak against my servant,

Moses?" (Num. 12:8). He delivers them from every trial: "Thy God, whom thou servest continually, he will deliver thee" (Dan. 6:16). They will receive His highest honor, His regal name, or divine monogram, inscribed upon them: "His name shall be in their [his servants'] foreheads" (Rev. 22:4). Best of all, He has reserved them a special place, especially near Him, in New Jerusalem: "His servants shall serve him; and they shall see his face" (vv. 3–4). Is any existence more enviable than this in time or eternity?

With Christ's words, example, and parables before us, as well as the characteristics and benefits of God's servants, isn't it time for a change? Isn't it time for us to become serious about servantship?

Chapter 22

DON'T REMIND HIM OF THE DEVIL!

ROVERBS 14:3 WARNS, "In the mouth of the foolish is a rod of pride, but the lips of the wise shall preserve them." Or, "A fool's talk brings a rod to his back, but the lips of the wise protect them" (NIV). Paraphrasing, this says:

> The boastful, arrogant, defiant, or rude words of proud, self-confident fools call for a "rod of pride" [a beating or whipping caused by pride], but no such punishment befalls God-fearing souls who speak humbly.
>
> —AUTHOR'S PARAPHRASE

The theme of this wisdom saying is *proud versus humble speech*. Jesus taught, "Those things which proceed out of the mouth come forth from the heart [mind]" (Matt. 15:18). So inflated words invariably arise from proud thoughts incubating in conceited hearts; wise, humble words spring from modest thoughts gestating in meek hearts. Scriptural history confirms both Christ's comment and Proverbs 14:3.

Nabal, Pharaoh, and King Nebuchadnezzar lived relatively calm lives until they thought, meditated, and spoke proudly against God and His people. Nabal haughtily maligned David—God's submissive, worthy servant and anointed king—as a rebellious, worthless servant and anarchist: "Who is David?...There are many servants nowadays who break away, every man from his master" (1 Sam. 25:10). When God righteously demanded, "Let my people go," Pharaoh spoke with rude defiance: "Who is the LORD, that I should obey his voice...I know not the LORD, neither will I let Israel go" (Exod. 5:1–2). Antiquity's proudest, Nebuchadnezzar spouted arrogantly against heaven not once but twice. When three Jewish youths refused to worship his idol for loyalty to their God, he spewed, "Who is that God, that shall deliver you out of my hands?" (Dan. 3:15). Later the self-centered sovereign took full credit for the kingdom God graciously gave him: "Is not this great Babylon, that I have built...by...my power...for the honor of my majesty?" (Dan. 4:30). And heaven heard them all.

Soon God's rod of discipline visited—with death strokes, military defeats, public humiliations, and loss of mental soundness—and remained, until their thoughts, minds, and words were humble again. All three discovered the great lesson Nebuchadnezzar stated for posterity: "Those that walk in pride he [God] is able to abase" (Dan. 4:37). Christ warned, "Whosoever shall exalt himself shall be abased" (Matt. 23:12) on not one but three occasions (Luke 14:11; 18:14). But it's not so with the humble.

Notably, no such "rod" fell upon Abigail or Daniel. Their consistently humble thoughts and words kept them from discipline. While Abigail's husband puffed arrogantly at God's anointed, she humbly prostrated herself at his feet: "Let thine handmaid be a servant to wash the feet of the servants of my lord" (1 Sam. 25:41). When Daniel could have taken credit for interpreting Nebuchadnezzar's dream, he meekly deferred the glory to God's wisdom and goodness: "There is a God in heaven who revealeth secrets. . . . This secret is not revealed to me for any wisdom that I have more than any living, but for their sakes . . . and that thou mightiest know" (Dan. 2:28–30). This shouldn't surprise us if we're becoming intimate with God.

Proverbs reveals, and all Scripture confirms, that, of all sins, God hates pride the worst: "These six things doth the LORD hate; yea, seven are an abomination unto him: *a proud look . . .*" (Prov. 6:16–17). Of all pride, God detests religious pride the most! All religious self-exaltation reminds Him most poignantly of His age-old, sanctimonious enemy, the devil. Isaiah 14, Ezekiel 28, and Genesis 3 reveal that he (Lucifer) harbored proud thoughts over his great wisdom, beauty, musical skill, and divine favor until, his heart filled, he spouted proud words of envious ambition, rebellion, and slander against God. The "rod" of expulsion fell swiftly!

Conversely, all genuine humility reminds the Father of Jesus, the meekest man to ever live and speak. He professed His humility: "I am meek and lowly in heart" (Matt. 11:29). And He possessed it, humbling Himself to become "obedient unto death, even the [lowly, shameful] death of the cross" (Phil. 2:8) to satisfy His Father's heart and save us. Jesus' words consistently reveal sober-minded thinking and meek, complete dependence on His Father: "I can of mine own self do nothing" (John 5:30), "but as my Father hath taught me, I speak" (John 8:28). And He's our Teacher.

Are we following His humble example? Casting down "every high thing" in our minds? Speaking meekly? If we think and speak proudly—with superiority, scorn, condemnation, prejudice, unforgiveness, or self-aggrandizement—we remind our heavenly Father of Lucifer and reap the rod. If humbly, He hears His Son in us and blesses us. So watch how you think and speak.

Don't remind Him of the devil!

Chapter 23

BE A COVENANTAL CHRISTIAN!

"E ARE THE salt of the earth," said Christ to every Christian (Matt. 5:13). This mountainous metaphor suggests many parallel truths. One clearly points to covenant making.

Present at every Middle Eastern covenant meal, salt was an indispensable part of ancient covenant making. The Arab expression, "There is salt between us," most often meant, "There is a covenant between us." The biblical expression a "covenant of salt" (2 Chron. 13:5) refers to a covenant as strong and enduring as salt. This speaks of an unchangeable, permanent agreement.

Like their mineral namesake, salty Christians voluntarily live by and remain faithful to solemn agreements and unbreakable vows made before God and man. They are consistently covenantal.

Before God, they live by the terms of the new covenant, the solemn saving and living arrangement God conceived and offered us through Christ's substitutionary sacrifice. Their covenant meal is the Lord's Supper. Every Christian who receives of the cup and the bread may say to the heavenly Father, "There is salt between us—a solemn agreement consisting of firm vows and sure promises," and then joyfully and devotedly live by the terms of that new covenant.

Before men, salty Christians gladly keep faith by honoring the terms of all their human covenants. If married, they live faithfully—lovingly, devotedly, and responsibly—with their spouses: "Let not the wife depart from her husband...let not the husband put away his wife" (1 Cor. 7:10–11). In their business affairs, they conscientiously observe the terms of their written and oral agreements, "heartily, as to the Lord, and not unto men" (Col. 3:23). In financial matters, they only make commitments they can honor and diligently honor every commitment they make, "owe[ing] no man any thing" rightfully due him (Rom. 13:8). As citizens, they obey the "covenants" of their nations, provinces, and cities, that is, their constitutions, laws, regulations, and court orders, obeying "every ordinance of man for the Lord's sake" (1 Pet. 2:13). As tradesmen or professionals, they willingly observe the codes and ethics of their trade or profession, "walk[ing] honestly toward them that are without [outside finished in spiritual growth and training. Such a heart will always be safe and at peace in God, even in crises.

This describes Christlike Christians, committed disciples whose hearts are redeemed, spiritually mature, and blameless. After their conversion, God steadily cleanses, reforms, and enlarges their hearts through steady devotion, teaching, counseling, and testing. In time they become "perfect," or spiritually mature: fully conformed to the image of history's greatest great heart—Christ! They live in blameless integrity by humbly examining themselves daily, quickly confessing and forsaking all sins. Let's get more specific.

Not trusting their own righteousness, great hearts receive Christ's righteousness by faith in His substitutionary death and resurrection. Like Asa, they "rely on the LORD" (2 Chron. 16:8) in every difficulty, trusting fully in His wisdom, power, and faithfulness. Sober-minded, they think humbly—not too highly of themselves, too little of God, or too lowly of others. Childlike in simplicity, they don't desire worldly sophistication, yet love and pursue excellence. God-fearing, they respectfully obey God's Word and guidance and are not consistently wayward or rebellious. Meek toward God, they're easily bent to His will. Loving integrity, their honest confessions and right choices free them from immorality, dishonesty, and hypocrisy. Fervent, they glow with Spirit-controlled, steady zeal for God and are rarely overheated, cold, or lukewarm. Focused on kingdom plans, they don't live for selfish ends. Faithful in duties, they don't ignore responsibilities or stop short in their work. Loyal to Jesus, love binds them to Him and His people—sacred ties they'll suffer for but never abandon. These great traits fill great hearts—hearts that are "perfect toward him." Ours can be one. How can we be sure?

The greatest great heart—Christ—is in us: "This mystery among the Gentiles, which is Christ in you, the hope of glory" (Col. 1:27). Our simple, consistent trust and obedience to God will release a growing manifestation of Christ's great heart in our lives. Our heavenly Father is yearning for this manifestation. His eyes are "flashing" and "searching back and forth" daily throughout every continent, nation, city, and church to discover great hearts. He wants to "display His strength" and "show His great power" on our behalf—breaking or softening adamant enemies, opening ways of escape where none exist, answering long-delayed prayers, converting hopelessly sinful "Ninevehs," raising churches and ministers long dead in unbelief and despair. Need this great help?

Be a great heart. By steady trust and obedience in every trial and triumph, release Christ in you and grow His great traits, practicing humility, reliance, integrity, fervor, focus, and loyalty. Then be confident His help awaits.

Give a great shout—"The LORD hath done great things for us, whereof we are glad!" (Ps. 126:3)—joyfully anticipating your great help for great hearts!

Chapter 25

HE WANTS US MERCIFUL

*I*N MATTHEW 12:1–14, Christ's shining mercy is set in sharp contrast to the Pharisees' dark meanness.

Matthew says that due to sheer hunger Jesus' disciples gleaned and ate some handfuls of wheat one Sabbath. Mercifully, Christ didn't object, since they weren't reaping the whole field but were just meeting their urgent bodily needs. But the Pharisees didn't see it that way. Mean-spirited, they instantly misjudged and condemned the disciples, and their lenient Master, for "harvesting" on the Sabbath.

Later that day a man with a paralyzed hand attended Jesus' meeting in the local synagogue. Sensing Jesus would heal him, the Pharisees asked Jesus if healing on the Sabbath was lawful, hoping for evidence to accuse Him of acting and teaching against Mosaic Law. Mercifully, Jesus healed the man. And, unmercifully, the Pharisees misjudged Him.

Yet Jesus graciously and patiently instructed His icy inquisitors in both instances, hoping to yet thaw their frozen love. Defending His disciples, Jesus reminded His biblically expert antagonists that David also technically broke the law when he fed his men priestly showbread as they fled from Saul. But since they were starving, God kindly excused them. Defending His Sabbath healing, Jesus claimed even Pharisees would promptly remove their animals from ditches or pits on the Sabbath to prevent their suffering. So surely He should help this man out of his "pit" of paralysis on the Sabbath. Thus He rested His case.

In His closing statement, our Advocate echoed God's call through Hosea for His people to have mercy: "I will have mercy, and not sacrifice" (Matt. 12:7). In other words:

> I want you to have and show mercy for the needy more than I
> want your sacrifices.
>
> —MATTHEW 12:7, AUTHOR'S PARAPHRASE

Here was the heart of the issue—and a cure for the Pharisees' sick hearts. If they had been willing to show mercy, Jesus concluded, they would not have "condemned the innocent" acts He and His disciples committed.

His message was not well received: "Then the Pharisees went out, and held a council against him, how they might destroy him" (v. 14). But we can receive it.

Through His Son's Hosea quotation, the heavenly Father is saying He wants not just the Pharisees but also us to be merciful. Why? There are at least five scriptural reasons.

First, mercy makes us like our heavenly Father. Jesus charged, "Be ye, therefore, merciful," then added, "as your Father also is merciful" (Luke 6:36). He also suggested ways we may exercise and grow mercy in our hearts: dealing generously with our personal enemies (v. 35); not misjudging, or judging people's actions prematurely, unfairly, or harshly (v. 37); not condemning, or rejecting as worthless and hopeless those who clearly sin or repeatedly fail (v. 37); forgiving people who offend, wrong, or reject us, releasing all anger and desire for redress (v. 37); and by giving, sharing money, materials, time, and other things with those in need (v. 38).

Second, mercy conforms us to Jesus' image (Rom. 8:29). This makes us His soul mates, or members in His bride church, and assures us we'll be taken in the Rapture.

Third, mercy pleases the Father's merciful heart. Pleased, He more readily and fully answers our prayers—and subdues our enemies: "When a man's ways please the LORD, he maketh even his enemies be at peace with him" (Prov. 16:7).

Fourth, giving mercy ensures we'll receive it. God's unchanging promise is, "With the merciful, thou wilt show thyself merciful" (Ps. 18:25). So if we're stubbornly unmerciful, though He wants to show us mercy, He can't. The Jews' persistent unmercifulness in persecuting Jesus and His church rendered them undeliverable when the Romans invaded Palestine in A.D. 70 to put down their rebellion. Honoring His Word, God abandoned those who abandoned mercy.

Fifth, mercy enables God to demonstrate His mercy through us. This in turn draws others to believe, love, and serve Him. It's a great day when we realize that "the goodness of God" through us "leadeth...to repentance" (Rom. 2:4). This shouldn't surprise us. It was the mercy, not the meanness, of one or more believers—in unrelenting intercession, patient sharing of the Word, frequent forgiveness, gentle forbearance, and so forth—that led us to repent and believe on Jesus. His mercy through us will do the same for even the most persistently sinful or troubled souls. Instead of seeing more of the dark meanness of this world, they will see in our lives the bright mercies of the Son.

So, "Be ye, therefore, merciful." As your dark indifference fades, the Son's mercies will rise and shine through you, illuminating for many the Father's will: He wants us merciful!

Chapter 26

HAVE YOU EXCHANGED YOUR STRENGTH?

*J*SAIAH 40:27–31 CONTAINS a message of hope and renewal for weary Christians. Isaiah's exhortation begins by describing Judah's righteous remnant in the monarchy's last days.

As the final years of Judah's apostasy wore on, the faith of many godly Jews grew utterly discouraged and exhausted as they watched their nation slip further and further into the deadly quicksand of sin and injustice. Prayer, fasting, protests—all seemed powerless to halt the downward spiral of idolatry and other infidelity to God and His law. And God's strange, long inaction heaped additional weights of doubt and despair on His faithful ones, leaving them weak with hopelessness. All evidence dictated that God had forgotten them and that their cause—restoring Judah to righteousness—was irretrievably lost. Weary in faith and frame, they cried, "My way is hidden from the LORD, and the justice due to me is passed away from my God" (v. 27). But Isaiah had a word for his discouraged brethren.

He reminded them that God, who created everything, still retains all knowledge and creative power and never becomes discouraged, tired, or faint: "Hast thou not known…[or] heard, that the everlasting God…the Creator of the ends of the earth, fainteth not, neither is weary?" (v. 28). The contrast was obvious: their strength can be depleted, but God's cannot! Not even a little. He's like a rock! What does this mean to Christians today?

Like the weary Judeans' spiritual strength, ours is exhaustible—but not God's. His is unflagging! And consummately compassionate, He stands willing and ready to impart His unfailing strength to every weary believer every wearisome day: "He giveth power to the faint; and to those who have no might he increaseth strength" (v. 29). Isaiah insists we receive these fresh impartations of strength since we all—even our strongest, the "young men"— at times grow weary with the injustices, difficulties, delays, and labors that try us and find ourselves ready to fall and fail: "Even the youths shall faint and be weary, and the young [strong] men shall utterly fall" (v. 30). Human strength, however great, remains exhaustible and thus sure to eventually fail under the rigors of prolonged heavy divine testing—unless we learn how to restore our depleted strength regularly. How do we do this?

Isaiah recommends we "wait upon the LORD" (v. 31). That is, we sit alone in His presence daily, preferably "early" (Prov. 8:17), confessing any sins and forgiving others, reading or studying His Word, praying, and worshiping Him with words of thanksgiving and songs of adoration. Sometimes we pour out our troubles before Him. At other times we sit still in submissive, silent awe. Then a heavenly wonder occurs: God's Spirit supernaturally permeates and ministers life to our spirit. Thus He refills His exhausted servant with His inexhaustible strength: "But they that wait upon the LORD shall renew ["change and renew," AMP] their strength" (Isa. 40:31). This supernatural *exchange* takes place "early" and whenever else we "wait" upon God. Thus we replace our insufficient human energy with God's all-sufficient power. Then we rise.

"They shall mount up with wings like eagles" (v. 31). As eagles "mount up" on warm air currents and glide easily above the countryside, powered not by the strength of their flesh but by the power of God's wind, so we rise and fly through the day, not by our energy but by the Spirit's strength. This happens daily—if our "waiting" is habitual.

In this "Laodicean" period, we must form the habit of waiting in God's presence daily. If we do so, despite the growing apostasy of our times, our personal walk and work will thrive. We'll no longer be easily discouraged or exhausted: "They shall run, and not be weary... walk, and not faint" (v. 31). Our new habit will release an ongoing miracle.

By receiving God's strength daily, we become like Him: inexhaustible! We now "run" through very active days of work or ministry and "walk" through long, dark trials of faith and endurance, without falling, because we find new strength and confidence every morning. Eventually, the wonder of it all dawns on us. Our days of discouragement are gone. Our hours wasted in anxiety are no more. Our weary weeks of doubt are passed. Our despair-induced panic attacks are history. Instead, our confidence in God is now steady and sure, a stable foundation for our work or ministry and an excellent life-witness for others. Why? We're drawing from a new Source daily—the ultimate Supplier of renewable energy!—who never fails: "I will never leave thee, nor forsake thee" (Heb. 13:5).

Have you exchanged your strength for His?

Chapter 27

BE HIS DELIGHTED DOORKEEPER!

*I*N PSALM 84, the psalmist proclaims, "I had rather be a doorkeeper [gatekeeper] in the house of my God than to dwell in the tents of wickedness" (v. 10). Clearly, he was content—sufficiently satisfied— to keep the gates of God's temple.

These "doorkeepers," also known as "porters," guarded, opened, and closed the gates to the temple courts daily. Usually Levites, these who "stood at the threshold" protected the courts from unauthorized entry and sometimes collected the people's tithes. While serving God in any capacity was an honor, gatekeepers held a rather humble position compared with other servants of God. They had very humble company: beggars also stood at the threshold of the temple courts! (Acts 3:2). There were other humbling factors.

When the Jews thronged the temple, they didn't come to see gatekeepers. They looked right past them, eager to catch a glimpse of the temple's splendid features: its gilded exterior, majestic steps, mighty pillars, beautiful doors, bronze laver or altar, porches, marble colonnades, and walls. Or they hoped to catch a glimpse of exciting things, such as:

- Israel's famous personalities (kings, princes, councilors) coming to worship
- The splendidly clad high priest
- A priest coming to or from ministering incense
- The Levites singing praises or helping the priests prepare offerings
- A prominent rabbi (Gamaliel, Nicodemus) sitting in Solomon's porch teaching God's law
- A prophet delivering inspired messages to God's people

Expectations such as these surely filled the people's minds as they entered the temple gates—and passed by the doorkeepers without a glance, greeting, or thought. Despite such inattention, our psalmist was a happy gatekeeper: "I had rather be a doorkeeper..." Why?

65

That was the duty, gifting, and place God chose for him. Whether others noticed or neglected, he knew God's eyes were watching. To Him alone he would one day give account for his gate keeping: Was he faithful, content, even joyful in the "day of small things"? Or did he despise and neglect his little-appreciated vocation? Wisely, the psalmist realized God would give him an eternal reward if he willingly and faithfully fulfilled his temporal ministry. He was so convinced he uttered our text, which seems to say:

> I would rather have the simplest, humblest duty in God's will
> than the most desirable or distinguished position outside it.
>
> —AUTHOR'S PARAPHRASE

Thus with the sword of happy submission to God's will he slew one of life's most vexing Goliaths, the ambitious discontent of pride. Like this psalmist, are you just a "doorkeeper"?

So am I. And so is every other Christian disciple and minister from the least to the best known. The only exceptionally notable person in God's current temple (the church) is *Jesus*, and the sooner we embrace this revelation the better. Why? Our heavenly Father has decreed, "No flesh should glory in his presence" (1 Cor. 1:29). So any prophet, preacher, or parishioner who thinks he is, or will become, the center of attention in God's temple is headed for a rude awakening. But the key question remains: Will we be content? Paul was: "I have learned, in whatever state I am, in this to be content" (Phil. 4:11). His teaching opens the door to our freedom.

By inspiration Paul taught, "Whatever ye do, do it heartily, as to the Lord, not unto men" (Col. 3:23). Are we "heartily" or hardly attending our "door," or the humble, unnoticed, thankless duty God has given us—hidden away in an office; riveted to an assembly line; saddled on a delivery truck; lashed to a desk with mountainous paperwork; fenced in on the farm or ranch; stuck on a struggling sales team; bound as a clerk in a store; besieged by babies, diapers, and milk; called to render "helps" to obscure ministries; planted in the pastorate of a small congregation? Whatever our "door," we must avoid entrapment by the father of prideful lies. He constantly tells us that if we only had a higher-profile, better-paying, more-appreciated, frontline position, we would be blissfully satisfied and want no more. What a lie! The truth is, if we won't be content with "whatever" God gives, we won't be content wherever we go. At this moment there's no place on earth where you can please, honor, and bear fruit unto God more than the place He has put you in. So don't leave your "gate."

Love it! And keep it, not with discontent but with delight: "I delight to do thy will, O my God" (Ps. 40:8). Others may not care, but the most important One in the temple is closely watching you and your "door." Be His delighted doorkeeper!

Chapter 28

WANT TO BE RICH?

F ROM TIME IMMEMORIAL people have rushed about daily buying, selling, and stealing to get "rich," or laden with surplus monies and materials. But there's another way to wealth.

King Solomon, the richest man of his day, declared that when God blesses His people, He makes them "rich." "The blessing of the LORD, it maketh rich, and he addeth no sorrow with it" (Prov. 10:22). The Hebrew word translated "rich" (*ashar*) means "to accumulate." Solomon asserts God gives this accumulation without excessive distress: "He addeth no sorrow with it." Thus he draws a contrast.

When worldly people acquire riches, their fortunes often come with much "sorrow"—excessive toil, broken relationships, anxieties, conflicts, and sometimes the guilt or legal consequences of wrongdoing. But when God makes someone materially rich, he or she is not burdened with this heavy and harmful baggage. God's riches are given by His grace and our just labors: "A faithful man shall abound with blessings" (Prov. 28:20).

While the Bible, especially the Old Testament, shows God enriching His people with worldly goods, it also persistently points us to higher ground. Here's another perspective on Proverbs 10:22: "The blessing of the Lord, *it* makes rich." Or, "The blessing of the LORD makes a person rich" (NLT). Or:

> To be "blessed"—lovingly granted insights, favors, and privileges—by the Lord [of all creation] is to be truly "rich," living the most valuable, noble, secure, serene, and enviable life possible.
>
> —AUTHOR'S PARAPHRASE

Indeed, to have God's loving approval and blessing on one's soul makes one truly, eternally wealthy, the enviable owner of a rich relationship, rare peace, and gratifying sense of fulfillment money can't buy, people can't steal, and time can't erode. This "accumulation" we should seek; without it we're poor no matter how many monies and things we own.

Jesus confirms this figurative interpretation of "rich" in His messages to the churches of Asia Minor. He described the Laodicean Christians, who were very wealthy in worldly terms, as being "poor." "Thou art…poor" (Rev. 3:17). Yet He said the Smyrnan believers, who were materially destitute and suffering intense persecution, were "rich." "I know thy…poverty (but thou art rich)" (Rev. 2:9). Why did He call these rich Christians "poor" and their poor brothers "rich"?

Being eternally rich, Jesus knew true riches. In His lifetime, Jesus persistently sought, acquired, and accumulated true riches. His treasure chest had fabulous wealth in it, spiritual jewels and heavenly valuables still available to us today:

- A God-fearing, humble heart
- Growing accurate knowledge of God's character, ways, and judgments
- Tested, proven faith in God's unfailing faithfulness
- Favor with God and favors from Him, such as answered prayers
- Ultimate security: the peace of God that passes human understanding
- The rapturous, blissful pleasure of sweet fellowship in God's presence
- Discernment of Satan's temptations, deceptions, and distractions
- The ability to hear the Holy Spirit's voice
- God's loving, wise guidance, corrections, and warnings
- Penetrating insight into the inner meaning of God's Word
- Clear understanding of God's plan for His people, one's own life, and one's times
- Growing wisdom, or the ability to make excellent decisions in the rapidly changing, confusing situations of life
- Loving friendship with other "rich" believers

Whenever bestowed, the true "blessing of the Lord" makes believers "rich" in these rare and invisible yet invaluable treasures. They are true riches.

Whenever God blessed men with vast worldly wealth in the Old Testament (Abraham, Isaac, Job), He always undertook to also make them spiritually rich. How did He accomplish this seemingly impossible task of making men materially and spiritually rich? He tested them over every material possession (and relationship) they had! Test by test, choice by choice, sacrifice by sacrifice, they proved to Him in real-life situations that, unlike the rich young ruler of Jesus' day, they put their quest to know Him and have eternal riches first. Consequently, in their fiery trials God opened their eyes to see what real riches were. Thereafter they never idolized or clamored for material wealth, though God delighted to give them "richly all things to enjoy" (1 Tim. 6:17). They coveted only eternal valuables—closeness to God and His spiritual riches—and let their worldly riches come or go as God pleased. You can be as rich as they were.

Just consistently put pleasing Jesus first in every decision and covet "the blessing of the Lord" above the things of this world. Jesus wants you rich! "I counsel thee to buy of me gold tried in the fire, that thou mayest be rich" (Rev. 3:18). Will you please Him?

Want to be rich?

Chapter 29

THE MIGHTY MUSTARD SEED

J ESUS' PARABLE OF the mustard seed describes something very minute becoming very mighty. Matthew recalls it:

> The kingdom of heaven is like a grain of mustard seed, which a man took, and sowed in his field; which, indeed, is the least of all seeds; but when it is grown, it is the greatest among herbs, and becometh a tree, so that the birds of the air come and lodge in the branches of it.
>
> —MATTHEW 13:31–32

Given good conditions, the Palestinian mustard seed develops into a large garden plant, actually a tree twelve to fifteen feet tall![1] Its branches reach out ministerially, providing nesting and perching places to birds and shade to animals and people. The tree's leaves and seeds also minister. Its leaves are cooked and eaten as greens, and when its seeds are ground to powder, they are used in seasoning and medicine.[2] Summing up, the mustard tree provides refuge, shade, nourishment, delight, and healing. What a transformation!

The mustard seed was small, but now it's large. It was lifeless, but now it's alive and growing. It was useless, but now it's useful. It was unimportant, but now it's important. It appeared to hold no promise, but now it's fulfilling its potential. Bestowing many benefits on many beneficiaries, it's the "greatest" tree in God's garden (Matt. 13:32). Why did Jesus say God's kingdom is "like" this mustard seed?

It parallels the growth of the kingdom's present form, the church. The Book of Acts and church history show the church becoming the greatest "tree of righteousness" in the garden of religion, more influential than any other "herb," or religious belief system, if not in the view of today's highly secularized world or our increasingly pluralistic society, then certainly in heaven's view—the perspective from which Jesus' parables spring.

Initially the ecclesia was minute among the world's mighty faiths and philosophies. Its Founder, a maligned, obscure Jewish prophet and convicted insurrectionist, had been slain, and, despite rumors of His resurrection, His surviving student-followers—a mere 120 hidden away in an upper room—had no prospects for growth. Then suddenly something supernatural happened.

God's Spirit filled them with His power, and they began growing—explosively! Like a mustard seed, the tiny group rapidly grew large. In just days its congregation increased to thousands; within weeks, to tens of thousands. It put out great "branches," or evangelistic or charitable outreaches through new churches, ministries, and ministers. Its apostles, prophets, evangelists, pastors, teachers, and other members touched the whole Mediterranean world within a century.

Down the centuries, this church tree grew human and organizational "branches"—missionaries, monasteries, monks, scholars, and writers—whose influence reached even further. Spreading good news, works, and prayers, they saved souls, preserved literature and knowledge, and built the core of Western culture.

Since the Reformation, more "branches"—translators, reformers, revivalists, educators, and charities—have blessed countless Christians and non-Christians through Bible translations, spiritual revivals, Christian colleges, orphanages, social programs, and their exemplary morality and work ethic. These branches grew nourishing "leaves" and "seeds," or Spirit-given works. These ministry outgrowths were life-changing books, sermons, doctrines, and plans for Christian communities to learn, live, and labor God's way. For five centuries God has used these spiritual "leaves" and "seeds" to nourish, heal, and delight the weak, sick, and lost. They've provided relief (shade) from the heat of life's stresses, shelter (nesting) from storms of adversity, and a sure standing place (perch) of faith in God.

Today Christianity is the "greatest" and only true faith in the religious garden. Yet it won't fill the world until Christ returns. Until then, the mustard seed pattern is being fulfilled wherever the "Seed" is "sown."

The "Seed" is Christ's life and Word in us. It's "sown" in our hearts, not just by our faith but by our spiritual "death," or sacrificial obedience. Whenever God's will crosses ours, if we submit and do His will, our self-will dies—and the Seed grows. As we continue obeying sacrificially, His life in us and in our churches, ministries, charities, and other Spirit-led works continues growing and branching out. Eventually a remarkable transformation occurs.

Our lives, churches, and ministries produce "branches," or spiritual and natural ministerial outreaches. We also grow "leaves" and "seeds," or Spirit-grown good works such as evangelism, teaching, helps, donations, and exemplary life-witnesses. Like the mustard tree's "leaves" and "seeds," ours benefit believers and unbelievers with spiritual and natural shelter, relief, security, nourishment, healing, and delight. Do you want this marvelous God-honoring, kingdom-building transformation in your life, church, or ministry?

Sow the minute but mighty Seed of Christ by sacrificial obedience. From now on, don't just study it; plant the mighty mustard seed!

Chapter 30

Jesus' Crucial Challenge

JESUS ISSUED A crucial challenge in the Sermon on the Mount: "Seek ye *first* the kingdom of God, and his righteousness" (Matt. 6:33). Are we responding? Let's consider His key words.

To "seek" is to earnestly search for, go after, or pursue. A highly active word, there's nothing apathetic or passive about "seeking." To seek "first" is to do so before other things and as one's highest priority. God's "righteousness" refers to His standard of what is right in every setting or issue as stated in the Bible. God's "kingdom" is the realm of His authority, where He is glorified and His will obeyed. Jesus taught frequently about God's kingdom.

"The kingdom of God cometh not with observation…behold, the kingdom of God is in the midst of you [who believe]" (Luke 17:20–21). Here He declared presently His "kingdom" exists, not in any visible political state but in and among people who surrender to His Lordship—born-again Christians! We seek this hidden, spiritual kingdom "first" by making it our top priority to:

- Maintain and grow God's kingdom in us
- Strengthen it in other believers
- Enlarge it by converting nonbelievers
- Glorify it by honoring the King

We'll address only the first point. Is it our top priority to maintain and grow God's kingdom in us by developing our personal relationship with the King? Or are other interests "first"? Jesus isn't first in many Christians' hearts, decisions, or schedules, but neither is He last. Usually He's somewhere near but not at the top of our priorities. Why isn't He our top priority? Several reasons are likely.

We may still have worldly heart idols. In these lukewarm times we may never have seen a Christian who puts Jesus first in everything. Or we may have seen those claiming to, whose zeal was excessive and fanatical, so we drew back. Or we may never have been taught how to seek the kingdom "first."

Here's the way. We seek the King first every morning, feeding on His Word, praying, and worshiping Him before doing anything else—and long enough to get our souls settled, strengthened, and ready for the day's stress. In every situation we first "give thanks" to God (1 Thess. 5:18). We seek His help first concerning every need or problem before seeking human counsel or assistance (Phil. 4:6–7). We put God first in our friendships, turning from unbelieving to believing companions. We put God's holiness first, confessing our sins quickly and thoroughly to the God of truth. We put God's fear first, choosing to stand in awe of Him, His power, and His judgment rather than dread men's opinions.

Furthermore, we put God's guidance first, trustingly following His Spirit's leading, even when nothing else is clear. We put God's chastening first, humbly receiving His correction, whether by His Word, voice, counselors, or corrective circumstances, and quickly making changes to please Him. We put God first in our finances, cheerfully giving tithes and offerings. We put God first in our viewpoint, accepting everything, even our crosses, from Him and prayerfully seeking His purposes in even our worst troubles. We put God first in worship, habitually praising and worshiping Him daily, whatever our circumstances, and refusing to ever be offended with Him. These are practical ways we maintain and grow Christ's kingdom in our souls "first."

Kingdom-first living also involves putting selfish interests and other people in a newly enlarged second place in our hearts. Are we prepared to say no to others and ourselves in order to say yes to Jesus' crucial challenge? Are we ready for the reproaches, ridiculing, and head-shakings that come when our choices and commitments to please Jesus mean others' wishes, and ours, are denied or deferred? Will we please God and pray for those who misunderstand us? Or will we please them and pray Christ will somehow accept second place? Too many Christians choose the latter option. But Christ's challenge remains: "Seek ye *first*..." Our response is vitally important.

We're not going very far in God until we put Him first, not passively but passionately. And practically. And permanently. Are you tired of ordinary Christianity and ready to step boldly into extraordinary Christianity? Heed Christ's challenge. Reprioritize your life. Seek the King and kingdom interests "first." All kinds of good blessings—every human and spiritual need, including fresh life, flowing joy, and a new, satisfying, energizing sense of God's approval—await your bold step. Don't take my word for it.

Take the King's: "Seek ye first the kingdom of God...*and all these things shall be added unto you*" (Matt. 6:33). Respond to Jesus' crucial challenge.

Chapter 31

ARE YOU CONSIDERING THE POOR?

*I*N PSALM 41, David describes God's blessing on any person who "considers the poor" (v. 1, ESV). He says God will shower the charitable with mercies as rich and varied as those he has given the poor. Let's examine them.

In divine reciprocity, God "protects" the charitable person and "keeps him alive" in his "day of trouble" (vv. 1–2, ESV), just as he has done for the "poor." In His faithfulness, God "will deliver" (v. 1) him from all his troubles, rescuing and releasing him just when he can bear no more. In His mercy, God "wilt not deliver him unto the will [desire] of his enemies" (v. 2), who maliciously long for his demise. In His compassion, God sends agents to nurse him back to health when he is sick: "The LORD will strengthen him upon the bed of languishing... [and] make all his bed in his sickness" (v. 3). He sends others to comfort him when he is wounded by the betrayal of close friends or relatives: "Even my best friend, the one I trusted completely, the one who shared my food, has turned against me" (v. 9, NLT). And His blessings flow on.

In His redemptive love, God quickly forgives him when he confesses his sins: "I said, LORD, be merciful unto me... for I have sinned against thee" (v. 4). By His grace God infuses him with firm moral integrity to stand, upright and uncompromised, in any temptation: "As for me, thou upholdest me in mine integrity" (v. 12). In His benevolence God bestows many other life benefits and advantages upon him until he is abundantly "blessed upon the earth" (v. 2). Others recognize and speak of this, to God's honor: "He shall be called blessed upon the earth" (v. 2, NAS). In His sovereign power, God "raise[s]" him from sickness to service and from humiliation to honor, and as his enemies watch, he assumes an admirable place and duty among God's people (v. 10). Lastly, God joyously gives the greatest benefit He can bestow, more intimate fellowship with Him in His presence—forever! "Thou... settest me before thy face forever" (v. 12); or "you have brought me into your presence forever" (NLT).

Why this mighty outpouring of benefits? This psalm's central figure has "considered" and benefited "the poor." Who are these "poor"?

In the Old Testament, the word *poor* is translated from several Hebrew words conveying the thoughts of poverty, lowness, weakness, or oppression.[1] They all describe a lack of something necessary to human health and happiness, such as money, respect, strength, or justice. By every definition, then, the poor are *needy*.

They are literally poor, or needy in monies or material things. Or they are figuratively poor, in one of several ways. They are prisoners or shut-ins, and therefore needy in freedom. They are sick, and hence needy in health. They are emotionally or mentally troubled, and so needy in mind. They are ignorant or ill-taught, and therefore needy in knowledge. They are hardened or bitter, and so needy in heart. They are isolated or persecuted, and thus needy in friends. They are discouraged, and so needy in hope. They are lost, or saved but still carnally minded, and thus needy in spirit. They are confused or hindered because of foolish decisions, and so are needy in wisdom. These are the "poor" we should consider.

As with Lazarus and the rich man, God puts these needy people at our "gates," or in our daily circumstances, to see if we will "consider" or ignore them. Are we responding as Psalm 41 suggests?

That requires not just thought but action. After thinking about the needs of the poor at our gates, we need to do something about them. We should recognize and remedy their needs by both spiritual and practical means. Spiritually we should intercede for them, taking their names and needs before God in persisting daily prayers of faith, offered according to the Word, in the Spirit, and with thanksgiving. Practically, acting alone or with others, we should give them precisely what they need—money, materials, assistance, the gospel, friendship, wise counsel, nursing, protection, forgiveness, instruction, and so forth.

As we consider the poor in these ways, a wondrous twofold enrichment follows. God's love in action through us enriches the poor at our gates with many blessings—and draws them to our Blesser. The Blesser then enriches us with the wonderful benefits of Psalm 41—and leaves us breathlessly worshiping at His feet. Wonderstruck, we'll cast our crowns before Him, declaring and singing, "Thou art worthy, O Lord..." (Rev. 4:10–11). Who's at your gate today?

Are you considering the poor?

Chapter 32

HAVE YE NOT READ?

HEN JESUS' ENEMIES charged Him with misconduct in Matthew 12:1–8, He retorted by charging them with insufficient study of the Scriptures—not once but twice! In His first response, He recalled the biblical history of David: "Have ye not read what David did?" (v. 3). In His second, He referred them to the Pentateuch: "Have ye not read in the law?" (v. 5). Spirit-led, He then cited two perfectly accurate biblical examples to invalidate their accusations and validate His actions. Thus He checked their attack and held His ground nobly. This was no isolated occurrence.

It was one of His characteristic ways of handling His rude religious opponents. He did the same thing five other times in the Gospels when they doggedly tried to prod Him to say something, anything, they could use against Him. Let's review them.

When the Pharisees asked His opinion on divorce, Jesus responded, "Have ye not read?" and referred them to the first marriage in Genesis (Matt. 19:4). When they criticized Him for letting the people praise His miracles, He said, "Have you never read?" and sent them to the Psalms (Matt. 21:16). When they challenged His authority to teach in the temple courts, He responded with, among other things, another appeal to Psalms, "Did ye never read in the scriptures?" (v. 42). When they asked about marriage in eternity, He responded, "Have ye not read?" and quoted from Exodus (Mark 12:26). When they asked how to receive eternal life, He retorted, "How readest thou?" and asked them for an answer from the Law (Luke 10:26). Surprisingly, His antagonists were not dummies but doctors!

They were the most well-educated religious experts of His day, the vaunted "lawyers" or "scribes"—professional scholars, teachers, and judges! Yet despite their hyper-diligent studies of the Scriptures and its rabbinical interpretations, they lacked insight and wisdom because they generally failed to live what they learned.

It's stunning that a lowly Galilean manual laborer could reference and apply Bible verses, principles, and history to confute their arguments, silence their test questions, and expose their misjudgments. It proves Jesus—who consistently obeyed His Father—knew God's Word better than the experts! As God's Son, this was expected; as a man, this presents us with a challenge.

If we too are to master God's Word and subdue our clever adversaries, we must "study to show thyself [ourselves] approved unto God" (2 Tim. 2:15). Jesus did so. He apparently studied Scripture regularly in His local synagogue in Nazareth and seasonally in the temple courts, though never attending rabbinical schools—as His foes acknowledged with amazement: "How knoweth this man letters, having never learned?" (John 7:15). To follow His example, we need a better command of pertinent Bible facts than our enemies. To gain this, we must seek to be not familiar with the Word but "mighty in the Word."

The Alexandrian scholar Apollos was "mighty in the Scriptures" and "instructed" (Acts 18:24–25), or biblically well read and orally taught. He helped the Corinthians "much" in public debates with their Jewish antagonists (vv. 27–28). "Fervent in spirit," Apollos was, like Jesus, obedient to the Scriptures he studied. His teaching significantly "watered" the Corinthian church's growth (1 Cor. 3:6, 8). Do you want to be "mighty in the Scriptures"?

Then stop wasting time and commit that time "wholly" to prayerful Bible reading and study: "Give thyself wholly to them" (1 Tim. 4:15). Cultivate love for God's Word: "His delight is in the law of the Lord" (Ps. 1:2). Like Mary, make "that good part, which shall not be taken away" your top priority, or first interest and pastime (Luke 10:42). Like Jesus, combine your study with obedience; only "doers of the word" fully grasp and wisely use it (James 1:22). Persist in your studies through setbacks and persecution. Sustained study will stimulate your intellect and ennoble your spirit, as it did for the Bereans, who grew "more noble" than those who neglected study (Acts 17:11). Your mind will also become "stayed" on God, secure and full of "perfect peace" (Isa. 26:3). Like Apollos, you'll grow "mighty in the Scriptures," ready to help Christians "much." And like Jesus, you'll eventually know God's Word better than your adversaries, even if you never attend Bible school or seminary—or never debate scholars!

Few of us are so called and gifted. But every Christian needs a full, rich knowledge of God's Word to exhort, counsel, discern heresy, examine prophecy, recognize misapplied Bible principles and parables, and avoid unbiblical fads and movements. We'll have it, if we diligently, prayerfully, and obediently study God's Word. I think I hear Jesus.

He's asking, "Have ye not read?"

Chapter 33

GOD'S ENABLERS

MATTHEW 13:53–58 REVEALS that when Jesus visited Nazareth, He was eager to save, heal, deliver, and bless. But He couldn't. Why? He found no enablers.

Instead, the Nazarenes disabled His good plan for their city. Jesus ministered, but only a little, as His miracle-working ability was held in check: "He did not many mighty works there" (v. 58). He only relieved a few minor ailments: "He laid his hands upon a few sick folks, and healed them" (Mark 6:5). Thus Jesus' fellow citizens proved they were indeed the descendants of their infamous forefathers, who tragically "limited the Holy One of Israel" in Moses' day (Ps. 78:41). The Nazarenes' failure to enable Jesus' ministry was tragic, but it was no enigma.

Three causes are clearly stated or described:

1. CARNAL REASONING. Despite the Spirit bearing witness to Jesus' heavenly words (Matt. 13:54), they concluded no local man could be Messiah. He wasn't from Bethlehem (vv. 55–56)!

2. AN OFFENDED SPIRIT. They were insulted (v. 57) by this uneducated carpenter's arrogant claim to be God's Son. He was Joseph's boy, and not even a Pharisee (vv. 55–56)!

3. UNBELIEF. They refused to believe His powers were divine since the authorities called them demonic (Matt. 12:24), and others assumed they were magical (Matt. 13:58).

While these crippling forces often work simultaneously, they also work separately, and it only takes one to disable Jesus' work in our lives, churches, or cities.

Our proud reasoning may reject the Spirit's repeated witness or refuse to put childlike faith in God's character or promise. If so, carnal reasoning—"thine own understanding" (Prov. 3:5)—will rob us. Or we may get offended (insulted, hurt, angry) with the Lord for sending us difficulties, defeats, delays, or losses. If so, offense will rob us. Or, weary with long, hard tests, we may quit believing God is still going to lovingly and faithfully deliver us. If so, unbelief will defeat us. Any one or combination of these disablers will hinder what Jesus stands ready and willing to do in the "Nazareth" of our personal lives. Three countermeasures help us escape these pits.

First, we should submit our intelligence to God's Word and guidance, remembering His thoughts are infinitely higher than ours (Isa. 55:8–9). Receiving God's help by faith requires childlike trust that He'll keep His promises even when reason says, "No way!" "…where there is no way. Yet setteth he the poor on high from affliction" (Ps. 107:40–41).

Second, we should refuse to be offended with Jesus, no matter how offensive the people or situations we meet. Jesus said, "Blessed is he, whosoever shall not be offended in me" (Luke 7:23). God sometimes lets the worst things hit His best people so, as with Job, He can make them better—purer, humbler, more trusting, discerning, fruitful, and like Jesus—and qualify them for rich rewards in this life and the next. However hard our trials, we mustn't harden our hearts.

Third, we should examine our hearts daily, alert for the onset of doubt, double-mindedness, apathy, and non-expectation—praying without expecting answers. Those who expect nothing receive what they expect.

If we faithfully practice these countermeasures, we'll never limit God. To the contrary, we'll *un-limit* or release Him to do on earth exactly as He does in heaven. No longer God's disablers, we'll become His enablers, those who facilitate, not frustrate, His plan and always help and never hinder His miracles. We'll enable Him to do whatever He wills, whenever He wills, wherever He wills, and to the fullest possible extent. William Carey did this.

When English Protestants cared little for foreign missions, Carey challenged them to evangelize faraway peoples, helped form the English Baptist Missionary Society (1792), and volunteered for service in India. Despite fragile health, a troubled wife, difficult sons, an unfaithful associate missionary, and no converts for seven years, Carey kept rejecting carnal reasoning, offense, and unbelief. Thus instead of disabling God's plan for his mission, he enabled it. After seven years his breakthrough came—a first convert! Carey went on, primarily through his extensive translation work, to do great things with and for Jesus in India and set a foreign missions example for the ages. His motto? "Expect great things from God; attempt great things for God."[1] What we expect, we enable.

Carey expected great things from Jesus—and got them! The Nazarenes expected nothing—and got it! These represent two kinds of Christians: enablers and disablers, Careys and Nazarenes. Believe God and His promises! "Didn't I tell you that you would see God's glory if you believe?" (John 11:40, NLT). This will disable your non-expectation and enable you to become one of God's enablers!

Chapter 34

THE LAVISH LANGUAGE OF LOVE

*L*OVE DRIVES OUR fellowship with God and offense halts it. In Psalm 73, Asaph describes these two powerful emotions working in his heart. Let's ponder his profound yet practical preaching.

Asaph begins by sharing candidly with the reader his offense with God. Everywhere he looks he sees the triumphing of evil men and the trials of good men: "I saw the prosperity of the wicked" (v. 3). The more he considers the "things seen," the more he envies sinners—harboring angry discontent at their having what he keenly wants—and regrets his repentance, faith, and obedience to God's Word and correction. "Verily, I have cleansed my heart in vain," he cries out as the deception of offense takes hold (v. 13). Then he visits God's "sanctuary," where heaven's Word illuminates earth's darkness (v. 17).

There God's truth awakens him from his nightmare of doubt, disappointment, and deception:

> Only when I came into God's holy place did I finally understand what would happen to them. You put them in slippery places and make them fall into ruin. They are suddenly destroyed. They are completely swept away by terror! As someone gets rid of a dream when he wakes up, so you, O Lord, get rid of the thought of them when you wake up.
>
> —PSALM 73:17–20, GW

The enduring Word reminds this short-sighted songwriter that he, not the wicked, is in the blessed, preferred position. He has a rich, satisfying, eternal relationship with God. Proud, disbelieving, self-serving sinners, though comparatively trouble-free for now, are actually in the worst conceivable position! At any moment they may die and fall headlong into a vortex of unending desolation and torment, never again having a chance to know the wonderful God he knows, follows, and enjoys daily!

Reawakened to reality, thankful, and freshly inspired with adoration for his Redeemer, the psalmist then uses some of the most eloquent language in the Bible to describe his sorely tested but surviving love for Him who is Love.

Ponder this exposition of his lavish love talk:

- "Truly God is good to Israel, even to such as are of a clean heart" (v. 1). O Lord, You are good, so good, to all who submit to Your salvation, instruction, and correction. My faith was right! I fling away all my doubts and reaffirm my confidence that nothing but good awaits those who trust and obey You!

- "I am continually with thee" (v. 23). Lord, I have something much better than worldly riches, success, and influence. It's You, Your sweet personality, kind acts, and precious, nourishing words of truth. I enjoy Your presence and my communication with You continually.

- "Thou hast held me by my right hand" (v. 23). Lord, what a tender lover You are. When I'm baffled or worried, You reassure me by "taking my hand," or quickening portions of Your Word that remind me that there is nothing and no one to fear, because Your strength, wisdom, and favor are with me, and nothing and no one can stand before You. "There is no wisdom, nor understanding, nor counsel against the LORD" (Prov. 21:30).

- "Thou shalt guide me with your counsel" (Ps. 73:24). Your unerring Word and unfailing voice show me the right way every time I face confusing crossroads in life. I'll never lack the insight I need.

- "And afterward receive me to glory" (v. 24). And after this life, You'll receive me warmly in heaven, where I'll behold Your beautiful face and revel in Your glorious realm.

- "There is none upon earth that I desire beside thee" (v. 25). There is no other person, leader, object, or goal in this fallen world that captivates my adoration. I am permanently, passionately love-struck, blind to all suitors and deaf to their appeals.

- "God is…my portion forever" (v. 26). Lord, You are my richest reward, my prized inheritance. Streets of crystal-clear gold, gates of pearl, walls of jewels, many mansions, legions of saints and angels—all these wonderful blessings are mine, yet they pale when compared to living close to You forever!

- "It is good for me to draw near to God" (v. 28). Lord, considering these insights, I declare a new supreme purpose: drawing near You every day, pleasing You in every issue, and preparing to walk and work with You forever! Help me hold this fast. Amen, so be it.

This isn't the language of a cold-hearted, proper Pharisee who sees his relationship to God in dry, legal terms: "redeemed," "justified," or "sanctified." They're the passionate words of a soul madly in love with God. Ponder them.

Be gripped, inspired, and changed by the lavish language of love.

Chapter 35

Spiritual Success

*E*very Christian is called to successfully minister Jesus—to this world, the church, his (or her) family, neighbors, city, nation, and so forth. For this, we must understand spiritual success.

Embedded in our old nature, worldly success is the aim of the natural man. It consists of things the present social order values most: power, position, accomplishments, wealth, and fame. Prideful and selfish, our old nature seeks success in popularity, material things, income, recognition, and reputation. The natural man prefers and pursues this crass outward show rather than a noble divine calling. His is a work of human ability, not of the Spirit's gifts and strength. His coveted gains are visible, never spiritual. His goals are immediate, never eternal. He focuses on this world, forgetting the next. Ignoring the Bible's revelation of heaven's will and values, he measures success solely by worldly ends and standards. Too often Christians, and even ministers—whose minds, values, and standards should be renewed by God's Word—judge success by these worldly standards instead of setting their sights on spiritual success as Scripture reveals it.

Spiritual success focuses on receiving and retaining God's favor. It is measured by biblical not societal standards. Briefly, its goal is fulfilling God's will. Jesus professed, "My food [satisfaction] is to do the will of him that sent me, and to finish his work" (John 4:34). And He made good on His profession. All His earthly life Jesus ignored worldly success and pursued His Father's will, completing it with His last act and words: "It is finished" (John 19:30). The natural man scoffs at these lofty, otherworldly ideals and their Professor, but Christians should study and seek them. To spiritually minded Christians, success is *fully being and doing God's will*—being all He wants us to be and doing everything He charges us to do in life.

This success involves simple things, such as faithfulness, truthfulness, steadfastness in adversity, and humility in victory. It is motivated by love for Jesus, not self, and moves us to serve His people, not our pleasure. Desiring it prompts us to seek eternal rewards, not temporal honors. We seek to build lasting character, not false reputations. Ruled by Messiah rather than mammon, we covet more of the Spirit, not more money. We dream not of being blessed but of being a blessing, not of comforts but of comforting others. We realize real success occurs whenever God is honored, His truth is proclaimed, His love is demonstrated, His authority is established, and His callings are faithfully pursued by individuals, churches, and ministries—irrespective of other measures of success.

When Jesus finished His course of ministry, His heart was filled with the joy of spiritual success. He reported His success in His final, "high priestly" prayer: "I have finished the work which thou gavest me to do" (John 17:4). A few hours later—betrayed, arrested, convicted, whipped, publicly humiliated, and nailed to a cross outside Jerusalem—Jesus didn't look successful. To Herod, Caiaphas, the Pharisees, and the people, He was just another miserable Messianic pretender. Even Jesus' disciples feared He, and they, had failed. But Jesus was a roaring success. So was the apostle Paul.

Yet when Paul's execution drew near, from every worldly perspective he too seemed a total failure. Many of his Christian friends and coworkers had forsaken him. He was not financially wealthy or accepted by Roman high society. He was not politically influential. He held no high office in any legally recognized religious body. His ministry achievements went unnoticed by the public. Though inspired and extensive, his writings were not acclaimed by Roman philosophers or educators; when he spoke briefly in Athens, the intellectuals there politely but promptly dismissed him. Though he planted numerous churches, he never founded any great universities, libraries, or religious institutions. Yet Paul's last words to Timothy, and to us, were not the sad concessions of a failure but the glad declarations of a spiritually successful soul. Not tragically but triumphantly he wrote, "I have fought a good fight, I have finished my course, I have kept the faith. Henceforth there is laid up for me a crown [reward]" (2 Tim. 4:7–8). Why the optimism? Paul knew his life had fully been, and he had fully done, God's will. Do you know this?

You can. Consider well the differences between worldly and spiritual success. Forget the former and focus on the latter. Pursue it. Practice it. Persevere, leaving others to think and say what they will, until one day you too say, "It is finished. I have finished my course!"

In that day, like Jesus and Paul, you'll be a roaring spiritual success!

Chapter 36

STANDING FAST AT THE FINISH

*U*NQUESTIONABLY, THE HARDEST part of long trials of faith and patience is finishing well. Three spiritual giants—Nehemiah, Elisha, and Elijah—encountered great struggles at the end of epic trials of faith and endurance.

Just before Nehemiah finished rebuilding Jerusalem's walls, a prophetess delivered a frightening false prophecy to him: "Let us meet together in the house of God, within the temple...for they [your Samaritan enemies] will come to slay thee; yea, in the night will they come to slay thee" (Neh. 6:10). Paid by Nehemiah's enemies, she hoped he would panic, take refuge in the holy place (breaking God's law), and bring reproach on himself and God's work. But he discerned the deception and held fast at the finish.

After enduring the long, cruel siege of Samaria, and only hours before God's deliverance arrived, Elisha suddenly faced a hasty execution order from discouraged and desperate King Jehoram: "God do so and more also to me, if the head of Elisha...shall stand on him this day" (2 Kings 6:31). But while Israel's prince and people panicked, "Elisha sat [still, trusting God] in his house" (v. 32)—and delivered yet another inspired message, this one promising God would deliver the very next day (2 Kings 7:1). So he too held fast at the end. But others didn't.

Years earlier the mighty prophet, Elijah, stumbled at the end of his greatest trial. For three and a half years Elijah stood firm like a towering rock of righteousness while a floodtide of idolatry swept over God's land and people. With exemplary faith and courage he rebuked Israel's idolatry, called it to repent, announced God's judgments, and awaited patiently God's appointed time for revival. Finally God released him to challenge Ahab and execute the false prophets of Baal: "Go, show thyself unto Ahab" (1 Kings 18:1). When God answered Elijah's public prayer with fire from heaven, suddenly, the entire lukewarm nation repented and re-pledged its allegiance to Jehovah: "The LORD, he is God; the LORD, he is God" (v. 39). At last God's—and Elijah's—time had come! Israel was ready to walk with God!

But Satan wasn't finished. His agent Queen Jezebel shot her swift and deadly poisoned "arrow"—a death threat to the true prophet who dared to defy her false ones: "So let the gods do to me, and more also, if I make not thy life as the life of one of them [Baal's slain prophets] by tomorrow" (1 Kings 19:2). Then the unthinkable happened. God's man of faith fled in fear: "When he saw that, he arose, and went for his life" (v. 3). Just when Elijah's long-awaited day of fulfillment was dawning, he ran away from his enemies—and his divine destiny to lead his nation in revival! How tragic! As fearless and faithful as Elijah had been during his ministerial "race," he faltered at the finish line.

These three examples demonstrate a distinct pattern: Satan habitually attacks long-tried saints just before their final victories. Nehemiah's wall was virtually finished, Elisha's siege was at an end, and Elijah's national revival was at the birth—then came the enemy, either subtly or savagely. Does this speak to you?

Have you been faithfully building a "wall"—a church, mission, ministry, family, business, etc.—in response to God's call? Have you endured a long, exhausting "siege" of hindrance caused by stubborn enemies who oppose or slander you on every side? Have you been steadily praying and fasting for a heaven-sent revival in your nation despite its unwise leaders, idol-loving public, and apathetic churches? Then don't be surprised if Satan uses anything or anyone to try to trick, trouble, or discourage you just before your breakthrough. His purpose is to shock, shake, and move you to fear, unbelief, or offense at God. Or better, to make you quit and flee God's work at the very dawn of its fulfillment. Have none of it!

Instead, "have faith in God" (Mark 11:22). Faithful, He always finishes whatever He begins. Compassionate, He always releases His praying captives. Just, He diligently rights every wrong in the end. Almighty, He can raise even the worst sinners and deadest Christians to abundant life. So keep working faithfully on your divinely commissioned "wall." Stay close to God in your long, difficult "siege," whatever hardships come. Continue petitioning and believing God for a surprising, undeserved national revival. Expect your awesome God to act awesomely: "By awesome things in righteousness wilt thou answer us" (Ps. 65:5). And having done all, "stand" (Eph. 6:13).

You stood firm at the beginning of your test. You stood steady in the middle. Now stand fast at the finish!

Chapter 37

IF PETER WALKED ON WATER...

THE REVELATION THAT Jesus walked on water is nothing new. Every informed Christian knows this. But Matthew 14:22–33 reveals something we may have overlooked: Peter also walked on water!

Matthew's eyewitness account plainly states, "And when Peter was come down out of the boat, he walked on the water, to go to Jesus" (v. 29). This physics-defying spectacle becomes even more amazing when we consider the waters upon which Peter walked. At the time, the Sea of Galilee was not placid but turbid. Because "the wind was contrary" (v. 24), the waves were large, violent, relentless, and life threatening. So the full revelation here is that Peter walked not on smooth but on stormy waters to go to Jesus. The Spirit of God is speaking to us here.

When used figuratively in the Bible, "waters" often symbolize trouble, and stormy or "deep waters" represent great trouble. When surrounded by overwhelming troubles, David wrote, "Save me, O God; for the waters are come in unto my soul....I am come into deep waters...let me be delivered from those who hate me, and out of the deep waters" (Ps. 69:1–2, 14). A disciple himself, Peter's stroll atop the roiling waters of Galilee represents overcoming Christian disciples walking closely with Jesus in steadfast faith, contentment, worship, and service while the stormy "waters" of severe or protracted tests buffet their souls mercilessly—and seemingly interminably. Some may reject this interpretation.

They may understandably claim that Peter's victory was too brief to be exemplary. After all, the point most often emphasized here is Peter's sinking, not his standing! Yet while his miraculous march atop the madness was minuscule, it was a miracle nonetheless and highly instructive to us. As Jesus accurately pointed out, if Peter had not doubted, he could have walked on the water just as easily and long as Jesus did. Forever? No, that would be fanatical and contrary to God's plan for redeemed mortals in this life. To the other side of the lake? Yes, that was very possible—if Peter stayed focused on Jesus and didn't "doubt."

"O thou of little faith, why didst thou doubt?" was Jesus' searching question to His stumbling student (Matt. 14:31). While Peter stayed focused on Jesus—the Word of God—he easily and steadily overcame the furious troubles. This spiritual victory continued as long as Peter kept the Word in the center of his viewpoint and the troubling wind-whipped waves on the fringe. But the "boisterous" whistling of the winds and roaring of the waves eventually turned his attention from the Master standing before him to the madness surrounding him. This simple shift was crucial, because it made him "doubt" (v. 31). "Doubt" here (Greek, *distazō*) means literally, "to duplicate," or figuratively, "to waver" or hesitate in thought or action.[1] Peter had already received a clear word of promise from Christ, "Come" (v. 29), which fully authorized his wondrous walk. But his shocking circumstances rattled him: "When he saw the wind boisterous, he was afraid" (v. 30). He began to "duplicate" his thinking, or rethink the matter and change his position after Christ had already spoken clearly. This doubt weakened his faith, strengthened his fears, and caused him to "sink" (v. 30). But all was not lost. Jesus mercifully lifted him back into the boat the moment he cried for help. And to this day, Peter's victory, though brief, challenges and comforts us.

His spectacular stroll dares us to ask, Are we overcoming our stormy trials? If not, why? Have we shifted our focus from Christ with us to the chaos around us? Are we sinking with doubt-induced fears? Are we failing due to stubborn sins or faults, such as unforgiveness, pride, strife, anger, neglecting fellowship with Christ, forsaking instruction, refusing counsel, overindulgence, carnal lusts, self-pity, and so forth? If we deny our faults, they remain—and we sink. But we can rise again.

Peter's victory comforts weary, wobbly, water-treading Christians by proving that, yes, every believer can rise above the worst spiritual storms and most persistent "waves." One long, meditative, believing look at Peter striding stably and upright on Galilee's stormy swells—his eyes riveted on Jesus and His promise—progressing steadily despite impossible odds, is enough to restore a healthy fighting spirit to the feeblest, most sunken-hearted Christian!

So let this message ring out: if Peter walked on water, so can you! Remember Peter's victory, renounce your doubts, refocus on Jesus and His promises, and rise from the depths of your timidity, despair, or panic to walk with God atop your turbulent test of faith!

And every time you're tempted to doubt, remember, "If Peter walked on water...so can I!"

Chapter 38

TRANSLATED OR TRAPPED IN TRAVAIL?

EFORE DEPARTING, JESUS solemnly charged His disciples to live in readiness for His sudden appearing to remove believers from this world just before the Tribulation period:

> Be on guard, so that your hearts will not be weighted down with dissipation and drunkenness and the worries of life, and that day will not come on you suddenly like a trap; for it will come upon all those who dwell on the face of all the earth. But keep on the alert at all times, praying in order that you may have strength to escape all these things that are about to take place, and to stand before the Son of Man.
>
> —LUKE 21:34–36, NAS

In this text, "Be on guard" calls us to sober, wise watchfulness, not over the affairs of nations, cities, or unbelievers, but over our own personal relationship to Jesus and our God-given responsibilities. "Your hearts…weighted down" refers to troubles excessively burdening or overwhelming our souls, or offending us with Jesus so that we stop trusting and communing with Him and fulfilling our calling. "Dissipation and drunkenness" refers to overindulgent or wasteful living that sometimes stems from discouragement over "the worries of life." But Jesus does more than charge us to be alert.

He shows us how. Avoid de-spiritualizing activities and pursue things that edify. Don't overindulge in carnal pleasures or permit unspiritual thinking, especially anxiety. Rather, indulge in God-things: prayer, Bible reading, good fellowship, thanksgiving, and worship—and obey God in daily tests! These activities keep us full of the Spirit who keeps us alert. Noncompliance leaves us unprepared and headed for a trap!

Jesus warned unprepared Christians will fall into a "trap" ("snare," KJV). A trap lies silent and undetected until activated—then it suddenly grips its victim without any chance of release. Specifically, the "trap" He warns of is the Tribulation, seven years of unparalleled worldwide judgment following the church's departure: "The hour of temptation, which shall come upon all the world, to try them that dwell upon the earth" (Rev. 3:10).

The apostle Paul compared the Tribulation to travail: "When people are saying, 'Everything is peaceful and secure,' then disaster will fall on them as suddenly as a pregnant woman's labor pains....And there will be no escape" (1 Thess. 5:3, NLT). These two symbols—traps and travail—share similar characteristics: a preceding quiet lull, sudden painful trouble, and no way out! In the Tribulation, all creation "travails," or writhes in the pulsating pains (wars, plagues) that will birth the new world order—Christ's thousand-year kingdom. Who'll be trapped in this travail?

"All them that dwell on...the...earth" (Luke 21:35), or everyone not ready for Jesus. They don't take His warning seriously or obey His instructions for readiness. Instead they "dwell," or focus excessively, on worldly issues, desires, and attainments, not kingdom truths, goals, and rewards. Wishful theology assures us they will all be nonbelievers, but Christ warned His *disciples*, not disbelievers. This implies if Christians "dwell" on present distractions all the time and Jesus not at all, we too may be left behind (Matt. 25:11–13). It's been said, "If we're caught up with Jesus now, we'll be caught up when He appears." But if we leave Him off now, He'll leave us behind later. So be ready!

"Keep on the alert at all times, praying" (Luke 21:36, NAS) is the first key to readiness. Draw close to Jesus regularly by prayer and self-examination. Then you'll "escape all these things that shall come to pass" in the Tribulation Jesus described (Luke 21:8–33, 36). (To "escape all" is to avoid a disaster, having no involvement in it.) Then you'll "stand before the Son of Man" in heaven when, after the Rapture, the bride church is officially "presented" to Jesus—transformed, translated, triumphant over this world, approved of God, and ready for eternal union, service, and rulership with her Husband-Lord. Paul revealed this heavenly "presentation." "That he might *present* it to himself a glorious church, not having spot, or wrinkle, or any such thing" (Eph. 5:27). (See Revelation 4–5.) When Jesus appears, you'll either be translated—caught up alive to heaven in a new immortal body—or trapped in travail. That's the truth.

Do you want truth or tickling? Many tickle ears by claiming there'll be no Rapture. Or, if it occurs, all Christians will be taken, ready or not. But the truth is Jesus promised to appear—"I will come again, and receive you unto myself" (John 14:3)—and repeatedly solemnly charged us to be ready. "Keep on the alert...that you may...escape all." Do you believe this truth?

Your answer will determine whether you're translated or trapped in travail!

Chapter 39

MAKE NO MISTAKE ABOUT IT!

*W*HEN STRONG OR persistent troubles meet us, we naturally and rightly wonder, Have we erred from God's will? Perhaps sometime, somewhere, somehow, what we thought was His leading was not. Prayerfully, we search our memory for answers.

We recall famous examples of Bible characters who reaped trouble for sowing disobedience. Jonah encountered a terrible storm at sea because he rebelled against God's guidance. When Christ's apostles impulsively launched out on an unauthorized fishing expedition despite His standing orders to "tarry," that night they caught "nothing" (John 21:3). Why? They were not in God's will. But there is another side to this issue.

Sometimes we meet sudden, sharp, or stubborn opposition when we're in the very center of God's will. The experiences of numerous biblical characters in both the Old and New Testaments establish this truth with equal authority.

The Old Testament reveals that God summoned Abram to leave Chaldea and sojourn in Canaan—and as soon as he did so, a famine visited Canaan. Joseph obeyed his father's call to visit and report on his brothers—and they promptly sold him into slavery. Moses obeyed Jehovah's dramatic call to return to Egypt and deliver his Hebrew brethren—but instead of Pharaoh releasing them, he increased their burdens. God led Moses to take the Israelites to the Promised Land through the wilderness—where they met not friends, joy, and blessings, but "fiery serpents, and scorpions, and drought" (Deut. 8:15).

The New Testament says Jesus "constrained" His apostles to enter a boat and row toward the far shore of Galilee—and that very night a powerful squall nearly sank their boat. An angel from God's presence released the apostles from prison with orders to "Go, stand and speak in the temple" (Acts 5:20)—yet when they returned to their temple ministry, they were promptly arrested and narrowly escaped execution. The Lord gave the apostle Paul a powerful vision expressly ordering him to Macedonia—where he found few open doors, converted just one woman, and was severely beaten and jailed without a trial. Thus the New Testament "amens" the Old: trouble also comes in God's will!

Have you experienced this in your life or ministry? Have you obeyed the Spirit's leading or call only to be rewarded with roadblocks, delays, perplexities, critics, and dogged opposition? Are you reeling with doubt and wondering if you were mistaken? Don't let the adverse "afterwards" of your obedience dismay you; calm down and prayerfully reexamine the "before."

Was your path scriptural, in line with God's written purposes, plans, and righteousness? If it's according to God's Word, it's according to His will. Or did the Holy Spirit seal His leading by strongly impressing your mind with timely portions of God's Word? The Spirit's witness is a surer indicator than your circumstantial woes. Was your original decision made in prayerful fellowship with Jesus and accompanied by sustained deep peace? When your choice is peaceful, your choice is perfect, because "all her [wisdom's] paths are [or bring] peace" (Prov. 3:17). Was your motive only to please the Lord? If He's pleased, don't worry who's displeased. Is your path in line with the calling, ministry, and gift God gave you? If you're following His call, He'll eventually turn everything against you for you (Rom. 8:28)! After taking this path, has God continued confirming that it's His will by blessing your private fellowship with Him, granting fresh insights from His Word, and releasing new rivers of inner peace daily, despite your outward perplexities, troubles, or opposition? If you have His confirmation, you have His confidence. So be confident!

You're not mistaken; you're marked! The devil has targeted you for attack because you're in God's will and pleasing Him. Or Satan's "rulers of the darkness of this world" (Eph. 6:12) are resisting because your life-witness or ministry is releasing the light of God's Word from the "lampstand" God has placed you on. The prince of darkness hopes to confuse, discourage, or move you to hinder or stop what God is doing through you. So ponder the source of and reason for your opposition: "An enemy hath done this" (Matt. 13:28).

Don't let him hinder or move you from God's will. Don't be doubtful; be determined! Don't be shaky; be steadfast! Don't neglect your gift; nurture it! Don't abandon your calling; abound in it! "Therefore...be ye steadfast, unmovable, always abounding in the work of the Lord, forasmuch as ye know that your labor is not in vain in the Lord" (1 Cor. 15:58). And be adamant!

Your life isn't a waste; it's a witness. Your labor isn't in vain; it's invaluable. Make no mistake about it!

Chapter 40

COME, HOLY SPIRIT!

*H*OW DO YOU change the spiritual and moral condition of this or any nation? For decades now the growing evangelical mantra has been *more political action*!

But I hear the distant echo of another chant. It's the voice of Scripture, first-century Christianity, and Christian history, crying in unison for *a visitation of the Holy Spirit*! Why?

This is God's biblical, timeless, and proven way. And it's the only way to change the soul of a nation. It's also the way He saved you and me. One day our spiritual and moral core was altered, not naturally, but supernaturally. When we read or heard the gospel—still "the power of God" to save! (Rom. 1:16)—the Holy Spirit visited us, convicted us of sin, and touched our dead spirits with living faith in Jesus. With our inner man divinely altered, we began discovering God's mind by studying His Word. Slowly our minds became renewed, and we began taking God's view of what is right—His purposes, values, and judgments. We began walking in this "righteousness" we received by grace through faith, manifesting more biblical living and decisions as more time and tests passed. Eventually, a thoroughly changed life resulted; from innermost to outermost, from being to behavior, we were a new person. Political parties and their platforms didn't do it. Elected leaders and laws didn't do it. Judges and court orders didn't do it. Ideologies and revolutions didn't do it. God did it—His way! "Not by [human] might, nor by [human] power [ways and means], but by my Spirit," and Word, our spiritual and moral condition was radically changed (Zech. 4:6).

This personal visitation of the Spirit parallels a national visitation. It's the only hope for national redemption. Jonathan Edwards, the leading theologian of the American Great Awakening, noted five distinguishing marks of genuine works of the Holy Spirit. He asserted that true heaven-sent revival:

1. Creates new respect and honor for Jesus in the community

2. Works against Satan's power and works of sin and worldly lusts

3. Creates new respect for the Bible as God's true Word

4. Is accompanied by "a spirit of truth," or humble honesty

5. Spawns new or renewed love for God and man[1]

Jesus, sin, the Bible, honesty, and love—indeed our relation to or practice of these things is drastically altered when the Spirit of God grips us. Born again, we're never the same again. This distinctively divine grip captivated whole communities and cities in past revivals, not through media-driven elections, legislatively driven agendas, or conservatively active justices, but through the intercession-driven evangelism of anointed heavenly messengers such as Edwards, George Whitefield, Charles G. Finney, Dwight L. Moody, Billy Sunday, and Billy Graham.

Mindful of this biblical and historical foundation, I pray daily for God to sweep through this nation (and all others) one more time before Jesus comes, solely for His honor, pleasure, and kingdom, with a mighty work of His Spirit, by grace giving conviction and repentance of sin and childlike faith in Jesus. Will God respond if we all pray this?

That depends on our spiritual condition. If we who know Him not only pray but also please Him, turning from everything in our lives that breaks His Word and grieves His Spirit, He'll answer. Two mighty trumpet-texts, from the Old Testament and New, sound this call:

> If *my people*, who are called by my name [today, born-again Christians], shall humble themselves, and...turn from their wicked ways...then will I hear [their prayers]...and will heal their land.
>
> —2 CHRONICLES 7:14

> Now repent of *your sins* and turn to God...then times of refreshment will come from the presence of the Lord.
>
> —ACTS 3:19–20, NLT

Can we hear God's trumpets?

Do you want God to change the spiritual and moral climate of our nation so that not merely our political agenda but His kingdom purposes—to save, teach, train, test, transform, and ultimately translate millions—may thrive worldwide in these last days? Then give God less politics and more penitence. Respond to His call to repent wherever necessary, even if others won't. Sign fewer petitions and pray more prayers. Stop asking, "Come, O presidents, governors, legislators, and judges," and start pleading, "Come, Holy Spirit!"

When He visits, He'll release many prepared spiritual leaders and accomplish in one brief season of heavenly revival what decades of worldly politics have failed to accomplish. Everyone won't be saved, but many will. The signs of the Spirit's work Edwards noted will appear again as God heals our land, spiritually and governmentally, from core to Capitol. Too simple?

That's the beauty of it: It is so simple! *Come, Holy Spirit!*

Chapter 41

THE OVERRIDING GOOD NEWS!

I HAVE GOOD AND bad news for Christians. Let's bravely take the bad first: our tests get harder, not easier, the farther we walk with Jesus.

Matthew 14:22–33 reveals that the second crossing of Galilee by the original disciples—our spiritual ancestors and biblical models in the Christian way—was more difficult than the first (Matt. 8:23–27). The latter test occurred at night, whereas the first took place in daylight. Jesus wasn't with them the second time, as He was the first, but was on a mountaintop, praying. Jesus didn't respond to His struggling disciples quickly in the second crossing, as He had earlier, but let them battle contrary winds and threatening waves most of the night. Matthew Henry noted, "Christ used [or exposed] his disciples first to less difficulties, and then to greater, and so trains them up by degrees to live by faith."[1]

Like theirs, our tests also become increasingly more demanding. Why? God uses testing to transform saved but stumbling babes in Christ into mature believers walking stably with God. Specifically, He uses our increased difficulties to:

- Exercise and build more faith—confidence in the unfailing faithfulness of God—in us, as Henry noted

- Stretch and increase our patience until it's "perfect and entire, lacking nothing" (James 1:4)

- Refine and purify our motives more deeply until God's purposes are ours

- Alter our attitudes until the mind of Christ is established in us

- Sharpen our spiritual discernment, vision, and hearing so we consistently sense, see, and hear God

- Increase our capacity to minister knowledgeably and compassionately

- Finish maturing our characters until they are conformed to Jesus' image

These things prepare us to be more like Christ so that, as His bride, we may blissfully live and work with Him forever! While heaven glories in this end, we often groan over its means. Why? No normal Christian wants harder trials.

But here's some overriding good news: *when our tests grow harder, God's grace grows stronger*! He promises to give obedient Christians whatever grace we need to overcome the tests He permits to perfect our faith and refine our characters. When the apostle Paul was besieged and almost overwhelmed by relentless adversities, Jesus revealed, "My grace is sufficient for thee" (2 Cor. 12:9). He performed as promised, giving Paul enough infusions of divine strength, ability, grace, wisdom, and favor to keep him moving forward in increasingly difficult challenges. Having repeatedly experienced Christ's unfailing grace and timely rescues, Paul encouraged the Corinthians, and us, to rest in Christ's utter reliability: "God is faithful, who will not permit you to be tempted above that you are able" (1 Cor. 10:13). So we need not fear when our crossings become more demanding.

Jesus' help will become more delightful! He'll do for us everything He did for His disciples in their second crossing. He'll visit us with greater regularity in our storms: "Jesus went unto them" (Matt. 14:25). He'll speak with greater clarity, and we'll hear His voice with greater confidence: "It is I; be not afraid" (v. 27). We'll see Him do greater—even impossible—things in our dark circumstances: "The disciples saw him walking on the sea" (v. 26). He'll enable us to do greater things than we've ever done before: "Peter...walked on the water" (v. 29). We'll cultivate greater peace as we repeatedly restfully rely on Him while surrounded by contradictory occurrences, reports, and feelings. Even when the spiritual winds are "contrary" and our troublesome situations "boisterous" and threatening, we'll still step out in faith when Jesus gives us His Word: "Lord, if it be thou, bid me come...and he said, Come" (vv. 28–29).

And if we fall, Jesus will "immediately" stretch out His hand to steady us by His Word, Spirit, and peace (v. 31). This will give us a greater awareness of how closely and constantly He watches over us. His correction will be greater, or more specific—"Why didst thou doubt?" (v. 31)—and our training deeper. Every time He ends a test, we'll rediscover that His power is greater than this world's greatest powers: "The wind ceased" (v. 32). Our worship will also be greater—purer, sweeter, and more satisfying to Jesus: "Then they…worshiped him" (v. 33). And our faith that He is indeed God's Son, our only Savior and all-sufficient Shepherd, will be greater, or more strongly and permanently established. We'll no longer hope but *know* He's who He says He is: "Of a truth [surely!], thou art the Son of God" (v. 33). So when harder tests overwhelm you, override them.

Remember and say, "When my tests grow harder, His grace grows stronger!" That's the overriding good news!

Chapter 42

ABOUT THOSE STORMY TESTS

*M*ATTHEW REPORTS THAT the turbulent storm that befell the disciples' second Galilee crossing came just after Jesus healed and fed a throng of over five thousand in the wilderness[1] and just before He healed "all that were diseased" in Gennesaret (Matt. 14:14, 21–22, 35). This storm wasn't accidental.

It was a divine appointment, with God and Satan each seeking different ends. God hoped the storm would educate and increase the disciples' confidence in Him. Satan hoped, however futilely, it would stop Jesus' growing ministry, which was liberating more people from his oppression every day. As Peter later noted:

> How God anointed Jesus of Nazareth with the Holy Spirit, and with power; who went about doing good, and healing all who were oppressed of the devil; for God was with him.
>
> —ACTS 10:38

Indeed, the "prince of the power of the air" (Eph. 2:2), or "ruler of the evil powers that are above the earth" (NCV), was storming mad that Jesus was busily blessing God's people. So he expressed his diabolical displeasure by enveloping Jesus' ministry team in an outburst of meteorological madness. As noted, they passed through these adversarial atmospherics just after one amazing ministry session and just before another. We should pause to consider this. We often see only the glamour of Jesus' ministry; it's time we also discern its grueling grind and grit. To deliver others, Jesus had to endure periodic distress.

On this stormy night, while His disciples struggled to keep their buffeted boat afloat, "Jesus went unto them, walking on the [churning] sea" (Matt. 14:25). Jesus walked about three and a half miles across a rough, vicious body of water to meet them and then land in Gennesaret, where He ministered to that community's sick (v. 35). Of these marvelous healing meetings one commentator notes, "Did these people know that He had come through a storm to meet their needs?"[2] Probably not. But the apostles knew.

Later, after the fledgling church's healing and preaching ministry reaped five thousand converts in Jerusalem, another "storm" beset the same disciples. This was not a meteorological but a religious disturbance, as the Jewish clerics united to persecute the new church's leaders: "They were confronted by the priest, the captain of the Temple guard, and some of the Sadducees....They arrested them and...put them in jail" (Acts 4:1–3, NLT). Thus Jesus' disciples walked in their Master's footsteps. Like Him, they endured Satan's stormy opposition because their ministry was blessing many. Others also trod this perilous path.

The apostle Paul famously encountered and endured many storms of persecution and tribulation on land and at sea in order to disseminate many powerful life-giving, faith-nourishing, character-building truths, gifts, and other blessings to the churches. When he arrived in cities to minister, he often did so freshly released from some turbid trouble, "in perils of waters...robbers...false brethren," which brought him "weariness and painfulness...hunger and thirst" (2 Cor. 11:26–27). One time Paul was tossed around for two weeks in a life-threatening hurricane and then shipwrecked before arriving on the island of Malta, where he healed and surely evangelized many: "The father of Publius lay sick...to whom Paul entered in, and prayed, and laid his hands on him, and healed him....Others also in the island, who had diseases, came and were healed" (Acts 28:8–9). Paul's spiritual understanding enabled him to endure these persisting perils. Do we share his insight?

Do we understand that our life works are really extensions of Christ's, that Christ lives in and ministers through us by His Spirit just as He did long ago? When the apostles launched into ministry, Jesus was there "working with them" (Mark 16:20). Luke unmistakably describes Jesus' ministry as not an end but a beginning—"All that Jesus *began* both to do and teach, until the day in which he was taken up" (Acts 1:1–2)—of an enduring work Christians continue and augment daily. But sharing His glorious work means enduring its grueling grind and grit.

If we feed God's people the bread of His Word, or minister healing to their bodies, or relieve their troubled hearts by the power and gifts of the Holy Spirit, we too must endure our share of satanic storms. Are we, our churches, and our ministries willing to endure these long, dark, dangerous, and wearisome gales to minister the Messiah's mercies on the "other side"? There, in our "Gennesaret," sick, famished, oppressed, misled, confused, and despairing people await the ministry of the Son of God through us. If we'll pay the price, whether before or after our times of ministry, God will see they get the blessing.

Now you understand about those stormy tests.

Chapter 43

AT TRIAL'S END

*T*HE CONDITION OF the apostles after their harrowing second crossing of Galilee is enlightening. After their stormy test, they reaffirmed their faith in Jesus' identity—"Of a truth, thou art the Son of God" (Matt. 14:33)—and also "came [near] and worshipped him" (v. 33). So at trial's end, the Bible focuses on two facts: their faith and worship.

The apostles' original belief that Jesus was God's very Son and their long-awaited Messiah was now tested, proven, and *established*—solid as a rock and no longer inclined to waver or change, whatever may happen! Their exclamation, "Of a truth," may be paraphrased, "You truly are who we thought You were!" Or, "Now we're convinced; what we believed about You—what John the Baptist witnessed by the Jordan—is true!" So their faith in Him shifted from a hopeful belief to a firm knowing. With the dross of doubt removed, their faith was pure as "gold tried in the fire" (Rev. 3:18). So was their praise and worship.

Like their confidence, their adoration of Him was now refined, increased, and fixed—constant and predictable, regardless of circumstances. From then on their verbal, musical, or bodily expressions of supreme love for Jesus were purer, or more sincere and heartfelt, and therefore more enjoyable to Him. Why? While the Lord appreciates and receives all sincere worship, He is most pleased by that offered by tried, refined saints. They have proven by sacrificial obedience in the turbulent adversities of life that they truly love Him first, before all other people and things. Since He knows He is most precious to them, their worship is most precious to Him.

Furthermore, when the "wind ceased" (Matt. 14:32), the apostles were also better fitted to minister and lead.

Second Corinthians 1:3–5 teaches that God puts Christians in troubling tests so that, after receiving His comforting wisdom, strength, and help in them, we will emerge "able to comfort them who are in any trouble" with the same truths and trust God gave us in our tests. So by enduring their stormy crossing in faith and obedience, the apostles received a new and deeper capacity to minister comfort, guidance, and correction to others in life's storms. Their extraordinary experiences helped them become "spiritually minded" (Rom. 8:6). They could now help less experienced, "carnally minded" believers see their troubles from a spiritual viewpoint— and survive, rise, and soar over them like eagles. So they were ready to lead.

By first exposing and then removing the apostles' fears in their stormy test (Matt. 14:26–27, 30–31), Jesus eliminated their spiritual instability. More stable, they could now lead other fearful believers without panicking, however rough the winds and waves! Those the apostles led would also stand strong, reassured by their confidence that, "of a truth," Jesus and His Word can be trusted. Acts confirms just how stable the apostles' leadership was during the turbulent early years of church history. The apostle Paul likened them to stone pillars: "James, Cephas [Peter], and John, who seemed to be *pillars*" (Gal. 2:9). They became stable as stone in the storm.

If we too endure our rough "crossings" in submissive faith and obedience, we'll emerge in the apostles' condition. Our faith will be confirmed, and we'll be much less, or not at all, intimidated by our next challenges or troubles. Our worship of God will be refined and in every way increased: more sincere, fervent, frequent, and inspired and filled with the Spirit—and more delightful to God! Our ability to minister to other tried souls will grow, and we'll successfully comfort and strengthen them in their stormy seasons. Thus we'll become stable leaders in these unstable End Times. The Rock in us will give shelter and strength to those whose faith is wavering with the winds of trial.

One writer notes:

> It is not generally the prosperous one, who has never sorrowed, who is strong and at rest. His quality has never been tried, and he knows not how he can stand even a gentle shock. He is not the safest sailor who never saw a tempest; he will do for fair-weather service, but when the storm is rising, place at the important post the man who has fought out a gale, who has tested the ship, who knows her hulk sound, her rigging strong...[1]

In these last days, do you want Jesus to prepare you, as He did His apostles, to help lead the ship of the church through her tempestuous earthly trials to the heavenly shores of the translation?

Then press on through your storms: "I press toward the mark" (Phil. 3:14). Good things await at trial's end.

Chapter 44

HE'S NEVER OUTDONE!

*I*NSPIRED AFRESH, THE prophet Isaiah wrote, "When the enemy shall come in like a flood, the Spirit of the LORD shall lift up a standard [a battle pole or ensign as a rallying point] against him" (Isa. 59:19). Or, when Satan comes flooding in on God's people with an overwhelming, seemingly insurmountable attack, God responds by sending His Spirit afresh to raise and rally His people and forward His cause anew. Thus, ultimately, God is never outdone by the enemy! Bible and church history confirm this.

The Bible says when Pharaoh moved like surging waters of death to kill the Hebrews' firstborn, God's Spirit raised Moses and inspired and empowered the Exodus: "He sent Moses, his servant, and…he brought them forth" (Ps. 105:26, 37). When the Jewish religious authorities suddenly overwhelmed the embryonic Jerusalem church with deadly opposition, the Spirit scattered its members, like spiritual seeds, to grow and bear fruit in new cities and nations—and a new, dynamic church was formed in Antioch: "At that time there was a great persecution against the church which was at Jerusalem; and they were all scattered abroad throughout the regions… [and] traveled as far as Phoenicia, and Cyprus, and Antioch, preaching the word" (Acts 8:1; 11:19).

Church history adds that centuries later, when Satan inundated the seventeenth- and eighteenth-century world with the false secular philosophies of the Enlightenment, chiefly deism (which teaches that God created the world but then abandoned it to its natural laws and never intervenes), God's Spirit responded by sending dynamic men, messages, missions, and movements: the Moravian missionaries, the Great Awakening, the Wesleyan revival, the evangelical emphasis on personal conversion, and the launching of Protestant missions worldwide. Thus the Spirit overreached through Zinzendorf, Edwards, and Wesley what Satan had done through Hume, Voltaire, and Rousseau. He was fulfilling His promise, "He shall set up an ensign [banner, standard] for the nations" (Isa. 11:12).

In the nineteenth century Satan planted his worst lie, Darwinism, in the world psyche. Faithfully the Spirit again countered by raising up Finney,

Moody, Spurgeon, and the Holiness, Higher Life, and faith-healing movements, to name a few. He also reintroduced and systematized the inspiring fuller doctrine of Christ's second coming, particularly the Rapture of the church, through Darby. Thus God rallied His embattled people and cause: "Behold, I will lift up mine hand…and set up my standard to the peoples" (Isa. 49:22).

In the twentieth century, when liberal theology and secularism came in on the church like a powerful tsunami, the more powerful Paraklētos raised more banner men, messages, and movements, including the Pentecostal, fundamental, evangelical, and charismatic movements. And our standard is still raised high for all—agnostics, atheists, adherents of false religions, apathetic churchgoers, and ardent Christians—to see in this twenty-first century. Why? God is never outdone!

Even in the world's worst hour, the Tribulation, God will lift a standard around which believers will gather and revive their faith!

Satan's most deceptive and convincing miracle, the raising of Antichrist from a "deadly wound," will be his ultimate envy-driven attempt to "go one-up" on God's greatest miracle: Jesus' resurrection. As His just judgment on those who persistently reject His Son, God will permit an unprecedented flood of satanic deception to sweep the earth, temporarily overwhelming the truth with the blind worship of the Antichrist. Paul prophesies:

> For this cause God shall send them strong delusion, that they should believe the lie [that the Antichrist's "resurrection" proves his deity], that they all might be judged who believed not the truth [previously persistently presented].
>
> —2 THESSALONIANS 2:11–12

But even in this, the world's darkest hour, God will raise one final standard to rally His people. He'll raise His "two witnesses" (Rev. 11:3) in Jerusalem, and, supernaturally protected, they'll denounce the Antichrist as an impostor and foretell Jesus' return to overthrow him and liberate the believing Jews he has driven into hiding. Their presence and prophecies will rally the faith of the hidden remnant and their sympathizers, until Jesus returns to earth—to raise His final standard around which all believers will rally a thousand years! Why? As Oswald Chambers said, "Everything the devil does, God overreaches to serve His own purpose."[1]

Have you experienced a "flood" of sudden, overwhelming opposition? Does it appear sure to sink your ship of faith? Or marriage? Or family? Or church? Or ministry? Then hold on. Don't react prematurely in passion or panic. Have faith in God, and look expectantly for His Spirit's response to your "flood." As surely as Isaiah is inspired and God is immutable, God's response will overreach Satan's challenge in your life. How can I be sure?

He's never outdone!

Chapter 45

THANKS FOR MY NEEDS, LORD!

N̲O̲ ̲O̲N̲E̲ ̲D̲E̲S̲I̲R̲E̲S̲ having needs of any kind—spiritual, health, material, family, business, or financial. We would all rather live without them, quiet, undisturbed, and satisfied. But needs are not our enemies; they're friends! They drive us to the Answer.

Against her will, the Syrophenician woman had a great need: her daughter was demonically possessed (Matt. 15:21–28). One day Jesus was ministering near the border between Israel and Phoenicia: "Then Jesus…departed into the borders of Tyre and Sidon [Phoenicia]" (v. 21). He may easily have come and gone without ever meeting this woman of faith, had it not been for her need. But driven by her daughter's desperate condition, the Syrophenician woman sought out the renowned Nazarene deliverer: she "came out of the same borders, and cried…Have mercy…my daughter is grievously vexed with a demon" (v. 22). When she found Him, she and her daughter found their immediate solace—"And her daughter was made well from that very hour" (v. 28)—and the living Solution to every problem. She had not only Jesus to thank for this discovery, but also her need. It led her straight where she otherwise wouldn't have gone—to Jesus! It's the same with us.

If Jesus hadn't created needs in our lives we couldn't meet with self-help, human assistance, education, psychology, or religion, we wouldn't have come to Him for salvation. And if He didn't create needs after our conversion, we wouldn't seek or know Him very well. (And I wouldn't be writing nor you reading this!) Then let's stop and ask: Would we rather be without needs or without Jesus? Without more needs or without more of Jesus?

We typically thank God for the solutions that meet our needs and terminate our trials. And we should! But we should also learn to habitually praise Him for our needs, those unexpected, unwanted, unrelenting difficulties that draw, pull, or drive us from "Phoenicia," the land of idols and ignorance of God, to "Israel," the land of the presence, people, and purpose of the one true God. Needs are the unrecognized catalysts of an ever-closer fellowship with Jesus, an ever-deeper knowledge of Him, and an ever-wider ministry with and for Him. But who creates our needs?

The devil? Certainly his dark designs and legions are involved, but our needs don't originate with our mean-spirited nemesis. Like our blessings, our troubles always come from the Lord: "So Satan went forth [to trouble and test Job] from the presence of the LORD...from the presence of the LORD" (Job 1:12; 2:7). Why does God send need-producing troubles?

Somewhere, sometime, someone is praying for us. So is Jesus, who "ever liveth to make intercession" for us (Heb. 7:25). Yes, it's true; the needs that drive us to Jesus arise not merely because Satan hates us but also because God's servants and Son are lovingly and unceasingly interceding for us. Intercession drives everything in God's kingdom and our lives, not just our triumphs but also our trials.

For instance, when we pray for people to be saved, Spirit-filled, sanctified, healed, delivered, matured, or more fruitful, the all-powerful Holy Spirit begins to create not only blessings but also needs in their lives. The blessings lead and draw them to Jesus: "The goodness of God leadeth thee to repentance" (Rom. 2:4). But the needs compel them to seek His face. They create holy pressures that constrain them to seek the holy One, who alone can fully help them. Then He saves them. Then He baptizes them in the Spirit. Then He heals or delivers them. Then He convicts them of running or wandering from Him. Then He convinces them of the danger of their besetting sins, rebellion, or stubbornness. Then, with their self-will broken, they're filled with the fear and faith of God. And a new, or renewed, relationship with Jesus is born.

As we continue interceding for these Christians, new needs arise. So they seek the Lord's help again—and pray. Then He answers again—and they believe once more. Convinced and inspired, they determine now to seek Him steadily, to pray and study His Word daily, drop distracting interests, examine themselves regularly, serve Him faithfully, worship Him often, walk in Jesus' ways, and thus prepare for His return. As this needs-prayer-answers cycle continues, they grow to know the Lord accurately, deeply, widely—and closely. Why? Intercession-driven needs have compelled them to seek, love, and walk with the Answer.

Are you persisting in intercession? Thanking God not only for your solutions but also for your needs and those your prayers create in others' lives? Since they send you and them to Him, pray, "Thanks for my needs, Lord!"

Chapter 46

COMPLETELY DEPENDENT!

*J*ESUS USED SOME amazingly accurate symbols in His teaching. For example, consider those found in His instructions to His original disciples in Matthew 10:1–42.

In that marvelous ministerial mandate, Jesus compared the first messengers of His Word, and by extension every disciple and Word-bearer throughout this age, to "sheep in the midst of wolves" (v. 16). By describing us as sheep and our spiritual antagonists as wolves gathered round us, Jesus strongly emphasized the hostile spirit of our antagonists, the lethal dangers of our present environment in this world, and our complete dependence on Him, our "good shepherd" (John 10:11). By choosing these symbols, Jesus linked us to David's shepherd song.

Psalm 23 gives us a fuller description of our total reliance on Jesus and His total care for us:

> The LORD is my shepherd; I shall not want. He maketh me to lie down in green pastures; he leadeth me beside the still waters. He restoreth my soul; he leadeth me in the paths of righteousness for his name's sake. Yea, though I walk through the valley of the shadow of death, I will fear no evil; for thou art with me; thy rod and thy staff they comfort me. Thou preparest a table before me in the presence of mine enemies; thou anointest my head with oil; my cup runneth over. Surely goodness and mercy shall follow me all the days of my life; and I will dwell in the house of the LORD forever.
>
> —PSALM 23

Our divine Shepherd, Jesus, provides "green pastures," or nourishing soul food taken in through meditation and instruction in God's Word. He leads us beside "still waters," quiet times of private prayer and worship in which we are refreshed by and refilled with the living water of His Spirit. He comforts us with His personal "staff," the reassuring touches of His sensed presence, and, when necessary, He reminds us of His benevolent authority by sending His "rod" of adversity, with its firm but loving strokes of correction. He graciously "restores our souls" when we're weary by arranging periods of bodily rest, recreation, and spiritual edification. He "leads" us in "paths of righteousness," or right paths, those He has chosen and prepared for His purpose and our good.

To this unfailing provision, He adds faithful protection. When enemies oppose us or our work, He tosses His "rod," discouraging or defeating them to defend us. He steadies us with sustained confidence, even in the darkest, longest, strangest, most hopeless "valley[s] of the shadow of death." So, in our lowest moments, we boldly confess victory over all need, foes, and fear: "I shall *not* want…I will fear *no* evil."

This protection leads to prosperity. The Shepherd grants us banquet "tables" of new blessings and fresh anointings of the "oil" of the Spirit for greater service, as our wolfish "enemies" look on, powerless to stop His favor or our praise, devotion, and service. Thus the "cup" of our circumstances "runs over" with His goodness "all the days of my life," even "forever"—if we stay near the Shepherd.

But if we stray, we stumble. And quickly! Though divinely chosen, favored, taught, trained, gifted, blessed, and anointed, sheep have no offensive weapons! Among ravenous, merciless, cunning wolves, unshepherded sheep can only do one thing: be devoured! We must remember this unpleasant fact. Why?

It's a necessary counterweight to Christ's chosen ones. Lest we swell with pride that He has chosen us to practice and proclaim His Word, He reminds us that, without His invincible help, we face impossible odds and sure failure: "Apart from Me you can do *nothing* [pleasing to God or enduring in His kingdom]" (John 15:5, NAS). Slowly but surely, the Shepherd's humbling warning infiltrates our proud, independent minds: In and with Him, possible! Without Him, impossible! The result is we're left exactly as He wants us—confident but not cocky, optimistic yet not presumptuous—as we go forth bearing His living Word to this dead world. Our faith is firm and our hope lively, yet we have no reckless sense of invincibility. We know that by ourselves we're defenseless sheep, not grizzly bears; vulnerable lambs, not voracious lions. We're wisely and healthily aware that dangerous wolves—false prophets, false teachers, hireling pastors, religious hypocrites, political frauds, envious Christians, hateful sinners, violent demoniacs, and malicious apostates—are eagerly waiting for us to break fellowship with the Shepherd so they (and their diabolical inspirer) can delight in our demise. This holy fear keeps us near our Good Shepherd. And safe, peaceful, and blessed.

And sure: we're not partially dependent on Jesus; we're completely dependent!

Chapter 47

NOT EVERY CROSSING IS STORMY

AFTER SPENDING THREE days busily healing and feeding multitudes on the eastern shore of Lake Galilee, Jesus and His disciples "sent the people home, and he got into a boat and crossed over to the region of Magadan" (Matt. 15:39, NLT). Considering how harrowing their two last crossings had been, I wonder if the disciples were a little anxious as they launched. Did they recall the howling winds and life-threatening waves and hold their breath? We don't know.

But we do know, unlike their two earlier crossings, and much to their relief, this crossing was calm and uneventful. Mark tells us Jesus and company quietly "entered into a boat...and came into the parts of Dalmanutha [or Magadan¹]" without incident (Mark 8:10). There were no high winds; violent waves; hours of wearisome rowing; long, dark terrorizing watches; ghostly appearances of Jesus; shrieks of fear; panic prayers; rebukes from Jesus; anxious bailing; wet clothes; shivering bodies; or sudden supernatural transportations to shore. None! To the contrary, this was God's peaceful sequel to their earlier stormy crossings. Earlier He gave them problems; now, peace.

This shows us that God can give us sweet serenity today in the very situations, relationships, or issues He severely tested us in yesterday. So when He calls, leads, or constrains us to again cross "Lake Galilee"—the scene of our past stormy experiences—we should not fear. Jesus may be ready to bless us there this year as much as He buffeted us last year. The apostle Paul's experiences illustrate this.

The first time Paul visited Lystra, he met a spiritual hurricane head-on! Pursued and maligned by former enemies, he was apprehended by the locals, stoned, and left for dead—only minutes later to rise and return into the city to recover and resume his mission (Acts 14:19–20). After further ministry in the region, he and Barnabas felt impressed to return again to Lystra. Lystra! Again! I'm sure red flags started waving all over Paul's mind. But sensing God's call and knowing the overriding need of the infant churches in and around Lystra, Paul bravely returned to his "Lake Galilee." "They returned again to Lystra, and to Iconium, and [Pisidian] Antioch, confirming the souls of the disciples and exhorting them" (vv. 21–22). But on this second visit, surprisingly, no opposition arose. Paul's "Galilee" was quiet and his "crossing" smooth. Instead of finding angry mobs and stones in Lystra, he found hungry converts and disciples. Instead of encountering bullies, he spent all his time edifying brothers.

A few years later, Paul felt divinely impressed to return to Lystra a third time: "Let us go again and visit our brethren in every city…and see how they do" (Acts 15:36). Again, undaunted, he launched and crossed his spiritual "Galilee." Surprisingly, this mission also was trouble-free—and profitable! It was then, in Lystra, that he met Timothy, who became his most valued friend, student, and co-minister (Acts 16:1–3). He also ministered throughout the greater region of Galatia without incident (vv. 4–5). Why?

It was a different time and season in God's plan: "To every thing there is a season, and a time to every purpose under the heaven" (Eccles. 3:1). Just as God gives Sabbaths from our work, so He gives rests from our trials. There are seasons when Jesus leads, calls, or "constrains" us to launch out onto rough waters to test, develop, perfect, and establish our faith in Him. Though we don't prefer these "Galilee" experiences, we need them. We'll never know God deeply, trust Him confidently, walk with Him closely, serve Him fruitfully, or worship Him perfectly without them. But thank God He also gives us sweet seasons of smooth sailing. Have we learned that our times and "crossings" are in His hands?

When He ordains trouble, there'll be no tranquility for a season. So, "count it all joy, when ye fall into various trials" (James 1:2). When He ordains peace, there'll be no persecution for a time. So praise Him when "he maketh peace in thy borders" (Ps. 147:14). What season are you in today?

Has Jesus called you to cross your "Galilee" again, to return to some place, deal with some relationship, or face some issue you would rather not revisit because of unpleasant past experiences? Are you worried more turbulence lies ahead in that place, with that person, over that issue? Don't be. Remember, the Master gives smooth sailing just as easily and frequently as stormy passages. Who knows, He may be giving you some surprisingly easy sailing, as He did the apostles and Paul. So bon voyage!

And praise Him that not every crossing is stormy.

Chapter 48

WILL HE LOVE OR LEAVE YOU?

*T*HOUGH KNOWN TO respond to everyone's needs, Jesus refused to respond to one group of supplicants.

When He arrived in Magadan, the Pharisees and Sadducees met Him requesting a "sign from heaven"—an attesting miracle from the skies, like those worked by Moses, Joshua, or Elijah (Matt. 16:1–4). His reaction was stunning. Instead of lovingly helping them, "He left them, and departed" (v. 4). How uncharacteristic! How un-Christlike! What caused Jesus to leave them instead of love them?

He didn't want to leave. They made Him leave by "testing Him" (v. 1). Let's see six ways they repulsed the Redeemer.

First, rather than humbly request help, they arrogantly demanded it: "The Pharisees and Sadducees came to test Jesus, demanding that he show them a miraculous sign from heaven" (v. 1, NLT). Jesus graciously granted thousands of miracles on an "in-faith" basis, but none "on demand."

Second, they didn't bow at Jesus' feet, acknowledging His authority over them, as other supplicants: "Jairus...fell at his feet, and besought him greatly" (Mark 5:22–23). Instead they put Him at their feet, or subject to their religious authority and approval.

Third, they didn't need a miracle but were just curious to see one. On this and other occasions Jesus called curiosity-driven wonder seekers by some very unflattering terms, such as "wicked" (Matt. 16:4) and "evil" (Matt. 12:39).

Fourth, for over two years Jesus had already given the Jewish people thousands of "signs," or miracles confirming His divine call and message: "Jesus went about all the cities and villages...healing every sickness and every disease among the [Jewish] people" (Matt. 9:35). So He had already overwhelmingly answered the Jewish leaders' request.

Fifth, they came to Him not in faith but in obstinate unbelief. Unlike Nicodemus, Gamaliel, Jairus, and other open-minded Jewish elders, these religious leaders were hardened with prejudice, adamantly determined to reject anything Jesus said or did, however biblical or benevolent.

Sixth, their request was hypocritical, a cheap religious act. The

Pharisees' and Sadducees' doctrines and declarations flatly contradicted their actions. The Sadducees were rationalists whose teachings denied the biblical revelation of the human spirit, angels, resurrection, and the supernatural in general. The Pharisees had already conferred and concluded that Jesus' supernatural powers were demonic and reported this widely: "He hath Beelzebub, and by the prince of the demons casteth he out demons" (Mark 3:22). For either group to approach Jesus and act as if a miracle might change their minds was a charade. Jesus refused to play along with their playacting.

So by testing Jesus in these ways they rejected Him and reaped precisely what they sowed: rejection! They rejected Jesus' signs on earth, so He refused them "signs from heaven." This left them, though hostile, in deep spiritual need and bondage. The times have changed, but human nature hasn't.

All the Jewish leaders' faults—demanding God's help, not bowing to Jesus' lordship, curiosity-driven sign seeking, ignoring what Jesus had already done in their lives, stubborn unbelief, hypocrisy, and false teaching—still occur among Christians. And all these forms of testing Christ's love and patience still cause Him to leave instead of love us. Rather than "signs from heaven," or answers to prayer, He gives us denials, leaving us in need, bondage, or oppression.

Has Jesus left you lately by withdrawing His presence ever so slightly or failing to answer your prayers? Is it because He's testing you, as He did Hezekiah (2 Chron. 32:31), or because you're testing Him? Essentially, "testing" God is trying to get Him to act at your initiative rather than you acting at His; or, asking Him to honor His promises while you dishonor His conditions; or, acting as the Jewish leaders did at Magadan. This always makes Him withdraw. If you're testing Him ever so slightly, stop! And start doing the opposite of the Jewish leaders.

Cease demanding and start humbly asking your heavenly Father for help. Honor Jesus' lordship by gladly serving His will without insisting He serve your selfish ends. Don't ask Him for anything just to satisfy your curiosity in miracles or extraordinary spiritual experiences; pray instead only for things you or others truly need. Renounce any stubborn unbelief—or Thomas-like refusal to trust God and His Word before seeing evidence of His action. Examine and, if necessary, alter your beliefs; identify teachings that, however long or widely held, plainly contradict Bible statements or promises, and reject them. Then instead of leaving you, Jesus will love you, draw near, and help you regularly with "signs from heaven." A choice looms.

It's your decision: "Be it unto thee even as thou wilt" (Matt. 15:28). Will He love or leave you?

Chapter 49

AFTER THE DARKEST VALLEY

P SALM 23 REVEALS that after the darkest valley, the brightest day dawns in our lives.

An inspired description of not only the Christian's Lord but also the Christian's life, Psalm 23 describes all the seasons in our walk with God. We first learn that our Shepherd provides all we need and declare confidently, "I shall not be in want" (v. 1, NIV). Then we learn to let Him restore our souls by resting and feeding in the lush "green pastures" of Bible reading and study, and by drinking the fresh, gentle, "still waters" of life in our pastors' and teachers' messages (vv. 2–3). Next we learn that we are here to honor "his name's sake," not ours, and so must choose "the paths of righteousness," or the ways that are right in His sight, in every decision (v. 3). Then, just as we learn to consistently recognize and follow His guidance, our life takes a surprising turn.

The good Shepherd leads us straight into a bad situation—a dark, cold, long, barren, hopeless "valley of the shadow of death" (v. 4), or "the darkest valley" (NLT). But this trouble is to test, not terminate us. We are to "walk through" this valley, not die in it. Yet in a sense we do die there. Our "flesh"—our old, independent, self-centered, self-confident, man-reliant ways of thinking, living, working, and ministering—dies a slow but sure death, after which new faith, strength, ways, purposes, and wisdom are born in its place.

Rising from the ashes of unspiritual living, we now learn to call and rely on the Shepherd "first" (Matt. 6:33) in every adversity and that His wisdom is always perfect and His methods the best. Soon we completely relinquish our private plans and start living for His kingdom purposes. Gradually our old fears fade too, and in their place a new indomitable confidence is born: "I can do all things [everything! anything!] through Christ, who strengtheneth me [with His supernatural, power, ability, grace]" (Phil. 4:13). We learn that as long as we stay close to the Shepherd, He stays close to us, comforting us with the "staff" of His manifest presence and defending us with the "rod" of His powerful intervention (Ps. 23:4). Boasting in Him, we defiantly declare, "The LORD is my shepherd...I will fear no evil" (vv. 1, 4), sure now that the Shepherd's faithfulness is unfailing, even in the darkest valley. But even these abysmally difficult periods end: "Surely there is an end" (Prov. 23:18).

As our low, dark hour of trial passes, our brightest day dawns, filled with the warm favor of divine Son-shine and its rich blessings. We begin finding new blessings "prepared before us" on the left and right. Soon we're feasting on a whole banquet "table" filled with rich blessings—and our spiteful "enemies" fall silent when they see the signs of the Shepherd's approval and the fresh "oil" of His Spirit's inspiration upon us (Ps. 23:5). Unable to contain our inner joy, the river of the Spirit within us begins flowing out: "my cup runneth over" (v. 5). We begin fulfilling our Abrahamic destiny to "be a blessing" (Gen. 12:2) as others are helped by the loving works and life-giving words that flow from our anointing. For the rest of our lives God's "goodness" and "mercy" track us; wherever we go, they "follow" (Ps. 23:6). We leave a lingering legacy of love—the Shepherd's goodwill and kind deeds flowing through us—in every life we touch. Yet there is a greater blessing.

"I will dwell in the house of the LORD forever" (v. 6). The key feature of God's "house," or temple, was His presence within. Without the glory, the temple would have been nothing, just another religious building. So to the psalmist, and us, to "dwell in the house" is to "dwell in the presence." And "in thy presence is fullness of joy" (Ps. 16:11). This is our greatest blessing, more of God! It is increased, enhanced, rapturous intimacy with Jesus—His peace deeper, His voice stronger, His Word clearer, His hand more evident, His anointings more frequent, and His strength more powerful! And these wonders are ours, not for a day, but "forever" (Ps. 23:6). They await us at the end of our darkest valley.

Is your valley of testing very low and dark? Psalm 23 prophesied you would pass this way. Jesus emerged from His darkest valley "in the power of the Spirit" (Luke 4:14). So will you! Don't give up; look up! The Son-shine of the Shepherd's favor and dawn of your brightest day await, after the darkest valley.

Chapter 50

IS YOUR SHIELD IN PLACE?

SALM 82 DECLARES when God's people judge unjustly, He eventually intervenes to judge justly.

This sobering song describes sin, oppression, and injustice among the redeemed, whom the psalmist Asaph describes as "the congregation of the mighty" (v. 1), "gods" (v. 1), and "children of the Most High" (v. 6). The pressing problem is God's disobedient children, "the wicked" (v. 2), who are persistently harming their vulnerable fellow believers, the "poor," "fatherless," and "afflicted" (v. 3). This has lasted so long "all the [vital social] foundations [including justice]...are out of place" (v. 5). These trouble-making tares among the wheat don't know God intimately and don't want to: "They walk on [stubbornly, willfully] in darkness" (v. 5). Sin has horribly hardened and blinded them.

Typically "wicked," they presume that good men, often naïve, will never detect their treachery: "Who will ever notice?" (Ps. 64:5, NLT). And they reason, gracious as He is, God will never punish them: "God hath forgotten...he will never see it" (Ps. 10:11). But they're wrong. God calls righteous leaders (the "mighty") to judge righteously: "Deliver the poor...out of the hand [oppressive control] of the wicked" (Ps. 82:4). And He adds a somber warning: if they don't, He will! He warns His wicked children, "I have said, Ye are gods...children of the Most High. But ye shall die like men, and fall" (vv. 6–7). Why does He call His people "gods"?

Compared to the unredeemed, who are mere unaided mortals, His people—Jews then, Christians today—enjoy a godlike status. Though earthbound, they are:

- Given heavenly wisdom, not left to human intelligence
- Blessed with satisfying divine fellowship, not just fickle human friendships
- Guided by a divine Shepherd, not short-sighted human counselors
- Supported by unfailing divine grace, not unpredictable human mercies

- Protected by an impenetrable divine shield, not limited human defenses

Jesus quoted and confirmed this: "Is it not written in your law, I said, Ye are gods?" (John 10:34).

Despite these superhuman favors, this psalm declares that if God's people persistently, impenitently sin, even His "divine" children may "die like men"—perish as impotently, insignificantly, and tragically as unsaved men neither watched nor shielded by God. King Saul illustrates this.

Though previously protected in battle, Saul was slain by the Philistines on Mount Gilboa, and his body was decapitated and desecrated. Of Saul's shocking, untimely death, David said, "How are the mighty fallen!...The shield of the mighty is vilely cast away, the shield of Saul, as though he had not been anointed" (2 Sam. 1:19, 21). Despite Saul's covenant, call, and anointing, God removed his "shield" of divine protection. Why? For years he envied, slandered, and labored to kill David. And despite many warnings and mercies, he had no intention of changing. So to save His poor, afflicted servant David from wicked Saul's hand, God intervened through the Philistines and judged justly. Do you know your shield?

It's not your attorney, money, family, friends, nation's military, or other natural defense mechanisms. It's supernatural—God Himself. "Thou, O LORD, art a shield for me" (Ps. 3:3). Specifically, God assigns angels to guard us and everything near and dear. Psalm 91 describes this and the Book of Job confirms it. "Hast not thou made an hedge about him, and about his house, and about all that he hath on every side?" (Job 1:10). But this godlike protection is not for everyone. It's only for Christians who humbly trust and obey God. "Sons [children] of disobedience" (Eph. 5:6) who, like Saul, presumptuously "walk on in darkness," risk having their shield removed at any time.

Thus God not only revives but also removes His people, albeit always with grief, only to relieve oppression, and only when no other alternatives remain: "The Lord killeth, and maketh alive" (1 Sam. 2:6). Though God used the Philistines to take Saul, He personally struck Nadab, Abihu, Uzziah, Nabal, Ananias, and Sapphira with terrible or terminal judgments. This isn't popular truth.

But it's vital. This generation needs to be told plainly what previous generations knew: persistently practicing sin negates new covenant benefits. Stubborn children of disobedience invoke the wrath, not the favors, of

God. We need to firmly believe both sides of the biblical coin of protection: God shields us, and sin exposes us. Surprisingly, this holy fear of the Lord boosts, not weakens, our faith. It repairs the sin-holes in our breastplate of righteousness and shield of faith and leaves our confidence in God rock-solid: "In the fear of the LORD is strong confidence, and his children shall have a place of refuge [safety, confidence]" (Prov. 14:26). So here's an unpopular but vital question.

Is your shield in place?

Chapter 51

MINISTERING TO LOST SHEEP

*J*ESUS REFERRED TO the Pharisaic and Sadducean Jews as God's "lost sheep" (Matt. 10:6). Indeed, they had wandered far from their heavenly Shepherd and His covenant and care.

Separated from God's true holiness, they were lost in sin. Separated from the leading of His voice and left to their ways, they were lost without guidance. Separated from the "staff" of His Spirit and His comforting, reassuring touches, they were lost in anxiety (Ps. 23:4). Separated from His "rod" of discipline, they were lost in their errors (v. 4). Separated from His "rod" of protection, and exposed to wolfish enemies, they were lost in danger (v. 4). Separated from His lush "green pastures" of truth, they were hungry, weak, and lost without knowledge (v. 2). Separated from His "table" of blessings and its funds and supplies, they were lost in poverty (v. 5). Separated from sweet fellowship with their fellow sheep, they were lost in loneliness. Seeing how lost they were, their merciful Shepherd drew near.

Upon arrival, He declared He was commissioned primarily to regather and restore Jacob's wandering sheep: "I was sent only to help God's lost sheep—the people of Israel" (Matt. 15:24, NLT). And He worked fast and faithfully to fulfill His commission, healing, releasing, correcting, exhorting, and teaching sheep after sheep. He found one possessed by thousands of demons and liberated him. He found a young lamb dead and raised and returned her to her father. He healed another sheep who was afflicted and financially drained for twelve years. He saved one from a stoning and instructed her to "sin no more" (John 8:11); and another from infirmity, exhorting him to "stop sinning or something worse may happen" (John 5:14, NIV). He liberated another long oppressed by a "spirit of infirmity" (Luke 13:11). His mere presence moved a rich sheep to stop stealing from his fellow sheep and "restore fourfold" (Luke 19:8). And He led countless other wounded, wayward Jews back to the fellowship, faithfulness, and fold of Jehovah. Our commission is like His.

"As my Father hath sent me, even so send I you" (John 20:21). As Jesus was sent to minister to Israel's lost sheep, mature Christian disciples are sent to minister to the church's lost sheep. These stray lambs are not "goats," or unregenerated unbelievers. They are born-again believers who, after receiving the Shepherd and entering His sheepfold, covenant, and care, wander away.

Some are degenerating Christians. They've lost their interest in the things of God and stopped going on in the way of life. They haven't fully turned back to their old life yet, but they're thinking about it. They've stopped restoring their souls daily by fellowship with Christ in His Word, prayer, and worship, and, lukewarm, are no longer focused on Him. Others are backslidden. Yielding to selfishness in the heat of trial, they have turned from their new, loving Shepherd to their old foolish sins and futile ends. Still others are apostate. Offended by long, hard tests, invasive corrections, or other difficulties or disappointments, they've fully forsaken the Word, ways, and person of the Truth, and now bitterly slander and resist His faithful sheep.

Some of these lost sheep attend church meetings regularly, though without receiving or ministering spiritual life. Others, though equally wrong in spirit, are more honest in behavior and avoid the sheepfold. But all share this common condition: they have wandered far from the Shepherd in their hearts and need to be restored to closeness with Him. How can we minister to them?

As God permits, we may offer lost sheep corrective counsel, graciously talking them back into the faith and fold by "speaking the truth in love" (Eph. 4:15). If this isn't possible, we may "go after that which is lost" (Luke 15:4) by persistently interceding: "If any man see his brother sin a sin which is not unto death, he shall ask, and he shall give him life" (1 John 5:16). Or we may speak commands of faith in Jesus' name to "bind" whatever binds them and "loose" them from it (Matt. 18:18). These prayers and commands are more effective when other intercessors agree with us, even as few as "two or three" (vv. 19–20). When new opportunities arise, we may further warn them of the consequences of wandering, specifically, loss of part or all of our rewards in Christ (2 John 8). We may also show kindness, so God's goodness through us may lead them to repent (Rom. 2:4). Then we should wait patiently, giving the Holy Spirit time to lead them home.

Look around. Everywhere the Good Shepherd's sheep are wandering—and He's grieving. Take His mantle, and mission, and minister to lost sheep.

Chapter 52

CONFESSING CHRIST

HROUGHOUT THE CHURCH Age, confessing faith in Christ has been vitally important. The apostle Paul certainly thought so.

Paul declared the confession of our faith to be an essential part of being born again. Without it we can't be saved "by grace...through faith" (Eph. 2:8). He explained to the Romans, and us, the simple mechanics of Christian conversion: (1) believe in Jesus, and (2) confess Him. "If thou shalt confess with thy mouth the Lord Jesus [Jesus as your Lord], and shalt believe in thine heart that God hath raised him from the dead, thou shalt be saved" (Rom. 10:9). The key thoughts in this verse are *believe-confess-saved*! Paul wasn't alone in emphasizing our confession of faith.

Jesus expects us to openly confess our faith in Him to other people. He identified the main obstacle that hinders us from confessing Him—fear of people's rejection, reproach, and reprisals. His instructions? "Fear them not" (Matt. 10:26). Then, to encourage and embolden us, He promised faithful confessors a wonderful reward: "Whosoever...shall confess me before men, him will I confess also before my Father" (v. 32). "Confess before my Father" means honorably present, recognize, and commend before all heaven. This means more than calling our names during the roll call of the redeemed. He'll also compliment our Christlike attributes and works before the Godhead, angels, and saints. No earthly honors or accolades compare with this heavenly honorarium! And it's ours, if we confess Him before men.

The basic requirement here is simple. Jesus wants us to say publicly that we believe in Him and His work to save us: we believe...Jesus is God's Son, He died for our sins, He rose for our justification, and, to put it in modern evangelical terms, He is now our personal Lord and Savior. This is confessing Christ by lip.

While this conviction and confession save us, Christ's challenge "confess me before men" implies more. There are other ways we may confess Christ, and should, if we want to please Him deeply and one day receive His full, enthusiastic confessor's commendation: "Well done, thou good and faithful servant.... Enter thou into the joy of thy lord" (Matt. 25:21). Not our words but our actions confess Christ, or declare by demonstration He is living and having His way in us, whenever we do the following.

We may confess Christ by leaving, or voluntarily abandoning, the places, associations, and relationships in which we formerly practiced sin of any kind. We may confess Him by lifestyle, or by not conforming to this world's secular beliefs and materialistic way of life but by instead transforming our life-goals, values, and daily habits to live humble, holy, Spirit-led, Christ-centered lives. We may confess Him by love, or by cultivating affection for Jesus by spending quality time alone with Him daily in devotional Bible reading, unpretentious prayer, and adoring worship; and also by loving and helping others, as He commanded: "A new commandment I give unto you, that ye love one another" (John 13:34), and "Thou shalt love thy neighbor as thyself" (Matt. 22:39). This confession of compassion convinces: "By this shall all men know that ye are my disciples, if ye have love one to another" (John 13:35).

Additionally, we may confess Him by loathing, or by hating sin while maintaining mercy for sinners: "Ye who love the LORD, hate evil" (Ps. 97:10). Knowing that Jesus hates sin and that apathy toward sin is therefore apathy toward Him and His will, we stand firmly against sin—first, in our lives; second, in the church; and third, in society. We may confess Him by labor, or by working wholeheartedly and steadily "as to the Lord" (Col. 3:23) in everything we do. We may confess Him by lending, or by reliving His life mission "not to be ministered unto, but to minister, and to give" (Matt. 20:28), as we look first to give or share rather than gain or hold. We may confess Him by lifting, or by promoting His name above all other purported deities as being the only true Savior and way to the Father. We may confess Him by lingering, or by waiting patiently for the Father's appointed time to fulfill His plans, bless our labors, answer our prayers, or release us from difficulties. (See Revelation 3:10.) We may confess Him by longing, or by desiring first to know Him more deeply, fellowship with Him more closely, obey Him more consistently, discern His hand and voice more frequently, and bear Him more fruit. This is our confession by life.

So confess Jesus by lip and by life! His highest commendation, and your highest joy, await—for confessing Christ.

Chapter 53

WILL YOU BE ENLARGED?

*I*N THESE PERILOUS times, God needs Christians with great hearts—believing souls enlarged by His Spirit to fully identify with His large purposes, plans, and passion for His people. But broadening our hearts won't be easy.

David testified God enlarged his soul by putting him through stressful situations: "Thou hast enlarged me when I was in distress" (Ps. 4:1). There are two valid interpretations.

One is whenever we're in distresses, God faithfully enlarges us, or releases us from our trials. The Hebrew describes someone who's trapped or limited in a narrow, tight place then suddenly released into a larger, roomier space.[1] "You have given me relief when I was in distress" (v. 1, ESV), or, "You have freed me from my troubles" (GW). This highlights how God gives us outward deliverance or release from trying circumstances. "God is faithful, who will…make the way to escape" (1 Cor. 10:13).

Another interpretation illuminates God's inner work—how He releases us from inner sin- and attitude-bindings and widens our hearts to be more Christlike in our thinking and living, all as we pass through tight places. He enlarges not our circumstances but our souls and our spiritual capacity, and not after but during (in) stressful tests of faith and patience. "*In* adversity Thou gavest enlargement to me" (Ps. 4:1, YLT).

One translation correctly endorses both views: "You have freed me when I was hemmed in and enlarged me when I was in distress" (AMP). While agreeing with both views, we want to focus on the second: the enlarging work God does in us during stressful tests as we continue trusting and obeying Him. This is clearly how He made David a greater man.[2]

After calling David, God graciously gave him a period of unchecked blessing and prosperity. Then He began enlarging him by putting him through a demanding decade of disillusioning rejection, demeaning reproach, discouraging delays, deflating humiliation, diminutive fruit, monotonous labors, and dangerous persecution. Yet there his dependency on, closeness to, communication with, and confidence in God were permanently forged. And David emerged "enlarged"—wide-hearted, humble, merciful, wise, taught of God, and ready for higher service.

No accident, this is also how God made Joseph's soul large, Paul's heart big, Moses' character colossal, and Daniel's inner man magnanimous. He put them into stressful trials, preserved, guided, and taught them and then later released them, enlarged and ennobled to lead. To deny this is to be unfaithful to the biblical record and its Inspirer's chosen method of making great souls.

Jesus used this method. He enlarged His disciples' faith during Lazarus' strange sickness and death, explaining, "I am glad for your sakes that I was not there, to the intent ye may believe [trust me more henceforth]" (John 11:15). He was "glad" at their stressful bereavement only because He knew that at trial's end, their confidence in Him and His help would be larger and stronger. Then they would be ready to help others restfully trust Him when for long periods His actions (or inactions) were unexplainable and their troubles unresolved.

Tests enlarge not only our faith but also our patience, love, loyalty to God, knowledge of His ways, and viewpoint on life, the church, and the world. But if we won't endure our tests, we remain small-hearted—set on our own little way, driven by our own little ambitions, and wrapped up in our own little world. And small-hearted Christians cannot be great leaders.

Try as we may, nothing else will enlarge us. Study, prayer, fasting, anointings, worship, laying on of hands, blessings, promotion, association with prominent leaders—none of these things by themselves enlarge us. We must go through the stressful challenges God sends. There our close fellowship and unerring communication with Him is founded. There our implicit trust in Him, His wisdom, and His ways is forged. There He takes away our smallness and gives us His largeness of heart: "God so loved *the world*" (John 3:16).

Today the church needs great hearts desperately. Why? Great blessings are coming—unprecedented outpourings of the Spirit, many conversions, marvelous deliverances, powerful healings, fresh revelations, the turning of nations—and with them, great trials. For these we need great leaders with large hearts. They alone can lead and teach us to do great things in great trials: "The people that do [deeply] know their God shall be strong, and do exploits [bold deeds]. And they...shall instruct many" (Dan. 11:32–33). Where are this generation's spiritually large leaders? Wherever and whoever they are, God is enlarging them.

Realizing this, they will look up and thank Him in their distress and let the enlarging go on. Will you be enlarged?

Chapter 54

GOT THE "RIGHT STUFF"?

JERICHO WAS ISRAEL'S first stop in the Canaan conquest (Josh. 6:1–27). The battle there was a divinely designed crucial test.

It would reveal whether God's people had the "right stuff," or character qualities necessary to rule the Promised Land. If they took Jericho His way, they had it. If not, they proved themselves unworthy to rule with Him—and worthy only to wander like their fathers' failed generation.

At Jericho they had to believe a God-given vision and promise. On the eve of hostilities, Joshua received a timely vision of Jesus, the Captain of Israel's hosts (Josh. 5:13–15), and with it a clear promise of victory: "I have given into thine hand Jericho" (Josh. 6:2). Would the Israelites trust the power of their heavenly Warrior and His angelic armies? Would they believe His Word guaranteeing victory? This faith in His faithfulness was the primary response God required. But there was much more.

They had to listen and take instructions well, as God's directives for victory were numerous and detailed. They had to be obedient, as victory would come only if they obeyed all God's orders. They had to submit to authority, obeying Joshua's leadership without resistance or resentment. They had to humble themselves, as their brave men accepted God's order to meekly march, not fight, knowing well they may be mocked as cowards by Jericho's warriors. They had to learn wisdom, by recognizing that God's way is always best—it was better that He fight for them than they fight for themselves.

They had to accept their individual callings, or God-given personal marching orders, and remain in the rank, position, and duty assigned them. They had to be patient, as victory would come in God's time, not theirs; not in one day, but seven; not after one circuit of the city, but thirteen. They had to control their speech by remaining totally silent while marching and shouting loudly only when prompted: "So the people shouted when the priests blew with the trumpets" (Josh. 6:20). They had to stop complaining continually and start praising God continually by offering a vicarious, in-strumental "sacrifice of praise" (Heb. 13:15) through their priests' constant trumpeting (Josh. 6:13). They had to guard God's presence in their lives by placing the ark of the covenant (God's earthly throne) in a protected position in their column with guards before and after. They had to overcome baffling contradictions, as for seven days and twelve circuits all their efforts produced no visible changes; Jericho's walls and warriors looked the same on the seventh day as on the first! They had to be diligent, rising early with Joshua to make the most of every day: "They rose early about the dawning of the day" (v. 15). They had to take proper rests, returning to their camp after each day's march: "They...returned into the camp; so they did six days" (v. 14). They had to alertly watch and pray for God's signals as they awaited Joshua's inspired command, "Shout" (v. 16).

They had to confidently confess their faith by shouting their victory before Jericho's walls fell: "When the people heard the [long, sustained] sound of the trumpet...the people shouted with a great shout" (v. 20). They had to mortify covetousness by not taking any spoils; Joshua's clear orders were, "All the silver, and gold, and vessels of bronze and iron, are consecrated [dedicated exclusively] unto the LORD" (v. 19). They had to fear the Lord by obeying Joshua's warning to not touch the "accursed thing" (spoils dedicated to God) lest they be judged. They had to further love their brothers by avoiding the spoils so that their selfishness would not "trouble" and "curse" their congregation (v. 18). They had to endure hardship, since the last day required seven times more physical exertion, willpower, and mental focus than the previous six: "On that day they compassed the city seven times" (v. 15). They had to accept God's judgments by slaying all the people of Jericho whom God had justly condemned, though to many this may have seemed unfair. They had to have and show God's mercy by sparing Rahab and her household, though some were likely tempted to despise them. So they showed God they had the "right stuff." Their characters were mature and ready to rule.

Is yours? The One with the "right stuff" indwells you. Your "Jericho," or present crucial test, is designed to mature and manifest His character in you. By consistently complying with God's instructions, you show Him you're ready to rule with Christ, not wander in worldliness. At Jericho the Israelites proved they were ready. What about you?

Got the "right stuff"?

Chapter 55

JESUS TELLS ALL!

*I*N MATTHEW 10 Jesus gave His original twelve disciples—the first Word-bearing Christians—a vital talk as He sent them forth to spread His message and ministry in Galilee: "These twelve Jesus sent forth and commanded them, saying…" (v. 5).

Faithfully, He spoke of things both advantageous and adverse, but more of the latter than the former: twenty-six of this chapter's forty-two verses deal with the unpleasant aspects of being His messengers. Here He addresses not only the original disciples but also every other "Word-bearer," or Christian minister or disciple who loves, lives, and spreads God's Word, from Pentecost to the Rapture. Let's examine His talk more closely.

How thorough He was! Not one hard fact was hidden. How blunt He was! Not one shocking statement was softened. Like an officer giving soldiers a battle briefing, Jesus laid out every difficulty and danger they could possibly face on their mission—citywide rejections, enemies with venomous hatred and ravenous revenge ("serpents, wolves"), scandalous public hearings, brutal whippings, cruel betrayals, forced flights, widespread hatred, vicious epithets ("Beelzebub"), shocking executions, anguishing family divisions, and other "crosses" (vv. 14–39.) The message was clear: Bearing His Word to the world would not be easy. It would be supremely challenging and demand total commitment to Him. Some would not make it through to the end of the mission. Why did He tell all?

Why not spare them full disclosure? Why not share just the positive aspects and let them discover the negative later? While Jesus didn't identify His reasons, four seem certain.

First, by disclosing their adversities, Jesus intended to dissuade insincere followers. The Messiah was not about to commission a "mixed multitude." If their motives were selfish, He wanted to weed them out early, before they made trouble for His committed ones.

Second, He didn't want His disciples to be naïve. They must not have inaccurate imaginations or grandiose illusions about New Testament ministry. Their outlook must be realistic, not rosy; grounded, not giddy. This would keep them from falling headlong into discouraging pits of disillusionment.

Third, He didn't want His Word-bearers to be overwhelmed with offense when Satan viciously attacked them through the rejections or persecutions of disbelieving family members or corrupt religious and political leaders. By forewarning them, He forearmed them. They were bolstered and braced for the enemy's swift arrows and blitzkriegs.

Fourth, as Matthew Henry noted, Jesus meant to strengthen His disciples' faith. When His problematic predictions came to pass, they could pause, ponder, and realize more deeply that, if He could so clearly foresee the future, He was truly God—knowing all, controlling all, and lovingly guiding all for their ultimate good! Thus they would trust Him all the more in their troubles.

Early church leaders followed Jesus' method. The apostles told all to their students and fellow ministers. Paul informed the Ephesian elders he had given them full disclosure: "I have not shunned to declare unto you all the counsel of God" (Acts 20:27). He also warned them to expect invasions of spiritual wolves and uprisings of self-serving ministers in their congregations: "I know this, that after my departing shall grievous wolves enter in, not sparing the flock. Also of your own selves shall men arise...to draw away disciples after them" (vv. 29–30). Peter frankly forewarned Christians everywhere to expect fiery tests: "Think it not strange concerning the fiery trial which is to test you" (1 Pet. 4:12). He further warned that wolfish, greedy false teachers would infiltrate, mislead, fleece, and bring reproach upon God's flocks: "There shall be false teachers among you...[and]...make merchandise of you" (2 Pet. 2:1–3). Are we following the apostles' method?

Do we give full disclosure to newly converted Christians? To newly ordained ministers? Or do we only share the advantages of walking and working with Jesus—having biblical insight, divine provision, divine health, angelic protection, spiritual authority, the power of faith, the joy of fellowship, the delight of worship, the marvel of the Spirit's power and gifts, and so forth? Truly, all these blessings and more are ours as we bear God's Word to the world! But we mustn't hide the adversities attached to these advantages. Jesus didn't. But His marketing skills weren't as good as ours.

"Come see the world!" read the US Navy recruitment posters of yesteryear. "Be all you can be!" is one of the Army's more recent pitches. Wouldn't it be nice if they added, "And be shot at—and possibly imprisoned, wounded, killed, maimed, despised by many foreigners, and appreciated by few Americans"? That's not good marketing, but it's our Master's way.

Isn't it time we follow His method? Jesus tells all!

Chapter 56

HE'S PREPARING HIS WAY...AGAIN!

EFORE JOHN THE Baptist's ministry, God desired to visit His people, reveal His glory among them, and save many through them, releasing them from Satan's oppression and establishing them in close fellowship with Him. But His way was blocked. Why?

The people of the holy One were too unholy. Their consistently sinful attitudes and actions made it impossible for the sinless One to come live and move among them. For the moment.

Enter John the Baptist—predestined, prophesied, prepared, anointed, and sent with messages from God—to remove the blockage and build a "way," or spiritual road, for God's desire. John was "the voice of one crying in the wilderness, Prepare ye the way of the Lord" (Luke 3:4). It wouldn't be easy to awaken and reform God's sleeping, stubborn, Pharisaically mis-led flock, but God sent John to do it. And do it he did, not by his human wisdom, ways, or willpower but by the almighty power and wisdom of the Spirit of God resting upon him (Zech. 4:6).

Simple and direct, John's constructive criticisms (Luke 3:10–14), given to correct the Jews' sinful attitudes and actions, had four essential goals. They are described figuratively in Luke 3:5 (NKJV):

1. RAISE VALLEYS. "Every valley...*filled* [and thus raised]..."
   "Valleys" speak of low or insufficient faith or self-esteem. Fear, oppression, condemnation, doubt, hopelessness—all these low conditions had to be lifted by trusting God, receiving His forgiveness, hoping in His promises and prophecies, and understanding one's honorable place, gift, purpose, and worth in God.

2. LOWER MOUNTAINS. "Every mountain...*brought low*..."
   "Mountains" here speak of uplifted attitudes. All the people's "pride of life"—vanity, nationalism, prejudice, sectarianism, boasting, religious ambition, envious competition—had to be lowered, or replaced by sober, humble, childlike, and egalitarian attitudes.

3. STRAIGHTEN CROOKED PLACES. "Crooked places…*made straight*…" Every crooked, or twisted, practice had to go—illegality, injustice, immorality, unethical behavior, and anything less than "his righteousness" (Matt. 6:33). Now they must straighten up, or walk and talk righteously.

4. SMOOTH ROUGH PLACES. "Rough ways *[made] smooth*." Rough ways are unloving dealings. All callous, curt, disrespectful, spiteful, or vengeful words and works must be replaced with mercy, patience, forgiveness, refusal to prejudge or condemn others, and "speaking the truth in love" (Eph. 4:15). Then they could live and work together smoothly, unified by the "bond of perfectness" (Col. 3:14).

Once these wrong attitudes and actions were changed, God's spiritual highway was in place. His visitation quickly followed, revealing the glory of God—the wonder of *Jesus living and ministering among them* in the fullness of His truth, power, compassion, and grace—for all to see. Through Scripture we still see this glory today.

In these last days God wants to visit His people again—not Jews but Christians. He yearns to send Jesus to us before He comes for us. He wants His earthly glory to dwell with us before we go dwell with Him in heavenly glory. So He's sending ministers with messages of correction to make a way for Him to visit us. It won't be easy to change us (1 Pet. 4:18), but God's Spirit is upon His "Johns" to do so. As we let their corrections change our wrong attitudes and actions—raising our valleys, lowering our mountains, straightening our crookedness, and smoothing our rough ways—we build God's spiritual highway. His visitation will soon follow. That's good news.

Here's more. We can let God prepare His way in us, even if others won't let Him. And we can do so in our church, even if other congregations prefer to remain uncorrected and unprepared for revival. How illuminating!

This explains why you're being tested as you are, why the messages you're hearing or reading often convict you, why the counsels you're receiving urge changes in key areas of your thinking and behavior. The Spirit that sent John is calling you: "Prepare ye the way of the Lord" in your life and in your church! Get ready for revival! Let Jesus come to you before He comes for you, and live with you below before you live with Him above. Let Him humble your pride, raise your confidence in Him, straighten your twisted ways, and smooth your rough words or ways. Then you will be a spiritual highway by which He may come to fellowship with you and minister through you His convicting voice, reviving Spirit, guiding Word, healing touch, and inspiring hope. And His glory will shine again, not from Galilee but from your soul, your church. Don't block God's way. Build it! Today! Why?

He's preparing His way...again!

Chapter 57

How Soon We Forget!

AVID EXHORTS US, "Forget not all his benefits" (Ps. 103:2). Yet we too often fail to do this very thing.

How quickly we lose sight of the signs of God's faithful love and fall back into the old habits of…anxiety, tormented with fears of failure until tangible answers manifest…discontentment, neglecting what we have because we covet something more…gloom, depressed with non-expectation when we should be joyful with anticipation! In this fault we mirror the ancient Israelites.

Though God had shown the children of Israel astounding signs in Egypt, a stunning intervention at the Red Sea, and daily wonders in the wilderness, the psalmist sadly noted, "They soon forgot his works" (Ps. 106:13). Consequently, Moses' generation stagnated and never grew to spiritual maturity. Instead of giving God glory, they gave Him grief. God mourned, "I was grieved with that generation, and said, They do always err in their heart, and they have not known my ways" (Heb. 3:10). That generation was not the only one to lose its holy recall.

Jesus' disciples also quickly forgot His loving wonders. Though they had seen Jesus multiply meager food supplies to feed a multitude of five thousand only weeks earlier,[1] when a new need arose to feed less people—about four thousand—they seemed stricken with amnesia. Dismayed, the disbelieving disciples exclaimed, "From where should we have so much bread in the wilderness, as to fill so great a multitude?" (Matt. 15:33). More than silly or stupid, this reaction was sinful. We too suffer from the sin of forgetfulness.

It's amazing how quickly we lose appreciation for what the Lord has done for us—last year, last month, last week, yesterday, thirty minutes ago! Why do we so quickly forget our Father's favors and His Son's sweet mercies?

We fail to do three things consistently: thank, think, and tell. We don't thank the Lord sufficiently for His gracious blessings or answers to prayer whenever they land on the shores of our lives. We don't spend enough time quietly meditating on them, considering at length what God did, and why, and how gracious and faithful He is to do so. And we don't testify of them enough or, in some cases, at all, though Jesus has appointed us as "witnesses unto me" (Acts 1:8). To correct these deficiencies, here are three recommendations.

First, we should form a habit of thanksgiving: "Give thanks in all circumstances, for this is God's will for you" (1 Thess. 5:18, NIV). On this foundation of general thanksgiving, we should build a house of specific thanks. Whenever God's blessings arrive, we should immediately stop and thank Him, before telling others, and offer additional thanks for several days. This ingrains gratitude in our hearts.

Second, we should take time to ponder "his benefits"—thoughtfully recalling our need, our prayer, and how the Lord responded, often in ways "exceedingly abundantly above" our requests (Eph. 3:20). Paul advised Timothy, and us, "Meditate upon these things" (1 Tim. 4:15). Scripture urges us to, "Remember the LORD thy God" (Deut. 8:18). This worshipful, repetitive remembrance cultivates enduring grateful memories of God's touches in our lives. We need to grow in this grace: "My people doth not consider [think sufficiently]" (Isa. 1:3). Or, "My people don't recognize my care for them" (NLT).

Third, we should testify of God's faithful help to other believers (not unbelievers, Matt. 7:6), in meetings, conversations, and correspondence. "Let the redeemed of the LORD say so" (Ps. 107:2); or, "Has the LORD redeemed you? Then speak out! Tell others" (NLT). This seals our memory of our "benefit"—and Benefactor!

These three exercises will save us from forgetfulness. Thereafter, we'll think and behave differently.

In tests, our cries of panic will become songs of praise. Instead of sinking with anxiety, we'll rise with expectation that God will do again what He did before: "The LORD who delivered me out of the paw of the lion, and…bear, he will deliver me out of the hand of this Philistine" (1 Sam. 17:37). When new blessings are delayed, rather than complain, we'll stand still in patient thanksgiving, content with the gracious benefits and Benefactor we already have and enjoy. Instead of stumbling in the weakness, confusion, and depression of worry, we'll "run, and not be weary" (Isa. 40:31) in the strength and joy of faith, knowing we'll see God work again in our life soon—today, tonight, or tomorrow! Instead of stagnating, we'll grow to full spiritual maturity. Instead of grieving our heavenly Father, we'll glorify Him.

And He'll shout for joy, "How well they remember!" And we'll never again moan, "How soon we forget!"

Chapter 58

HAVE YOU RECEIVED THIS POWER?

*Y*E SHALL RECEIVE power, after the Holy Spirit is come upon you," said Jesus to His original followers (Acts 1:8). And from Pentecost to the present, everyone receiving the Holy Spirit has indeed received power. But what kind?

The pat theological answer is power for service. While true, this definition is simply too limited to be accurate. *Power* is translated from the Greek *dunamis*, meaning "miraculous power or ability."[1] The New Testament also renders *dunamis* as "power [of God], mighty works, a miracle, strength, virtue."[2] Jesus said we receive this power by receiving His Spirit. Clearly, the power of God's very Spirit—His distinctive divine strength and ability—imparted to us is much broader and more diversified than power or strength for service. Let's get specific.

It, rather He, is the power to overcome sin, or our sin nature—our proud, stubborn, inborn preference for defying, or doing without, God.

He's the power to overcome our sins—the wrong acts and omissions arising consistently from our sin nature that cause us to offend God and others and oppose ourselves.

He's the power to be Jesus' witness, not only declaring but also demonstrating how great He is: "After the Holy Spirit is come upon you…ye shall be witnesses unto me" (Acts 1:8).

He's the power to seek Jesus first, or "seek ye first the kingdom of God, and his righteousness" (Matt. 6:33), daily and in every decision.

He's the power to recognize the Bible is God's counsel and accurately interpret, apply, and obey its instructions in spontaneous daily situations.

He's the power to see the ultimate worthlessness of worldly wealth and goals and the true riches of biblical values and ends.

He's the power to break the strongest unholy, harmful habits and form even stronger holy, helpful ones.

He's the power to be thankfully content in every circumstance, advantageous or adverse, and steadily pursue our work with energy and excellence, not to please people, but "as to the Lord" (Col. 3:23).

He's the power to know, love, and walk closely with Jesus in a world that rejects and mocks Him and churches that often follow Him afar off.

He's the power to pray privately, simply, and effectively to God anywhere, anytime, about anything, and know He answers.

He's the power to worship God daily "in spirit and in truth" (John 4:24), ever rediscovering that "in thy presence is fullness of joy" (Ps. 16:11).

He's the power to "be still, and know" (Ps. 46:10) when and what God's still, small voice is speaking to your heart.

He's the power to teach, preach, or share God's Word with timely and lasting inspiration and to minister truths Christians loathe—sin, self-examination, chastening, judgment—as easily as those they love.

He's the power to discern false teachings and teachers and recognize true prophets and prophecies.

He's the power to give thanks, worship, and intercede for others effectively in an unknown prayer language perfectly understood by God and aligned with His will.

He's the power to minister precious gifts or operations of the Spirit to reassure, correct, warn, or guide believers in difficult times.

He's the power to stand firm against sin, false teaching, and compromise in the church and, if necessary, separate from sinning or hypocritical Christians—yet retain mercy and pray for them daily.

He's the power to be different without being unfriendly, to be misunderstood without becoming self-conscious and defensive, to seek the highest standards without being proud or cynical.

He's the power to accept rejection from family or friends for Jesus' sake, without succumbing to anger, retaliation, resentment, or self-pity.

He's the power to endure long, fiery trials of injustice without collapsing, corrupting, or compromising for false peace.

He's the power to steadily pursue a ministry in the face of steady opposition and ultimately finish your course.

He's the power to love the unlovable, to patiently bear with fools, frauds, and fiends who persistently try you or pitilessly betray or persecute you.

He's the power to see the invisible, "We wrestle…against spiritual wickedness" (Eph. 6:12), and believe the unbelievable, "The things which are impossible with men are possible with God" (Luke 18:27), and be sure of the uncertain, "I know whom I have believed" (2 Tim. 1:12).

This, and nothing less, is the wondrous power Jesus offers us through the full anointing, or baptism, of the Spirit (Acts 1:5). More than strength for service, *dunamis* empowers every part of our being and living. Upon arriving in Ephesus, the apostle Paul asked some purported believers, "Have ye received the Holy Spirit since ye believed?" (Acts 19:2). Wisely, they received (vv. 6–7).

Have you received this power?

Chapter 59

THE RIVER OF LIFE—FLOWING THROUGH YOU!

*J*ESUS SAID A river of life flows from everyone who believes on Him and receives His Spirit: "He that believeth on me, as the scripture hath said, out of his heart shall flow *rivers of living water*...this spoke he of the Spirit, whom they that believe on him should receive" (John 7:38–39).

Notice this river is described in other Bible references: "as the scripture hath said." Primarily, He spoke of Ezekiel 47:1–2, where the prophet foresees an ever-increasing, life-giving, fruit-creating watercourse flowing from the millennial temple in Jerusalem. The characteristics of this future physical river describe the present spiritual river of which Jesus spoke. Let's review them.

Divine, the river of life originates in God's "house" (v. 1), or temple, where King Jesus' presence will dwell. So it springs from God's presence, the only source of heavenly life and revival. If after receiving the Spirit's fullness we spend time in God's presence daily, meditating in His Word, praying, and worshiping, the river of life steadily flows into us. Our bodily "temples" then become secondary sources of the river of life in this world—and the life steadily flowing in steadily flows out to bless the human "landscape" around us. If we stop drawing near, the river and its outflow dry up.

Growing, the river becomes deeper as it flows, "to the ankles...knees...loins...to swim in" (vv. 3–5). As a river's depth increases, so does its force or power. The longer we continue our daily visitations in Jesus' presence—weeks, months, years—the deeper and stronger the outflow of the Spirit's power.

Creative, the river produces new life and fruitfulness in the barren "desert" (Arabah) and fruitless (Dead) "sea" (vv. 6–9). As it penetrates the arid Arabah, trees begin growing and bearing fruit on its banks. When it touches the Dead Sea, it desalinates its barren waters presently too salty for fish. Soon it too is fruitful with a "very great multitude of fish" (v. 9). Similarly, the Spirit's river in us creates spiritual life and fruitfulness in people, families, churches, cities, and nations previously dead and barren toward God. Amazingly, "everything shall live where the river cometh" (v. 9), and a "very great multitude" of disciples appear and thrive.

Enduring, the river will long sustain its fruit—"very many" fish from the revived sea and nourishing, healing "fruit" from the desert trees "every month" (vv. 10–12, NAS). The Spirit flowing through us also sustains life. In us, it feeds the "fruit of the Spirit" (Gal. 5:22–23) and the fruit of Spirit-led works, words, and ministries. Through us, it continues drawing and netting lost souls and feeding and healing hungry, wounded Christians.

Compassionate, the river will "go down" to the lowest places (v. 8). The Dead Sea is earth's lowest elevation,[3] yet this river will touch and revive it. The Spirit's reach through your witness, words, and prayers will save even the lowest sinners and most depressed, hopeless backsliders.

Victorious, the river ultimately cannot be "passed over" (v. 5). While ankle-, knee-, or waist-deep, it can be easily forded. But once its waters are fully "risen," no one can walk over it any more. When spiritually shallow, the river in us is easily "passed over." Our enemies frequently overcome us, and Christians sometimes overlook our spiritual gifts and ministries. But when we're deeper and stronger in God, we're no longer "passed over"— overcome or ignored. Our adversaries continue resisting but no longer cause us to stumble. We overcome their wiles and wounds and keep faithfully trusting, obeying, and serving God. And the river of ministry flowing from us is eventually recognized and used to help bless others.

Universally available, this river of life will flow through anyone who persistently obeys the lessons of Ezekiel 47 and Jesus' instructions.

So "thirst" for more of Jesus, "come" near Him, and "drink" in the water of the Spirit daily through Bible meditation and study, prayer, and worship (John 7:37–39). Refuse to let the deadness and lowness of your tests (deserts) and the barrenness of churches (Dead Seas) discourage you. Stay linked to the Source—communion with God—and keep refilling your temple with living water daily until the river of the Spirit grows deep and strong. Whatever the cost, stay obedient to God; disobedience quenches the river. Whatever conflicts, contradictions, or offenses come, hold fast your faith. To keep the river flowing, you must keep believing: "He that *believeth* [continues to believe] on me...out of his heart shall flow rivers" (John 7:38). Then wherever you go or pray, the river flows. And "every thing shall live where the river cometh" (Ezek. 47:9)!

Jesus and Ezekiel agree on God's will: the river of life—flowing through you!

Chapter 60

WORSE THAN ABORTION!

ESPITE THE US Supreme Court's 1973 landmark decision and the loud voices of the largely feminist pro-choice movement, abortion remains today what it has always been: cold-blooded murder! However rationalized, it is the cruel killing of unborn yet living people created in God's image. It's hard to overstate the enormity of this national sin; the figures are staggering.

According to the National Right to Life Committee (NRLC), some 1,212,000 abortions were performed in the United States in 2008.[1] That's a shocking 101,000 per month, or 3,320 per day! This government-sanctioned mass murder is nothing less than an American holocaust. Despite the public's general indifference, our heartless repetitive practice of feticide remains an abomination to God and anyone who embraces the biblical value of human life. But calm your righteous indignation for a moment while I tell you about an even more shocking sin.

This stunning evil is a church sin, not a societal sin. It is committed only by Christians, never by unbelievers. It is a crime of the body of Christ, not the body politic. The ecclesia will answer for it, not the nation. Ministers should rally to stop this horrific transgression, not congressmen. Millions of born-again believers are guilty of it, including many who justly protest abortions. The sin of which I write is spiritual abortion, the deliberate cutting short of God's plan for the life of Jesus implanted in us when we experience salvation, or spiritual rebirth.

God plans for the life or nature of Jesus in us to first receive power. This occurs when the newly born again Christian is baptized with the Holy Spirit: "Ye shall receive power, after the Holy Spirit is come upon you" (Acts 1:8). God's plan can't prosper without God's power. He then intends for the Christ life in us to steadily grow. This occurs as we are nourished, by much Bible reading and study; taught, by receiving many teachings from gifted pastors and teachers; guided, by elders' counsels and the Spirit's leadings; and rigorously tested, by Satan's relentless challenges, tricks, and temptations. As this continues, Christ's character image—His love, truth, holiness, humility, and faithfulness—matures in us and manifests with increasing regularity. We recognize our gifts and callings and faithfully pursue them to enlarge, edify, or establish Christ's kingdom, or sphere of authority, in individuals and churches. When crosses and thorns come, we accept them and go on in our devotion and duty. And our destiny—to participate in the great climactic work of the Church Age: preparing Christ's bride, His overcoming church, for His appearing! Thus Christ's life in us runs its full course, helps build His kingdom, and glorifies God! This is God's plan fulfilled.

But many Christians are frustrating His plan. They're neglecting spiritual growth and indulging sin and selfishness. They're abandoning teaching, ignoring counsel, and evading testing. Jesus' life in them—unnourished, undeveloped, and unrevealed—is weakening, withering, and wasting away. Instead of Christ's character manifesting, their old satanic nature and ways are growing: pride, envy, contention, greed, lust, etc. They think only of their nation, not Christ's kingdom; of time, not eternity. They're unconcerned with their or their church's readiness for Jesus' appearing. They're pursuing their plans and ignoring God's. Thus they abort, or cut short, the development of Christ's life in them and spoil God's plan by a criminal negligence equivalent to murder. As horrible as physical abortion is, this spiritual abortion is even more horrific.

Consider these facts. Physical abortion wastes fallen humanity. Spiritual abortion wastes redeemed humanity. Physical abortion wastes Adam's seed. Spiritual abortion wastes Christ' seed. Physical abortion is performed by people living in darkness. Spiritual abortion is performed by people who have the Light of the world and His Word. Physical abortion robs babies of temporal life, liberty, and happiness. Spiritual abortion robs believers of eternal rewards, honors, and joys. Physical abortion burdens our consciences. Spiritual abortion grieves the Lord. Physical abortion is the murder of people formed in God's image. Spiritual abortion is the murder of God's image formed in people. It's Calvary all over again—man puts God to death—but at the hands of Christians, not Jews or Romans. Physical abortion is America's scandal. Spiritual abortion is the church's scandal. Are we righteously indignant about it?

We Christians vociferously protest physical abortion in this nation, as we should. But shouldn't we be even more committed to ending spiritual abortion in our own lives and churches? Let's start protecting the right to life of the unborn and the "first-born" in the wombs of our souls (Rom. 8:29).

If we don't, we'll be guilty of a crime worse than abortion!

Chapter 61

THE SECRET OF VICTORY

HY DID GOD order the Israelites to not fight at Jericho but simply carry the ark around the city seven days (Josh. 6:1–25)? He wanted them to learn and send an important message about the secret of victory. The symbolism here is rich.

The name of the ark was significant. It was the ark "of the covenant," and so speaks of God's covenant—or enduring, solemn agreement—with the Israelites. Its promises and obligations bound God and His redeemed people together in a unique way of life and worship. The ark's contents were also illustrative.

The ark contained the stone tablets inscribed with the Ten Commandments, which Moses brought from the holy mount. They speak of the authoritative commands of God's Word.

There was also a bowl of manna, the Jews' heavenly food, preserved from their wilderness period. This symbolizes the spiritual nourishment of God's Word.

Furthermore, Aaron's rod was in the ark. This speaks of the supernatural, life-giving, beautifully transformative, fruit-bearing power of the Holy Spirit. His power had miraculously revived Aaron's dead, unattractive, barren stick and transformed it into a living, beautiful, fruitful work of God overnight!

The ark's lid, or "mercy seat," was God's earthly throne, and thus His seat of judgment. Its name, "mercy seat," speaks of God's tender mercies and prophetically of His "throne of grace" (Heb. 4:16), where we request His heavenly mercies and help with all our earthly problems.

Since God's manifest presence rested on the mercy seat, wherever the ark was, God's presence was. So God ordered the ark placed in a protected position in Israel's procession, with armed guards going before and after (Josh. 6:8–9). This symbolizes guarding God's presence in our lives.

Usually, the ark rested in the tabernacle's innermost chamber, or "most holy place." Since the tabernacle was Israel's worship center, the centrally located ark was at the heart of Israel's worship. So it symbolizes our praise and worship. Two other facts loom.

First, the Levites carried the ark around Jericho. This represented upholding the covenant it represented, carrying out or living by its obligations. Second, they did so seven days (v. 4). A perfect number, seven symbolizes perfection or spiritual maturity. So the Israelites carried the ark until they were mature—consistently obedient—in their covenant faithfulness and spiritual walk.

While these symbols spoke loudly at Jericho, the Israelites were silent! God ordered them not to speak during the seven-day march (v. 10). Why? They would testify by their actions, not their words. Though inaudible, their profession of faith was clear and full.

Their actions proclaimed:

- Our weapons are not carnal but mighty through God, not natural but supernatural! We'll win this conflict not by fighting in our strength and wisdom but by carrying the ark—or upholding, or keeping, our covenant with God. We won't just talk about our covenant; we'll live it, and our actions will speak louder than our words. As we keep our covenant obligations, our God will perform His covenant promises…and give us victory.

- By feeding daily on the manna of God's Word, we'll grow steadily stronger in faith and hope. By obeying the commands of His Word, we'll live righteously and enjoy the strong security of His protecting armor. We'll trust the rod of His Spirit's supernatural power; He'll revive us when we're weak and reveal His Son's beautiful nature, fruit, and good works in us.

- We'll keep the ark of worship at the center of our lives, blessing God and eliciting His favor and assistance by thanking, praising, and worshiping Him daily. By watching our hearts "with all diligence" (Prov. 4:23), we'll guard God's presence in our lives, ensuring continual access to the fullness of joy and peace found only there. We'll depend upon God's mercy, confessing and forsaking our sins quickly at His mercy seat and calling boldly for His help in every challenge and conflict. And we'll practice these disciplines "seven days," or until we walk in them with perfect consistency, "perfect and complete in all the will of God" (Col. 4:12).

- As we thus faithfully carry God's ark—carrying out His covenant—He'll faithfully bring down every wall hindering us. In His time and way, we'll prevail, not by contending with you, but by cooperating with Him.

That's the secret of victory Israel learned, lived, and taught us at Jericho. Have you learned it?

If you're locked in a challenging conflict at some imposing, impassable "Jericho," don't foolishly fight your enemies and carry sinful burdens of strife, anger, and anxiety. Wisely carry the ark—uphold your covenant obligations and expect God to keep His—and teach others the secret of victory.

Chapter 62

ARE YOU WALKING WITH GOD?

*L*ET ME ASK a vitally important question: Are you walking with God?

I didn't ask if you are born again, attend church, give tithes, support missions, have a creed or confession, believe the Bible is inspired, or engage in Christian ministry. Many Christians meet these conditions yet do not walk with God. They are like Jacob, not Enoch. Let me explain.

Quietly yet profoundly, Genesis 5 notes, "Enoch walked with God" (v. 22). And to hook even the most inattentive reader, it repeats this titanic truth: "Enoch walked with God" (v. 24). Why this statement? Why the repetition?

It reveals Enoch was a thoroughly changed man. The record doesn't state, "God walked with Enoch," conforming Himself to Enoch's habits, values, and preferences. Instead it says, "Enoch walked with God," implying Enoch didn't demand that God please him, but rather lived to please God. Hebrews reveals, "Before his translation he had this testimony, that he pleased God" (Heb. 11:5). Enoch conformed to God's thoughts, standards, and ways. Rather than make God search for him, Enoch sought God's presence and fellowship daily. His attitude and actions pleased God greatly. How do we know?

Before the great flood, God took Enoch bodily to heaven: "And he [Enoch] was not; for God took [translated] him" (Gen. 5:24). Enoch was the only believer taken up ("raptured," if you please) before the first worldwide judgment. Thus he symbolizes overcoming Christians whom God will "take" before the last worldwide judgment, the Tribulation. Like Enoch, they'll walk with God, live to please Him, and be taken by Him.

Though Isaac often recited Enoch's exemplary story to young Jacob, its theme apparently never sunk in. Jacob's early life was the opposite of Enoch's. Though redeemed, Jacob chose not to walk with God but to call God to walk with him. His prayer-vow at Bethel exposes his unchanged heart and self-centered, materialistically driven life:

> Jacob vowed a vow, saying, If God will be with me, and will keep me in this way that I go, and will give me bread to eat, and raiment to put on, so that I come again to my father's house in peace; then shall the LORD be my God.
>
> —GENESIS 28:20–21

The repeated "me's" and "I's" are illuminating.

Jacob wasn't interested in changing his values, goals, or lifestyle, nor in pleasing or serving God. That God should walk beside and, as a supernatural Helper, serve him seemed a much better idea. Thus the covenant he proposed at Bethel.

It decreed Jacob would continue ruling and guiding his life and going wherever he pleased: "in this way that I go." God's part was to come along to provide specific benefits. They were:

- REASSURANCE: "be with me"
- PROTECTION: "keep me"
- FOOD AND CLOTHING: "give me bread…raiment"
- GUIDANCE/RECONCILIATION: "so that I come again to my Father's house"
- SECURITY: "in peace"
- PROSPERITY: "of all that thou shalt give me"

That was the deal. If God performed acceptably, Jacob would retain Him as his deity of choice: "Then shall the LORD be my God." And, as a token of his magnanimousness, he would give God 10 percent: "Of all that thou shalt give me I will surely give the tenth unto thee" (v. 22). But no more!

Amazingly gracious, God listened to this and mercifully blessed Jacob for a season despite his selfishness. Later He sent His rod of chastening and evoked deep, lasting changes in him. But for most of his life, Jacob, though saved, was a "me" man, distinctly unchanged—and distinctly unlike Enoch.

Are we more like Enoch or Jacob? Are we learning to walk with God in His biblical standards, kingdom purposes, and spiritual life habits? Or only praying for Him to walk with us, to come alongside us with blessings and benefits while we serve our ends in life? It's time to stop pleasing ourselves and start pleasing our heavenly Father, as Enoch did. And Jesus—"I do always those things that please Him" (John 8:29). It's time to stop asking

God to serve our plans and start serving His. No small thing, this is what makes real disciples and saints. It also determines if we'll be sure or sorry.

Because he walked with God, Enoch was sure God would keep him from the flood. When Jesus appears, He'll take "Enoch" Christians—who walk with Him. Jacobs, though saved, can't be sure they'll escape that final hour that's coming on "all the world" to finish testing Israel and the nations (Rev. 3:10). They'll be sorry. Will you be sure or sorry?

Again, I ask: Are you walking with God?

Chapter 63

SHIELDED BY HIS FAVOR

RAISING GOD FOR His many blessings, King David stated, "Thou, LORD, wilt bless the righteous; *with favor wilt thou compass him as with a shield*" (Ps. 5:12).

Truly, favor with God is like a large shield protecting us on all sides from life's harmful spiritual arrows, or sudden bitter words or plots; and swords, warlike actions that wound and divide; and spears, other offenses and attacks thrust upon us.

Shields provide protection and security in conflicts. To be "compassed" with a shield is to be covered and surrounded with protection. Thus shielded, believers are secure whenever Satan attacks them through adversarial people or adverse circumstances.

Several translations of Psalm 5:12 confirm this:

- "You protect them like a soldier's shield" (NCV).
- "You surround them with your favor as with a shield" (NIV).
- "You cover them with favor as with a shield" (NRSV).

Specifically, the spiritual arrows, swords, and spears of life are swift, cutting, or piercing troubles: persecution, slander, bereavement, injury, divorce, betrayals, job loss, bankruptcy, foreclosure, disasters, poverty, failure, etc. From these satanic weapons we all need protection. God's protection highlighted in Psalm 5:12 is His favor. God's favor is the loving approval, generous goodwill, personal preference, or high regard He has for and shows us by the favors—mercies, gifts, assistance, or honors—He bestows.

Usually this comes to us through people God puts in our lives. He puts His favor for us in their hearts—then they love, protect, defend, support, assist, or comfort us in our adversities. Thus His loving approval is embodied in and expressed through them. He gives this favor when we start desiring it.

When we determine to please God, He delights to favor us. And His help always comes just when we need it. When competing to become Persia's new queen, "Esther obtained favor in the sight of all them that looked upon her" (Esther 2:15). Many Bible characters enjoyed similarly timely shielding.

155

God gave Joseph two shields. His first was the Egyptian official, Potiphar. Soon after Joseph's brothers shot him with arrows of betrayal, God caused Potiphar to favor and promote him: "And Joseph found grace in his sight…and he made him overseer" (Gen. 39:4). This kindness kept Joseph from being injured by his brothers' cruelty. Later Potiphar's wife slashed out at Joseph with swords of false accusation and unjust incarceration. This would have killed him, if God hadn't intervened, giving him "favor and wisdom in the sight of Pharaoh" (Acts 7:10).

Ruth also had divine shields. Boaz's kindness saved her from the pitiless, piercing spear of poverty. She said, "Let me find favor in thy sight, my lord; for thou hast comforted me" (Ruth 2:13). And Naomi's wise counsel kept Ruth from folly and ruin, leading her instead to "rest" in a blessed marriage: "Daughter, shall I not seek rest for thee?" (Ruth 3:1).

David's shields were six hundred fighting men. Their faithful companionship and valor supported him when King Saul's armies relentlessly pursued him with literal arrows, swords, and spears (1 Sam. 23:13, 26)!

Daniel too had two shields: the chief eunuch, Ashpenaz, and his assistant, Melzar. Together they kept Daniel from being expelled from Nebuchadnezzar's three-year training program: "Now God had brought Daniel into favor and compassion with the prince of the eunuchs" (Dan. 1:9).

When the Samaritans shot hidden arrows of subtle false accusations at the Jewish remnant rebuilding the temple, God gave them open favor with Darius I, who not only protected but also promoted and provided for their work (Ezra 5-6)!

The apostles were shielded by Gamaliel, whose wise and timely defense—"refrain from these men, and let them alone" (Acts 5:38)—rescued them from the Sanhedrin's swift sword of execution.

John the Baptist's shields were the common people. They protected John from Herod's revenge until his time came: "When he [Herod] would have put him [John] to death, he feared the multitude, because they counted him as a prophet" (Matt. 14:5).

Jesus enjoyed the same shield. The people often stood between their Messiah and His madly envious religious enemies: "The scribes…sought to lay hands on [arrest] him, but they feared the people" (Luke 20:19). Church history continues this story.

God's favor moved Constantine to help the persecuted church; Frederick the Wise to hide Martin Luther; Zinzendorf to give shelter to the

Moravians; the English working class to support Methodism; Moody and Scofield to promote Darby's teaching; and Hurst to "puff" Graham's ministry. And the story goes on.

Whoever seeks God's favor will receive it—through the people He appoints. And no weapon formed against them will prosper. They'll finish their work and days shielded by His favor.

Chapter 64

SMITTEN TO FLOW

O F GOD'S DEALINGS with Israel in the wilderness the psalmist wrote, "He opened the rock, and the waters gushed out; they ran in the dry places like a river" (Ps. 105:41).

Historically, the reference is to Rephidim. Only days into their wilderness experience, the newly saved Hebrews encountered a critical problem: "There was no water for the people to drink" (Exod. 17:1). But, as always, the Redeemer had a remedy. He instructed Moses:

> Thou shalt smite the rock, and there shall come water out of it, that the people may drink.
>
> —EXODUS 17:6

When Moses did so, indeed, the water came gushing out, ending the crisis. But not its prophetic message.

Prophetically, the rock Moses smote represented Christ, the Rock of our salvation, whom God smote on the cross so we could receive not only Christ's forgiveness and nature but also His full, rich, "gushing" baptism with the spiritual water of life, the Holy Spirit. Nothing else can fully slake the deep burning thirst of our sin-parched souls. Jesus said, "Whosoever drinketh of the water that I shall give him shall never thirst [again]" (John 4:14). The Gospels and Acts describe our Rock's smiting and gushing.

An eyewitness, John recalls after Jesus expired, a Roman soldier pierced His side with a spear and "immediately blood and water came out" (John 19:34, NAS). This "sudden flow of blood and water" (NIV) was a sign of things to come. Christ's sacrifice would release a river of sin-washing blood and another of soul-comforting Spirit. And soon.

"When the day of Pentecost was fully come" (Acts 2:1), the real living water, the Holy Spirit, gushed out of Christ, the heavenly Baptizer, and filled the 120 in the upper room. Peter said, "Being by the right hand of God...he [Jesus] hath shed forth this, which ye now see and hear" (v. 33). This accomplished God's purpose: He had smitten Jesus, "that the people may drink" (Exod. 17:6). The Spirit has been quenching Christians' thirst ever since, in their initial baptism and countless daily refillings. And from them, rivers of the Spirit's comforts and blessings have gushed to sustain, refresh, inspire, and guide people in the desert of this world. The Rock foretold this.

He prophesied, "He that believeth on me, as the scripture hath said, out of his heart shall flow rivers of living water" (John 7:38). We know these rivers are the Spirit's flowing works, because the next verse specifies, "This spoke he of the Spirit, whom they that believe on him should receive" (v. 39). But what releases the Spirit's wondrous ministry through us?

Jesus said faith is one requirement: "He that believeth in me…" Exodus reveals another requisite: we must be smitten. Our heavenly Father uses our sufferings for Christ's (not sin's or folly's) sake to smite the Rock in us so the rivers of life in Him may gush out. Every time we're smitten, more spiritual water is released to bless others through our conversation, evangelism, counsel, teaching, or life witness. Extraordinary rivers are released by numerous or severe smitings. Church history confirms this.

John Wesley was smitten often by Anglican rejection, violent mobs, and a troubled marriage. Young Charles Spurgeon was smitten when one of his largest meetings was interrupted by a false fire alarm sparking a panic that left seven people trampled to death. Charles Finney and Adoniram Judson were each deeply wounded by the deaths of their beloved wives. William Seymour was smitten when the California church that called him as their pastor locked him out after his first sermon. These blows increased the rivers of blessing flowing from these human channels. Heavenly jolts continue today.

When smitten by disruptive visitations of injustice, slander, rejection, resistance, betrayal, bereavement, abandonment, or failure, remember, though Satan brought it, it's God's stroke. He's smiting the Rock in you so the Spirit's river of life may flow more freely and "the people may drink" of its blessings. This can't happen if He only sends you blessings and prosperity. If you accept the blow, give thanks, and keep drinking in living water daily in Bible meditation, prayer, and worship, even broader rivers of spiritual blessing will flow through your life-channel—words in season to the weary, wise counsels, timely encouragements, spiritual insights, gentle corrections, excellent teachings, charitable gifts, hospitality, or helps. Many thirsty ones will be refreshed. So choose.

Do you want to be comfortable or Christ's channel? Jesus could have refused His smiting—but Pentecost would not have occurred. You can refuse yours—but the Spirit won't flow through you. Don't disappoint the Rock; delight Him!

Praise Him for letting you also be smitten to flow.

Chapter 65

THE SUBSTITUTIONS OF GOD

*T*HE WRITER TO the Hebrews reminds us that God sometimes removes things to put better things in their place: "He taketh away the first, that he may establish the second" (Heb. 10:9).

Specifically, the passage explains how God removed the Jewish system of animal sacrifice to establish a better and final Sacrifice, Jesus (vv. 1–16). Mere animal sacrifices couldn't accomplish His desire to make worshipers "perfect," or perfectly related to Him, fully sanctified, and spiritually mature. But the new Sacrifice is both willing—"Lo, I come to do thy will, O God" (v. 9)—and able: "He is able also to save them to the uttermost that come unto God by him" (Heb. 7:25). So God substituted a Savior who accomplished His will for a system that didn't: "He taketh away the first [sacrifices], that he may establish the second [Sacrifice]" (Heb. 10:9). This principle of divine substitution is not limited to sacrifices, priesthoods, and covenants.

It also applies to people, redeemed and unredeemed. Consider the Bible's convincing testimony.

God didn't hesitate to remove Gentiles from their positions if they interfered with His plan for His people. Disobedient Vashti is put out of her privileged Persian queenship and obedient Esther is called in—divinely positioned to deliver God's people in their coming crisis. Thoughtless King Belshazzar is deposed and thoughtful Darius the Mede assumes his throne—to graciously favor and honor Daniel and his God.

He also frequently "putteth down one, and setteth up another" among the redeemed (Ps. 75:7). Backslidden Eli and sons fall in battle, and God raises Samuel to assume their ministry—and model and teach righteousness to His offended, confused people. Stubborn King Saul is rejected from Israel's kingship, and humble David is anointed to replace him—and feed and lead Israel in the ways of the Good Shepherd. Christ-rejecting Israel is dispersed for its rebellion, and the Christ-worshiping church assumes its privileged mission—to carry out God's plan to save the nations.

Covetous, contentious Judas falls from his apostleship, and contrite Paul rises to take his place—Christ's willing and wise apostle to the Gentiles. Paul declines unfaithful Mark's application for a dangerous mission and later selects Timothy—who, as Paul's associate minister, faithfully helps him overcome and finish his course. Paul's aide, Demas, walks out of his life and Onesiphorus walks in—to "often refresh" (2 Tim. 1:16) him with visits and mercies Demas should have rendered.

Though occurring in different times and circumstances, all these substitutions had one common thread: God replaced someone who didn't do His will with someone else who did. "The same yesterday, and today, and forever" (Heb. 13:8), He still replaces His contentious servants with cooperative ones.

At this very moment, all over the world, God is removing from offices, churches, ministries, missions, and relationships people who, despite His patient, gracious dealings, stubbornly refuse to do His will, and He's replacing them with others who will gladly and ably do it. Why? They're "better"—more humble and responsive to Him. As Samuel told King Saul: "The LORD hath torn the kingdom of Israel from thee...and hath given it to a neighbor of thine, who is *better than thou*" (1 Sam. 15:28).

Both sides of this principle are working in our lives. If we're humbly and faithfully doing God's will, He's preparing us to assume higher places presently occupied by those who are proud, stubborn, or unfaithful; or by others whose season of service has ended. Conversely, if we're persistently unfaithful in our present callings, responsibilities, and privileges, God is quietly preparing "better" souls to replace us. This should stir holy fear and hope.

We should fear God—stand in awe of His awesome power, sovereign authority, and sure warnings—knowing, if we contend, He has others who'll cooperate. They're ready to take our relationships, jobs, duties, offices, ministries, missions—and rewards! Jesus urges us not to abandon our rewards and privileges to others: "Hold fast that which thou hast, that no man take thy crown" (Rev. 3:11). John agrees: "Look to yourselves, that we lose not those things which we have wrought, but...receive a full reward" (2 John 8). Obstinate Christians may hinder God's work temporarily, but ultimately it will go on—without them!

Simultaneously, we should hope to become a substitute. We should believe that if we faithfully serve God, He'll eventually grant us a better place someone vacated or took for granted: "Friend, go up higher" (Luke 14:10). So three things remain.

Fear God—don't forfeit your place! Have hope—prepare to be a substitute! Silas did, "and Paul chose Silas, and departed..." (Acts 15:40). And believe—be confident in the substitutions of God!

Chapter 66

FAITHFUL—WITH OR WITHOUT EVIDENCE

*T*HE REGULARITY AND depth of our private fellowship with God determines the strength of our personal relationship with Him. The strength of that personal relationship in turn determines how useful our life works will be to God and His kingdom.

Realizing this, Satan attacks us with contradictions, delays, disappointments, reproaches, and offenses, sometimes very bitter, persistent ones, with one prime objective in view—to break up our fellowship with God. If he achieves this fundamental break, several things naturally follow. Our soul will grow weak and our usefulness to God will begin spoiling. Our ability to help build and strengthen His kingdom—sphere of loving authority—in other lives will gradually diminish. Our twofold fruit, of the Spirit (Gal. 5:22–23) and of good works, will wither on the branches of our life until they stop manifesting. Thus Satan's plan will succeed and God's fail in our life.

Lusting to lead us down this road to ruin, Satan will eventually ask God's permission to strip away part or all of our blessings, comforts, or joys. If God lets him, it's only to test us.

This make-or-break testing started long ago when Satan said of Job, "Doth Job fear God for nothing?" (Job 1:9). His insulting insinuation was clear: Job—and all God's people—only serve God for the blessings He gives. Take away their blessings, Satan wagered, and they'll "curse thee [God] to thy face" (v. 11). They'll become hurt, disappointed, and angry over God's treatment of them and fall away from lovingly seeking and faithfully serving Him. "When affliction...comes on account of the Word, at once he is caused to stumble [he is repelled and begins to distrust and desert Him Whom he ought to trust and obey] and he falls away" (Matt. 13:21, AMP).

In Job's case, God let the enemy "clean house" for a season, as every blessing near and dear to Job was systematically and cruelly removed: possessions, children, health, the loving support of his wife, and even the strengthening fellowship of his friends. Only Job's spiritual life was left untouched, so that, if he would, he could still fellowship with God while passing through his valley of weeping. As David later wrote under similar circumstances, "As for me, I

163

will behold thy face in righteousness; I shall be satisfied when I awake, with thy likeness" (Ps. 17:15); or, "As for me, I will continue beholding Your face…I shall be fully satisfied, when I awake [to find myself] beholding Your form [and having sweet communion with You]" (AMP).

At issue was this: Would Job be the same man when stripped of all his blessings? Would he continue to thrive spiritually? Would his love for God be undiminished and his service unchanged? Satan hoped that Job's sudden, strange adversity (which God said was "without cause," Job 2:3) would end his close fellowship with God. If so, he would never resume his previously wide and effective ministry, which Eliphaz described: "Thou hast instructed many, and thou hast strengthened the weak hands. Thy words have upheld him that was falling, and thou hast strengthened the feeble knees" (Job 4:3–4). Quenching such a river of life would deprive God's people of much edifying teaching and comforting counsel, and, to some degree, diminish God's kingdom. Hoping this would not happen, God released Job into his valley of testing.

In that howling, hellish examination, Job suffered numbing shock, bitter grief, deep disappointment, persisting perplexity, and unimaginable emotional and physical agony. With these afflictions occurring in rapid sequence, he had no relief from pain. Bowed by their crushing weight, he cried out, questioned, complained, and contended, but he never stopped believing in God's faithfulness, love, power, and purpose in his life. At his lowest moment he declared, "Though he slay me, yet will I trust in him" (Job 13:15). So he triumphed over his trauma, disproved Satan's claims, and emerged as faithful without evidence of God's blessings as he had been with them. Case closed!

But our cases are still open. What if God lets us experience some, even one, of Job's troubles? He knows we'll seek and serve Him when we're prosperous, popular, and successful, but will we be the same worshipers when we're cut back, reduced, and stripped of all evidence of His approval—with no sign of relief? Will we cling to God or, offended, fall away? Draw back to spiritual infancy or go on to full maturity? Will we prove ourselves faithless or faithful? What will our case file's final report say of us?

Are you suffering in some cruel crucible? Stay close to God, and faithful—with or without evidence of His blessing!

Chapter 67

AS THIS LITTLE CHILD

*I*T WAS AN exciting time. Very exciting! Despite persisting opposition from the Jewish leaders, Jesus was drawing, healing, teaching, and feeding massive crowds. And rumors were flying.

Though He had twice informed those closest to Him of His soon-coming sufferings, talk persisted among the crowds, and hope among Jesus' growing band of disciples, that God's earthly kingdom would appear any day. Caught up in the moment, the Twelve begin daydreaming about their position, power, and prestige in Jesus' administration. Their résumés were indeed impressive.

The King had handpicked them and taught and counseled them extensively. They had now been His constant companions for over two years. They had taught His messages and ministered His healing power all over the nation. Three of them had only recently witnessed His stunning divine glory on a nearby mountaintop. Clearly no one else's claims rivaled those listed on their ministerial résumés. Surely they would sit high in His kingdom. Very high. So they proudly reasoned, and asked, "Who is the greatest in the kingdom of heaven?" (Matt. 18:1), eagerly anticipating appointments to high offices and honors.

But Jesus' answer laid them low (vv. 2–4). Very low! He said their concept of greatness and His were totally different. If they hoped to even *enter* much less rule His kingdom, they would first have to totally change their values. To illustrate He "called a little child…and set him in the midst," and then said, "Except ye be converted, and become as little children, ye shall not [even] enter into the kingdom of heaven" (vv. 2–3). His call for them to become "converted…as little children" refers primarily to the pivotal spiritual conversion that we call the new birth. As Jesus informed the learned rabbi Nicodemus, "Ye must be born again" (John 3:7). But here Jesus was also referring to something more, not just to a sudden spiritual quickening but also to an abiding mental conversion. Succinctly He was telling His associates they must totally change their way of thinking—"be…transformed by the renewing of your mind" (Rom. 12:2)—especially their concept of greatness. To Jesus, and His Father, greatness is childlikeness.

Like good children, childlike Christians are not driven by worldly ambition to seek top positions, but are rather willing to be equal with others. They are soft-hearted, without hard or bitter attitudes. Their ways of thinking and living are simple and uncomplicated, not overly sophisticated or complex. They are quick to believe God's Word, not skeptical or rationalistic. They are slow to anger, not hasty in spirit. They are merciful, not malicious; forgiving, not vengeful. They are driven by love for God and His people, plan, and glory, not by lust for power and its wealth, fame, and pleasure. Rather than worry and fight their way through problems, they prayerfully and restfully rely on their heavenly Father for provision, protection, guidance, and favor. They befriend believers of all races, nations, socioeconomic groups, and cultures without prejudice or snobbery. They thank God repeatedly for the simplest provisions and pleasures, and they refuse to complain however adverse their circumstances. Summing up, they're not proud but humble.

Jesus cites this crowning virtue as the prime requirement for advancement in His kingdom: "Whosoever...shall humble himself as this little child, the same is greatest in the kingdom" (Matt. 18:4). His thinking is the exact opposite of this world's. Here the proud, loud, and self-assertive rise and dominate the meek. But in Jesus' kingdom, He raises the meek, faithful, and God-serving to rule over the proud. This may seem novel, but it's not. God has always raised the humble, not the haughty, to high position and power.

Israel's first great leader, Moses, was "very meek, above all the men who were upon the face of the earth" (Num. 12:3). Its first king, Saul, was humble when God first chose him (1 Sam. 15:17). Its greatest king, David, was very humble when called into the royal family (1 Sam. 18:23). Its great prophet, Jeremiah, was very meek when God called him to high service (Jer. 1:6). To learn more about childlikeness, we should study their biblical records. And also, look around us.

Jesus took a little child and "set him in the midst" of His proud, ambitious disciples as a living demonstration of childlikeness they could observe and ponder. Thus they learned and eventually lived it. Jesus still does this today. Faithfully He places near us—in our home, neighborhood, workplace, or church—at least one Christian who demonstrates the greatness of childlikeness.

Are you learning from Jesus' teaching, biblical examples, and childlike ones near you? Will you be "as this little child"?

Chapter 68

SEE THROUGH TO THE SOURCE

KNOWING WELL HOW vital faith is, God is always working to enlarge our faith. Our confidence in Him must not remain small.

Small faith sees God in pleasant occurrences only, but large faith learns to see Him in every situation. Even when it doesn't yet understand what He's doing, or why, large (or growing) faith still acknowledges His presence, control, and loving plan. Why?

God has commanded us to do so, for our good and growth. Proverbs 3:6 states:

> In all thy ways [paths, situations] acknowledge [be aware of] him...
>
> —KJV

> In all your ways know, recognize, and acknowledge Him...
>
> —AMP

> Have mind of Him wherever you may go...
> —A NEW TRANSLATION, JAMES MOFFATT

> In every situation, good and bad, be aware God is there, in full control, working out His wise and loving plan for you through every person and event you meet; and communicate this awareness to Him...
>
> —AUTHOR'S PARAPHRASE

Thus we acknowledge God in two ways: (1) by realizing He is present and at work, and (2) by telling God we realize this. The first is a realization; the second, a communication. We may do the latter by saying, "Thank you, Lord," or, "I acknowledge You, Lord," or, "Lord, I know You're in this," or something comparable.

As a man, Jesus obeyed this command. He saw His Father's hand in everything that touched His life, from His long, low season of submissive training and service in Nazareth, to His high and lofty ministerial success in Capernaum. He acknowledged His Father habitually, even in His shocking betrayal and crucifixion—"The cup which my Father hath given me, shall I not drink it?" (John 18:11); and, "Thou [Pilate] couldst have no power at all against me, except it were given thee from above" (John 19:11).

With clocklike consistency Jesus did two things in every new situation. First, He accepted that His Father sent the situation, good or bad, fair or unfair, for a good purpose. Second, He reacted to it, meekly or boldly, passively or actively, precisely as His Father dictated. Whatever kind of situational package life delivered to His doorstep, Jesus saw through its human deliverer to its heavenly Source. Why? His faith was large—as large as it gets.

Let's follow His example. Let's enlarge our faith by acknowledging our heavenly Father's presence, control, and wise and loving purpose in everything!

For instance, when we receive income, profits, or provisions, let's see not only the human buyers, donors, or providers but also our Father. "Thank You, Father, for these sales, salaries, or gifts!" When we receive advantageous opportunities, let's see not only the friends who facilitated them but also the Lord. "Thank You, Lord, for this open door!" When people favor us, let's see not only their natural graciousness but also the underlying supernatural grace of Him who "make[s] all grace abound toward you [us]" (2 Cor. 9:8). "Thanks, Jesus, for causing this person to receive, befriend, or bless me!" And let's treat trouble the same.

When adversity visits, let's see not only earthly troublemakers but also the heavenly character Builder. "Thanks, Father, for sending me these opportunities to become a fully developed overcomer!" When people reject us without cause, let's see not only human pettiness but also God's larger purposes. "Thanks, Lord, for taking this friendship so I'll rely even more on sweet fellowship with You and Your faithful ones!" Whenever our plans or prayers are delayed, let's see not only human hinderers but also the divine Scheduler. "Thanks, Father; it's not Your time yet, and Your time is always best!" (See Ecclesiastes 3:11.)

Indeed, whoever or whatever touches your life, see through them to the Source: "Thus saith the LORD...this thing is from me" (1 Kings 12:24). When you understand what's happening, praise God; when you don't, trust Him. If you know nothing else, know this: "We know that God causes all things to work together for good to those who love God...who are called according to His purpose" (Rom. 8:28, NAS). So give Him thanks by faith: "Give thanks whatever happens. That is what God wants for you in Christ

Jesus" (1 Thess. 5:18, NCV). Then react as Jesus did, according to your Father's directions. Obey His inerrant Word. If it's not specific enough, pray for guidance, then obey God's voice or providential signs.

Doing this consistently will make you "spiritually minded" (Rom. 8:6) and cause your faith to steadily grow larger—until it's as large as it gets. Conformed to Jesus' image, you'll detect the Father's touch in whatever touches you and always see through to the Source.

Chapter 69

AFTER THE FLOOD—FRUITFULNESS!

HEN NOAH FINALLY emerged from his long, dark trial in the ark, God conferred His full favor and fruitfulness on him and his family: "God blessed Noah and his sons, and said unto them, Be fruitful, and multiply, and fill the earth" (Gen. 9:1). Not only sweet, this divine benediction was also potent.

Power-packed, it exploded and blossomed into an ongoing worldwide fulfillment. Thus the end of Noah's long trial was also the beginning of a long period of amazing favor and fruitfulness. God did everything He promised as Noah's little family gradually repopulated the whole wide earth! What a satisfying reward this fruitfulness must have been to a family that had been so barren so long. Let's review their previous sad, lengthy desolation.

Genesis 6 describes that long, hard trial. The decline of the pre-Flood world began when, contrary to God's instructions, the righteous and unrighteous intermarried (v. 2). This led not to the conversion of the ungodly but to the corruption of the godly. Human thought and conversation became increasingly more godless and selfish until people pondered "only evil continually" (v. 5). Yearly society sank lower into a vortex of immorality and "violence," especially murder (v. 11). Eventually the world's cup of sin became filled. God strove with His people in their consciences, urging them to return to His ways, but to no avail. Reluctantly He appointed a time to end His grace and begin His judgment—120 years (v. 3). But before "the end of all flesh" (v. 13), God revealed to His righteous remnant His plan to flood the faithless and rescue the faithful.

That remnant was small: one man and his extended family! "But Noah found grace in the eyes of the LORD" (v. 8). While the world walked in sin, Noah "walked with God" (v. 9). And while the world fell away, Noah stood firm as a "preacher of righteousness" (2 Pet. 2:5), calling his peers to repent and escape the coming flood. He and his family suffered painful separation, loneliness, and mockery as they declared their faith by building an ark of deliverance amid the unbelieving and surely abusive populace. Carrying this heavy cross, they must have longed for the day they would enter the ark. But that day didn't end their testing.

Their year in the ark was another great challenge (Gen. 7–8). During the initial downpour, they lived in cramped quarters on limited rations without proper exercise, fresh air, or normal freedom of movement—and without seeing the sun, moon, or stars for five months! When God's release process finally began, it took seven months to unfold! Life in Noah's ark was hard, with all its fearful sights (floating corpses); restless, noisy animals; laborious chores; monotonous weather; and unique smells! During this stressful year, God mercifully gave Noah joyful flashes of hope when: the rain finally stopped; the ark rested on Mount Ararat; other peaks were sighted; the dove returned with new growth, "a fresh olive leaf in its beak" (Gen. 8:11, NLT); and when Noah saw dry ground for the first time in ten months! But, a disciplined follower of the Holy Spirit, Noah waited patiently until God's voice signaled His time to, "Go forth from the ark" (v. 16). So he endured his second extraordinary test.

After the Flood, God's blessing was extraordinary, not one or two but threefold:

1. "Be fruitful"—produce good fruit.

2. "Multiply"—produce continuing fruit.

3. "Fill the earth"—produce maximum fruit—to the limit!

Thus exceptionally favored and blessed, Noah's small but fully tested family left the ark and filled the world with its kind: "Of them was the whole earth overspread" (Gen. 9:19). So may we.

And so will we—if we endure our Noahic challenges. For that, we must stand firm while our world falls away from all semblance of righteousness and morality and its thinking becomes "only evil continually." While our nation walks in sin, we must "walk with God," preach righteousness and repentance, and endure painful, heavy crosses of separation, loneliness, and mockery. In our "arks" (trying circumstances), we must bear long "rains" (troubles), tolerate loud "noises" (reproaches), steadily pursue humble "chores" (vocational or ministerial duties), give thanks for "olive leafs" (hopeful signs), and wait patiently for God's word of release—while living, working, or ministering in a zoo of restless people whose imperfections test us as ours have God!

If so, God will say to us, "Be fruitful, and multiply, and fill the earth"

(Gen. 9:1). By our messages, missions, or missionaries, we'll go forth in the Spirit's power to reproduce our own kind—Christian disciples of strong faith and devotion—the world over!

Thus favored, after our "flood" we'll find fruitfulness!

Chapter 70

ACCOMPLISHED THIS "DECEASE" YET?

*D*URING JESUS' TRANSFIGURATION, the apostles overheard Moses and Elijah talking about the "decease" Jesus would accomplish. "Moses and Elijah...spoke of his decease which he should accomplish at Jerusalem" (Luke 9:30–31). How odd.

Typically, we don't consider dying an accomplishment. We accomplish tasks, goals, and victories, but not deaths! Yet Moses and Elijah saw Jesus' death as an accomplishment. Why? His death for our sins on the cross was the climax of the Father's will for Him, the central purpose of His life mission. By submitting to crucifixion, as unfair, cruel, and painful as it was, Jesus accomplished the last and most demanding part of His Father's plan. That Israel's two greatest prophets gushed about Jesus' death—not His heavenly teaching, powerful miracles, or compassionate healings—confirms that His death, not His ministry, was His greatest earthly accomplishment.

Similarly, our greatest earthly accomplishment will not be our visible religious works, ministries, or good deeds, though they're important. "The mark" or goal toward which we are pressing (Phil. 3:14), the great noble finish line of our spiritual life, is our "decease." It won't be accomplished at Jerusalem. Or on a wooden crucifix. Nor is it likely to involve physical death. Our glorious decease will be a spiritual death. This passing, for which heaven waits and wonders, is our full surrender of sin and self-will. Our transfiguring demise occurs in two steps or stages.

First, we die to our individual sins, the particular ways our old fleshly sin nature rebels against God's will. We surrender the secret besetting sins we've stubbornly held, realizing now they grieve Jesus and keep us from living every moment in the fullness of His Spirit. We also start habitually controlling our harmful emotions, confessing and forsaking wrong motives, and detecting and changing our bad attitudes—fixed patterns of wrong thinking and feeling toward people and situations.

Second, when God's desires and ours clash, we die to self-will, abandoning what we want to apprehend what He wants. God intentionally arranges circumstances to create these clashes of will, knowing we need them to die to self. If every situation goes our way, we'll remain saved but unchanged, still self-willed, self-seeking, and self-serving rather than Christ-serving. Dying to our sins is easy, but this death to self is the climactic, decisive battle of our souls. Sadly, few Christians accomplish this "decease." Have we learned how to "die"?

Christ showed us the way. When His and His Father's will conflicted, in childlike simplicity He first told His Father exactly what He wanted: "Father…remove this cup from me" (Luke 22:42). Then He put aside His preference to pursue His Father's preference: "Nevertheless, not my will, but thine, be done" (v. 42). He thoughtfully uttered these dying words three times—until His selfish will expired. As He emptied Himself, the Father refilled Him with overcoming grace: "There appeared an angel unto him…strengthening him" (v. 43). This Gethsemane way remains open.

When conflicted, follow it. Every time you choose the Father's will over yours, acknowledging but then relinquishing your delight for His, Father gives you fresh grace to do His will not just contentedly but joyfully. Every death to self-will births in you a new delight for Christ's will: "I delight to do thy will, O my God" (Ps. 40:8). His life, joy, and truth will flow not only into you but also through you to minister relief to desolate, desperate, and despairing people all around. The apostles Paul and John learned and lived this Gethsemane way.

When Paul was terribly vexed by all the trouble his demonic thorn in the flesh (2 Cor. 12:7) was causing, he prayed for deliverance three times, only to hear God say it was His way of keeping Paul humble. Immediately he surrendered his preference for tranquility to God's preference for humility. This "decease" brought fresh grace, and Paul subsequently endured his troubles "most gladly" (v. 9) and ministered even more revelations to the church! John loved ministering and fellowshiping in the churches of Asia. But when God handed him a cross of exile for the Word's sake, John yielded his preference for Ephesus to God's preference for exile. God immediately gave him fresh grace, and "in the Spirit on the Lord's day" (Rev. 1:10), John received the church's greatest, most comforting prophecy, the Revelation. Thus the apostles' "decease" to self brought new life to saints.

Yours will too. So when conflicted, take the Gethsemane way. Honestly tell Father your preferences, and repeatedly surrender them to His. He will give you fresh grace and new life, truth, and blessings for others. This will be your greatest accomplishment.

Have you accomplished this "decease" yet?

Chapter 71

IS YOUR FAITH LARGE OR LITTLE?

*M*ATTHEW 8 CONTRASTS large and little faith. After immortalizing the centurion's inspiring "great faith" (v. 10), Matthew describes the apostles' uninspiring "little faith" (v. 26). Let's consider the characteristics of each.

Great faith places full confidence in God and whatever He says—promise, warning, or prophecy. Like the centurion, it says, "Speak the word only, and [it will follow]" (v. 8). With childlike trust, it refuses to be discouraged by facts that contradict God's sayings, nor, being honest, will it deny them. It believes that the omnipotent God's will and Word are irresistible, that ultimately all the "things which are seen" (2 Cor. 4:18) will conform to the things said. And it trusts He'll explain every contradiction in His time and way.

Not so trusting, little faith is gripped and staggered by contradictory evidence. Relying more on reason than the Redeemer, it quickly doubts and soon forgets the greater, abiding facts: whatever has happened, Jesus is still present and all-powerful, and His character and promises, unchanged, are still true. Once we forget these weightier spiritual realities, unbelief sets in. So while God's faithful character and enduring Word win the hearts of "great faith" believers, contradiction-prompted reasonings intimidate those with "little faith" and shackle them in disbelief. They need a greater biblical focus.

Examples of great faith fill the Bible. The Israelites showed strong faith by trumpeting and shouting victory over Jericho for seven days—while its walls remained visibly unchanged. Why? God said He had given them the city and its walls would fall. En route to Rome, Paul showed immense faith by declaring he and his shipmates would survive a violent hurricane when "all hope" was "taken away" (Acts 27:20). Why? God's angel promised, "Paul, thou must be brought before Caesar; and…God hath given thee all them that sail with thee" (v. 24). When all physical evidence and past experience swore God's promise was false, Abraham "against hope believed in hope" (Rom. 4:18), confident he'd yet become a father of many nations, despite the persisting contradictions. Why? God had promised this, and Abraham was "fully persuaded that, what he had promised, he was able also to perform" (v. 21). God ultimately performed His promises to these because they kept trusting Him despite prolonged discouraging evidence. Thus He honored the faith that honored Him.

Matthew 8 confirms God will always honor great faith and dishonor little faith. Jesus publicly praised the centurion and implicitly promised him a seat at His marriage supper (vv. 10–11). Yet He rebuked His own apostles for doubting Him: "Why are ye fearful, O ye of little faith?" (v. 26), leaving them saved from the storm but ashamed in His presence. Here's food for thought: the measure of our faith will one day win us Jesus' personal praise—or rebuke! It's examination time.

Are we growing or starving our "measure of faith" (Rom. 12:3)? If we consistently feed our God-confidence with a steady diet of God's faith-building Word, strengthen it with prayer, train it by courageous choices in tests, and establish it by persevering through long contradictions, we'll develop great faith. If not, we'll consistently manifest little faith in every stormy test and at the end of life's crossing be left reprimanded and embarrassed by Christ, though saved by His grace. Ponder this now, while you can still build your faith.

And practice what you ponder. Believe fully only the faithful character and sayings of God—not the promises, visions, or plans of mere men. Ultimately, what heaven promises, not what humans predict, will prevail. See but do not focus on the facts that contradict God's revealed will, calling, or promise in your life, family, church, or nation. Ever remember, God can change things any moment: "Thou knowest not what a day may bring forth [birth]" (Prov. 27:1). All-powerful, He's irresistible and will do the impossible if you only continue believing Him: "All things are possible to him that believeth" (Mark 9:23). So keep relying on His truthful nature and true Word. Why? Faith matters!

Never succumb to the lie that your belief is unimportant. To the contrary, your choice to rely wholly on God's unfailing faithfulness is vitally important—to you, your family, God's people, and His plan. Believers receive answers and fulfillments that doubters delay and disbelievers forfeit. Jesus works wonders, not according to His power, but our faith. He charged the centurion, "Go thy way; and *as thou hast believed*, so be it done unto thee" (Matt. 8:13). He's charging you today.

So, "go your way!" And "have faith in God" (Mark 11:22), praying with expectancy, feeding your faith, and examining yourself regularly to see: Is your faith large or little?

Chapter 72

GROWING IN KINGDOM GREATNESS

*I*NSPIRED BY THE hope of Jesus' imminent kingdom glory—and theirs—the disciples asked Him, "Who is the greatest in the kingdom of heaven?" (Matt. 18:1). Matthew, Mark, and Luke dutifully note this.

That the Gospels record their question reveals that Jesus' original followers, like us, had worldly ambition. That Jesus so fully answered it proves that He wanted not only them but also us to know the answer. It states precisely how His Father will determine which Christians will be the "greatest"—of highest rank, authority, privilege, and influence—in His eternal kingdom. His answer, given here and elsewhere in the New Testament, was altogether otherworldly.

Jesus' kingdom will be utterly unlike any previous or present earthly realm: "My kingdom is not of this world" (John 18:36). To rule by His side there, we must live by His kingdom's values here. For that we must know them. Jesus' New Testament teachings reveal three prime requisites for advancement in His kingdom. These pillars of kingdom greatness are humility, servantship, and suffering.

Let's consider their main features:

- HUMILITY. "Whosoever... shall humble himself as this little child, the same is greatest in the kingdom of heaven" (Matt. 18:4). Jesus plainly says the humblest now will be the greatest then. Novel as it sounds, this isn't new. Not once but twice Proverbs declares, "Before honor is humility," implying before being honored in God's kingdom, we must be humbled here (Prov. 15:33; 18:12). And the Bible shows repeatedly that on earth God has always chosen the humblest people for the highest posts. Moses, David, Jeremiah, Paul, and even King Saul had sober, not swollen, self-views when divinely appointed and anointed.

- SERVANTSHIP. "Whosoever will be chief among you, let him be your servant" (Matt. 20:27). Ideal servants are passionately committed to serving their master's desires and ever looking to do so: "As the eyes of servants look unto the hand of their masters" (Ps. 123:2). Our Master's greatest desire is that we serve other Christians for His sake: "Lovest thou me...feed [nourish, nurture, help] my sheep" (John 21:16). Are we lovingly serving believers—by intercession, kindness, counsel, assistance, and fellowship—to Jesus' delight, or neglecting or abusing them to His grief? To serve His desires and their needs, we must set aside our desires and needs. Are we willing?

- SUFFERING. "Grant that these, my two sons, may sit, the one on thy right hand, and the other on the left, in thy kingdom.... Are ye able to drink of the cup...and to be baptized with [my] baptism?" (Matt. 20:21–22). When Zebedee's wife, Salome, openly asked Jesus to appoint her sons to His kingdom's highest positions, He immediately asked if they were prepared to accept His "cup" of sufferings for righteousness' sake and "baptism" of sacrificial death to self-will. Thus He revealed that the greatest in His kingdom will suffer, and die (figuratively or literally), to accomplish His will. Our willing acceptance of our cups and baptisms, and the number, severity, and duration of these crosses, these factors will determine our authority, privileges, and influence in the kingdom—forever! If we suffer here, we'll rule there: "If we suffer [for Him], we shall also reign with him" (2 Tim. 2:12). And the more we suffer, the more we'll rule. But if we refuse to suffer, we forfeit our authority: "If we deny him [to avoid suffering], he also will deny us [the right to rule]" (v. 12).

Jesus didn't select these pillars of kingdom greatness randomly. They are the pillars of His personal greatness—His character, teachings, and works. He was history's humblest man. He was God's most perfect servant. And He suffered most willingly, frequently, and severely to do heaven's will. Since Jesus will be the Greatest One in His kingdom, it follows that the subordinates He deems "greatest" will be those most like Him. They too will be upheld by the pillars of His greatness.

These pillars also support His present spiritual kingdom, the church.

If Christ (not merely Christians) raises a minister, he (or she) has first been established in humility, servantship, and suffering.

Does this illuminate your circumstances? Is the Greatest One making you like Him and His greatest ones? They are the humblest souls. Are your circumstances low? They are His most committed servants. Do you have some difficult sheep to serve? They are willing, experienced sufferers. Is your cup bitter? Your baptism of trouble overwhelming? Your cross painful, lonely, humiliating? Yield, pray for more grace, and let the Greatest One make you great. Be humble. Be His servant. Bear your sufferings willingly. And don't pity yourself.

Praise the King! You're growing in kingdom greatness!

Chapter 73

LOVING OR LOATHING HIS "LITTLE ONES"?

W HEN JESUS WANTED to show us how to be His humble disciples, He selected a little child as His example: "Jesus called a little child...and set him in the midst of them, and said...Whosoever...shall humble himself as this little child..." (Matt. 18:2–4). Then He proceeded to describe "little ones."

His sayings about little ones have two main applications. First, they speak of *child believers*, "one of these little ones [children in years] who believe in me" (v. 6). Second, they speak of *childlike believers* [childlike in spirit] of whatever age. Jesus occasionally addressed His disciples as "children," though they were all grown men: "Children, have ye any food?" (John 21:5). These two definitions give us a basic description of Jesus' "little ones."

Let's deepen and expand our understanding. More specifically, "little ones" are:

- Christians who are young in age. As implied above, child believers are important to God. They're developing adults, whereas adults are often undeveloped kids. When His disciples turned away parents bringing their children for His blessing, Jesus, "much displeased," commanded, "Permit the little children to come unto me" (Mark 10:14).

- Christians who are young in the faith or recently converted. These "babes in Christ" (1 Cor. 3:1), whether adolescent, adult, or aged, need special care. They need steady prayer, teaching, fellowship, encouragement, and guidance to escape Satan's snares; put down spiritual roots; increase in knowledge of God; build strong faith; overcome tests; and thrive as Christ's disciples.

- Christians of little spiritual insight, discernment, or wisdom. Still carnally minded, or viewing life from a solely natural viewpoint, their spiritual eyes and ears are not yet sharp and focused. Unrenewed in mind and slow or dull in spirit, they're easily deceived and misled.

- Christians of little rank or small influence in society or the church. These extraordinarily ordinary ones do not hold office, title, degree, or clout. They're of little education, income, culture, or social standing. Proud Christians callously overlook them, their needs, and their value.

- Christians of little grace or spiritual growth. Neither fruitful nor childlike, these childish ones are thorns incarnate. The diminutive grace and growth they exhibit make it hard to live, work, or fellowship with them.

- Christians of little faith. Whenever their faith and patience is tested, these habitually question, doubt, and panic rather than trust, praise, and overcome. Instead of standing fast, they crumble fast—and make extra trouble for others.

- Childlike Christians of whatever age. Surprisingly, the most spiritually mature Christians are childlike in spirit. Consistently they implicitly trust their heavenly Father, humbly obey His Word, submissively yield to His Spirit's guidance, and respond to every problem first "by prayer" (Phil. 4:6).

In Matthew 18, Jesus expressly commands us to be rightly related to all these, His "little ones."

He orders us to receive them as we would Him: "Whosoever shall receive one such little child in my name receiveth me" (v. 5). We should emulate their good qualities, especially humility: "Whosoever...shall humble himself as this little child" (v. 4). If they stray, we should seek to restore them by counsel and intercession, because "it is not the will of your Father...that one of these little ones should perish" (v. 14; see vv. 11–14). Never should we "despise" them, thinking little of or looking or speaking down to them: "Take heed that ye despise not one of these little ones" (v. 10). Most importantly, we must never offend them—cause them to stumble spiritually by setting a bad example or by treating them badly. In some of the most solemn language He ever used, Jesus warned, "Whosoever shall offend one of these little ones who believe in me, it were better for him that a millstone were hanged about his neck, and that he were drowned in the depth of the sea" (v. 6). How accurate are His teachings and warnings!

In our blind pride, we often devalue, overlook, or offend Jesus' little ones. Why? We're busy seeking, serving, and saluting "great ones"—anyone appearing successful, rich, popular, or important. Eager to appear polished professionals, we avoid childlike Christians. They're too unsophisticated. Our churches seek "great ones." Thus many "little ones" wander away without loving fellowship, counsel, or prayer. Focused on our adult world and woes, we neglect the child believers in our churches, schools, neighborhoods, and homes. This un-Christlike behavior causes to stumble the very ones we should help walk with God. But Jesus hasn't changed. While we steadily loathe His "little ones," He steadfastly loves them.

Matthew 18 is a reality check. Who are the "little ones" in your circle of contacts? Are you loving or loathing His "little ones"?

Chapter 74

CLEANSED AGAIN—FOR MORE USE AND GLORY!

*W*HEN JESUS WENT into the temple to cleanse it, He caused quite a disturbance.

Suddenly and vigorously, He "cast out" and "over-threw" everything contrary to His Father's will in the Royal Porch's thriving market and currency exchange (Matt. 21:12). Tables, chairs, coins, bird cages, animals, vendors—all these objects and people went flying or fleeing in every direction! He also stood in the Gentile's court to block people carrying merchandise through it as a shortcut across Jerusalem (Mark 11:16). After His chaotic cleansing session ceased, He calmly resumed using the temple!

The same day He healed the sick there: "The blind and the lame came to him in the temple, and he healed them" (Matt. 21:14). The next day He taught in Solomon's Porch: "He taught daily in the temple" (Luke 19:47). Enthusiastic praises filled the temple courts. "Even the children" entered the spontaneous shouts and songs, "Praise God for the Son of David" (Matt. 21:15, NLT). Thus His surprising correction and subsequent ministry led to more glory for God!

This was Jesus' second temple purging, the first occurring two years earlier. Why this second cleansing?

The first didn't finish the job. Spiritual compromise and corruption gradually revisited and repossessed the holy place. Godly, kingdom-building prayer declined, and ungodly religious profiteering increased. Selfish disorder replaced scriptural order, as God grieved. Jesus' second cleansing was a deeper cleaning—a thorough purging meant to remove not some or most but all of the corruption.

Though by week's end the Cleanser was crucified and the temple re-polluted, Jesus' goal was nevertheless briefly achieved. His deeper cleaning led to more use and glory. Rid of its core sins, the temple courts again yielded rich fruit: Jesus' heavenly teaching, compassionate healings, powerful deliverances, and soaring prophecies (Matt. 23:34–39). Most importantly, He and His Father were honored. There's a lesson for us here.

Every Christian is a spiritual temple, a God-indwelt place called to holy living and labor: "Know ye not that your body is the temple of the Holy Spirit" (1 Cor. 6:19). As with the temple courts, Christ wants to bear fruit and receive honorable worship from the courts of our personal lives. As He cleansed Herod's temple twice to finish this work, so He visits us...until the job is done. If His first purging, or season of spiritual cleansing and righteous training, does this, He stops disturbing and starts using our divinely reordered lives. If it doesn't, or if sin or selfishness later reasserts itself, He comes again, determined to cleanse us.

Without warning, through unforeseeable events, He overturns our comfortable state of spiritual or moral compromise and urges us to cast out things we hold and love more than Him: trust in money, carnal pleasures, excessive leisure, man pleasing, ambition, wrong relationships, and so forth. Or, if already cleansed in these issues, He may retest us to deepen our cleansing and strengthen our righteousness in these areas. Once His Spirit shows us these unauthorized people ("money changers") and objects ("tables") cluttering and controlling our hearts, we must deal with them. And quickly. We do so by humbly confessing our sins and letting them go to lay hold of Christ and His will for our lives.

Why is His cleansing so persistent? As with Israel's temple, the more He cleanses our personal lives, the more He uses us and glorifies Himself.

Increasingly our prayers enable spiritually blind Christians to see—their divine gifts and callings, sin's true nature, how to apply Bible truths, God's beautiful character, His hand working in their circumstances, Satan's deceptions and distractions, the right way at crossroads, fulfillments of prophecy, and the imperative of readiness for Jesus' appearing. Increasingly the truths, warnings, and encouragements we share will heal spiritually lame believers, and they'll walk—close to God; in His ways; on stormy waters; through valleys of Baca; through darkness, floods, fires—and not faint, all the way to New Jerusalem!

The more the Cleanser uses us, the more honor we yield Him. Increasingly people will praise not us but Him who has purged and used our humble "courts" for His highest purposes.

Has the Cleanser suddenly disturbed your "courts" again? Has He overturned your monetary or materialistic dreams? Called you to cast out your besetting sin? Blocked your path, preventing you from using His holy promises as a shortcut to achieving your selfish plans? Sent unauthorized possessions flying and wrong relationships fleeing? Ordered you to get your bodily temple and habits back into His divine order?

Yield, and let Him have His way. You're being cleansed again—for more use and glory!

Chapter 75

THE STUFF OF SCHISMS

*E*XPRESSLY AND EMPHATICALLY, Jesus desires that Christians be lovingly unified. His loftiest command and prayer confirm this.

On the eve of His passion, Jesus laid down His most solemn law to His disciples: "This is my commandment, that ye love one another" (John 15:12). Later that evening He uttered His final, high-priestly prayer for all His followers throughout this age: " [I will] that they all may be one [in spirit]...Father...perfect in [or perfectly united as] one" (John 17:21–23). Thus His last precept and petition were for our loving unity.

Ever His antagonist, Satan is determined to create the opposite: needless schisms, or divisions, among us. Some separations are necessary. When Christians stubbornly practice, promote, or condone sin or heresy, they force godly Christians to separate from them to prevent sin's growth and preserve the church's holiness. Though unwanted, these divisions are unavoidable and beneficial, furthering our fidelity, spiritual growth, and maturity. But Satan wants to create unnecessary rifts among the righteous.

These rifts create harmful incisions in Christ's body. Satan's favorite dividers are our bad attitudes—fixed patterns of wrong thinking or feeling toward other Christians! Among our divisive attitudes, two stand out: judging and envy.

Envy is unjustified anger at those who have what we don't have but want. Envy may arise over material things: money, possessions, cars, clothes, etc. Or personal blessings: spouses, children, friends, beauty, etc. Or non-tangible things: knowledge, favor, achievements, honors, etc. Or spiritual things: Bible knowledge, answered prayers, spiritual gifts, ministries, intimacy with God, etc. Envy moves us to criticize and avoid, not cherish and befriend, those we envy (Acts 7:9). It creates a subtle competition that spoils cooperation. Unchecked, envy will eventually sever the closest bonds: siblings, spouses, friends, congregants, ministers.

By "judging," we mean *misjudging*. Sound, fair decisions made prayerfully and patiently about our personal responsibilities are necessary. Impulsive, misinformed, unfair decisions, especially in matters that aren't our business and that move us to unfairly criticize or reject people, are unnecessary. And un-Christian. And divisive. We should be growing in merciful understanding, giving others the benefit of the doubt. But misjudging turns ministers of mercy into masters of misjudgment—and dividers of brethren!

Typically, we misjudge Christians by:

- Believing rumors without seeking facts
- Rejecting believers because we disagree with their opinions (yet can't name anyone we fully agree with on all issues!)
- Finding fault with their body, diet, or dress
- Disapproving of their pastor, church, or denomination (or non-affiliation)
- Considering them too worldly or spiritual; too lukewarm or zealous; too ignorant or intellectual; too poor or rich

What busy jurists we are! Our flawed "rulings" often spring from suspicions or scruples.

Suspicions—unfounded but firmly accusatory imaginations running free in our minds (sometimes mistaken for "discernment")—cause us to misjudge innocent Christians merely because they're suffering adversities. Job's friends *knew* he was a secret sinner—though they had no proof! Lacking facts, they built their house of rejection on a foundation of fiction.

Scruples are personal ethical or religious standards that, though not biblically commanded, we live by because we feel they're right. To have and live by scruples is acceptable; to reject others for breaking our scruples is not acceptable. It makes schisms, not unity. But "where the Spirit of the Lord is, there is liberty" (2 Cor. 3:17) in all matters not addressed in Scripture. Never mistake your scruples for God's Scriptures. Unless you want Jesus to judge you rightly for judging others wrongly, "judge not, lest ye be judged" (Matt. 7:1).

How happily united we would be if we exchanged our unofficial motto, "Judge, and be judged," for "Live, and let live!" Of all people, Christians should freely permit different opinions, lifestyles, manners of worship, and personal preferences if they don't clearly break Scripture. The alternative— fellowshiping only with others exactly like us—is unkind, unintelligent, and un-Christlike. In fact, it's antichrist...what the Savior loathes and Satan loves! It's also unnecessary.

Blissful, loving, fruitful spiritual unity among all believers is possible.

Before and as the Spirit fell at Pentecost, "all" present were in "one accord" (Acts 1:14; 2:1). The apostle Paul begs us to pursue and preserve the same unity: "I beseech you . . . that there be no divisions [schisms] among you . . . be perfectly joined together in the same mind" (1 Cor. 1:10). Psalm 133 hints that God will "command the blessing" of the "precious ointment" of the Spirit whenever and wherever believers "dwell together in unity!"

Do you want the blessing of the Spirit or the divisiveness of envy, misjudging, imaginations, suspicions, scruples? Seek loving unity, savor the stuff of Pentecost, and be done with the stuff of schisms!

Chapter 76

ON FREEDOM WAY

T HE FREEST MAN ever, Jesus pointed us with authority to the one and only road to spiritual freedom. How may we access this liberating way of life?

Repentance and rebirth put us on this path. We turn from the false hopes, pleasures, and bondages of sin to a new, delightful, and enduring personal relationship with Jesus, the Author of spiritual freedom. This profound change of mind and living leads directly to spiritual rebirth. The freest man Himself told a good man still bound by dead religion, "Marvel not that I said unto thee, Ye must be born again" (John 3:7). How may we go further in this liberating relationship?

We look for, focus on, and live in *truth* all our days. Jesus said this truth-centered lifestyle leads to full, rich, and lasting personal emancipation: "Ye shall know the truth, and the truth shall make you free" (John 8:32). It's wonderful that we may live daily free from the tyrannical control of selfishness and sin and their unseen master, Satan—if we know the truth. As Pilate asked, "What is truth?" (John 18:38).

Truth has several aspects. Truth is reality, any real facts or accurate knowledge. The queen of Sheba told King Solomon, "It was a true report that I heard in mine own land, of thy acts and…wisdom" (1 Kings 10:6). Truth is also honesty, or any sincere disclosure of one's true feelings, condition, or actions. Jesus told a Samaritan woman, "Thou hast well said, I have no husband…that saidst thou truly" (John 4:17–18).

But primarily, Jesus' reference to truth points to biblical truth. When promising truth would make us free, He prefaced it with, "If ye continue in my word" (John 8:31), thus linking truth with His Word. He later asserted in prayer, "Thy word is truth" (John 17:17). The Old Testament agrees. The psalmist called Scripture "the word of truth," adding, "Thy law is the truth," and "all thy commandments are truth" (Ps. 119:43, 142, 151). So the truth that liberates is chiefly the Bible, God's very Word. It is entirely real, accurate, and honest in its description of God and humanity, and their past, present, and future relations.

Since we know that truth frees us and God's Word is truth, the next question is, How? How does truth free us? Truth liberates us as, and to the degree, we do the following things.

Seek truth, prayerfully reading and studying God's Word regularly. Believe truth, committing your mind to full reliance upon the Word and the One who spoke it, without further proofs or reason. Confess truth, confidently speaking aloud the specific biblical truths and promises you believe and humbly acknowledging your true sins, thoughts, and feelings to God. Trust truth, persistently believing it "with all thine heart" (Prov. 3:5) when unbelieving critics arise presenting unexplained contradictions that ensnare many in doubt. Love truth, making it your heart's desire and sweetest delight, especially in bitter trials. Obey truth, submitting to and complying with it in your daily habits, priorities, initiatives, and reactions. Fear truth, believing God's warnings of the sure, self-opposing consequences of sin. Hope in truth, confidently expecting God to fulfill all His promises and prophecies in His time and way. Profess truth, when asked your beliefs, publicly confessing your faith in the Word in this faithless world. Pray truth, adopting inspired biblical prayers as your personal petitions for people, churches, and nations. And don't stop there; continue in His Word!

Minister truth, sharing with others precious biblical truths God has shared with you. Labor for truth, working to sow it in the church and world or help ministries doing so. Suffer for truth, accepting rejection for the Word's sake, remembering Jesus prophesied every disciple must "bear his cross" (Luke 14:27). Be loyal to truth, faithfully standing by, helping, and consoling those who suffer for it. Wait for truth, patiently pursuing your devotions and duties while God patiently "works all things together" (Rom. 8:28) for good and to demonstrate how true His truth is. Watch for truth, daily expecting its fulfillments in your life, church, and nation, and searching for them in history. And endure for truth, keeping "the word of my patience" (Rev. 3:10), or Christ's order to wait patiently for His help until His truth triumphs over all your tribulations and tribulators. Continuing in these things makes you increasingly freer—released from the self-opposing influence of sin, selfishness, and Satan, and free to increasingly know, enjoy, serve, and honor the freest One. This is Freedom Way!

It's God's appointed highway to full inner liberty. If you follow it, Jesus promised you'll become "free indeed" (John 8:36). Today get on Freedom Way!

Chapter 77

IN EVERY SITUATION

HE MOST ATTITUDE-, life-, and destiny-changing verse in the Bible, bar none, is:

In everything give thanks, for this is the will of God in Christ Jesus concerning you.

—1 THESSALONIANS 5:18

"Everything," also rendered "all circumstances" (NIV) and "whatever happens" (NCV), refers to every situation in our lives. Obedience is easy when our situations are pleasant, though we may forget to give thanks even then. But it's a challenge when circumstances are hard. We prefer to thank God after He ends our difficulties, but He wants us to offer thanks "in" every situation. All the spiritually great ones did so.

Three times a day Daniel "gave thanks before his God" (Dan. 6:10), whatever his circumstances. David vowed perpetual thanksgiving: "I will give thanks unto thee forever" (Ps. 30:12). Paul offered thankful worship while illegally beaten, placed in stocks, and jailed. While His best friend, Lazarus, was still entombed and lifeless, Jesus prayed, "Father, I thank thee that thou hast heard me" (John 11:41). This freewill thank offering in adversity pleases God, refills us with His Spirit, and imparts His overcoming viewpoint. We usually overlook thanksgiving because it's so simple.

God's command is, "Just give Me thanks"—not a roaring "Hallelujah Chorus," spirited Jericho march, or enthusiastic Red Sea dance. It's easy to quietly say, "Thank You, Lord." Any Christian of any age, education, skills, or wealth can do it. Why does God ask this?

First, it's His will: "This is the will of God." God wants us thankful and giving thanks all the time. The more we comply, the more we cultivate the habit of thanksgiving, a mind-set that looks for things to be thankful for in every setting—and finds them! Also, thanksgiving drives away complaining. Forming the habit of thanksgiving breaks the habit of complaining. Despising murmuring, God refuses to favor murmuring Christians. Their constant complaints imply He's a poor Shepherd or has erred in sending them difficult circumstances. Wherever God puts habitual murmurers, they'll search for causes to complain—and find them! Complaining sours our disposition, spoils our fruitfulness, and, if continued, ruins our Christian life-work and destiny. So God warns, "Neither murmur ye, as some of them also murmured, and were destroyed" (1 Cor. 10:10).

Second, every situation we meet is part of His plan for us, sent to bless, correct, or challenge us. It's obvious we should give thanks for His blessings. We should also thank Him for corrective or challenging circumstances because they purge us of faults and sins that offend God and others, prepare us for God's service, and win us the honorable distinction of "overcomer."

Third, thanking God strengthens our faith. By giving thanks, we acknowledge God's presence, hand, and control in our lives: "In all thy ways [circumstances] acknowledge him" (Prov. 3:6). This reminds us He's still "very present" (Ps. 46:1), all-powerful, faithful to His Word, and ready to help.

So give thanks in every situation: when your prayers are answered quickly, and when they're delayed; when God does as you ask, and when He overrules you; when friends lovingly support you, and when they cruelly betray you; when your income increases, and when it decreases; when you're healthy, and when you're sick; when your plans succeed, and when they're hindered; when your days are quiet, and when they're wild with activity; when your business, church, or ministry grows, and when it's stagnant or shrinking; when God's guidance comes quickly, and when you must wait for it. This is our daily sacrifice.

Hebrews urges, "Let us offer the sacrifice of praise to God continually, that is, the fruit of our lips giving thanks to His name" (Heb. 13:15). This "sacrifice of praise" is the Christian equivalent of Israel's "continual burnt offering" (Exod. 29:38–46). Just as Jewish priests offered God sacrificial lambs on their altar "day by day continually," so Christian believer-priests should offer Him sacrificial thank-offerings on the altars of our lips continually.

The benefits are wonderful, paralleling those of the continual burnt offering. God meets us, causing us to sense His nearness; speaks to us through His Word or counsel; sanctifies us, setting us apart to minister to and for Him; dwells among our congregations; and causes us to know confidently He's our personal God. All this is ours as we offer the sacrifice of praise "day by day continually."

Dynamic, these benefits will powerfully change our attitudes, daily lives, and eternal destinies. Giving thanks in every situation brings God into every situation—His presence, wisdom, strength, grace, victories, and honor! So why delay?

Let the offering begin. Now, just where you are, give thanks in every situation!

Chapter 78

SEEK THE INNER CIRCLE

ALL BORN-AGAIN CHRISTIANS have the same relationship with God but not the same knowledge of Him or fruitfulness for Him. Why? In a word, *fellowship.*

Some believers "draw near" (James 4:8) to fellowship privately with the Lord regularly, while others do so irregularly. Or rarely. Or never! Why is regular intimate fellowship with Jesus important? Our closeness to Him determines our knowledge of Him, and that determines our fruitfulness for His kingdom. The key links here are *closeness—knowledge—fruitfulness.*

When we walk closely with Jesus daily, God's Spirit blesses our study of His Word by giving us exceptional insight into Jesus' character, values, purposes, and ways of living and working. Only from this deeply rooted tree of knowledge grow Jesus' works and His Spirit's exceptional fruit—"love, joy, peace, long-suffering, gentleness, goodness, faith, meekness, self-control" (Gal. 5:22–23)—in our lives. If our close fellowship with Him withers, so does our knowledge of Him and fruitfulness for Him. Therefore some Christians have a superficial, incomplete, and unsatisfying knowledge of Jesus, while others enjoy an accurate, rich, and growing understanding. And, consequently, some are very fruitful, while others produce little or no increase for His kingdom. It's always been this way.

During Jesus' earthly ministry there were various circles of fellowship with Him, from the outer fringe to the inner circle. Let's examine them.

The outer fringe believers consisted of the local crowds. These people saw and believed in Jesus when His itinerant ministry visited their city, village, or region (Jericho, Bethsaida, Judea, the Decapolis) to teach, heal, or deliver. They drew near His presence, but only for a few hours, and their contact was public, not private. So they knew Him, but only in a very limited way.

Moving closer, there was the larger body of disciples. These deeply serious, fully committed, student-followers left their homes to accompany Jesus on His ministry tours. Many women who supported Jesus' ministry team financially were among them (Luke 8:1–3), and many men. "Of these men" who "went in and out among" the apostles' company from the "beginning" of Jesus' ministry, Judas' replacement, Matthias, was selected (Acts 1:21–22). These disciples experienced not one but many of Jesus' meetings, teachings, and miracles. So they knew Him better than the local crowds—but not as intimately as the Twelve.

The apostles were even nearer to Jesus. He handpicked them from the larger body of disciples to eventually continue His ministry (Mark 3:13–15; Acts 1:1–2). They too experienced many of Jesus' messages, mercies, and miracles. But, unlike other disciples, they had special access to Jesus, lodging, lunching, and lingering with Him daily, and frequently requesting and receiving special insights: "When they were alone, he expounded all things to his disciples" (Mark 4:34). So they knew not only the public but also the private Jesus; not only His great works but also His great heart. They closely observed His reactions to prosperity and adversity, fame and shame, and His private habits of prayer, worship, and meditation. So they knew Him better than other disciples. But even they weren't Jesus' closest followers.

That distinction belonged to His inner circle—Peter, James, and John. These three apostles enjoyed several intimacies denied the others. They alone witnessed the raising of Jairus' daughter, Jesus' wondrous transfiguration, and His intense agony in Gethsemane. Why these privileges?

From Jesus' perspective, He was preparing them to lead His church. Jesus knew well that extraordinary intimacy with Him would lead to extraordinary knowledge of Him and extraordinary fruitfulness for Him. He was right! Consider their exceptional fruit in spirit and works: they grew spiritually mature, evangelized and discipled thousands, wrote gospels and epistles, received visions and the Revelation, led the fledgling church, trained strong leaders, endured bitter persecution, and suffered martyrdom or exile.

But from our viewpoint, there's another reason they received the most special access to Jesus. They drew near Him most often. Why? They loved Him more: "Simon…lovest thou me more than these [disciples do]?" (John 21:15). They craved His Word, presence, and approval more. They cared more for His people and plan. My proof? They labored more for His gospel and kingdom—and suffered more! "We have left all, and have followed thee" (Mark 10:28). Let their example probe and prompt you.

Do you love Jesus more than others do? Enough to seek Him and His Word daily? To work "heartily, as to the Lord"? (Col. 3:23). To suffer for Him? May the Messiah use this message to stir you to no longer be content with the outer fringe or any intermediate circle of fellowship with Him.

Today, rise and seek the inner circle.

Chapter 79

POSITIONED FOR HIS BLESSING?

*M*ERE MORTALS CAN'T thrive without the Immortal's blessing. We either position ourselves for His blessing or endure an unsatisfying existence. What is God's blessing?

God blesses us by in some way bestowing good upon us. This good may be tangible: food, shelter, material goods, monies, protection, friends, children, and so forth. Or it may be intangible: peace, the sense of God's presence, biblical insight, divine guidance, infillings of the Holy Spirit, spiritual gifts, and so forth. As Creator and Sovereign of the universe, our heavenly Father doesn't have to ask for permission to confer these and other blessings on us. He just causes them to enter our lives, as He caused Jesus to enter this world.

"When the fullness of the time was come, God sent forth his Son..." (Gal. 4:4). This memorable verse describes the greatest blessing God ever gave this world: Jesus of Nazareth! Jesus was a unique blend of mortal man and Immortal God incarnate. A blessed people, many first-century Jews recognized Jesus as an extraordinary Blessing—and Blesser. So instead of bringing their infants to the local synagogue to receive their rabbi's traditional blessing,[1] they "brought unto him little children, that he should put his hands on them, and pray" (Matt. 19:13). When Jesus subsequently "laid his hands on them" (v. 15), as Son of man He asked Jehovah to bestow good upon them. But as Son of God, He did more. Rather than invoke a blessing, He initiated it. Instead of requesting, He released a fresh supply of divine good upon these infants—and represented it.

Jesus' messages, miracles, and exemplary life were the greatest manifestation of God's blessing on Israel. Wherever He went, worked, or prayed, great good followed! Peter described this, and Luke inscribed it, for the ages:

> How God anointed Jesus of Nazareth with the Holy Spirit, and with power; who went about doing good, and healing all that were oppressed of the devil; for God was with him.
>
> —ACTS 10:38

As God's "goodness and mercy" surely followed King David all his life (Ps. 23:6), so God's sure mercies and goodness followed Jesus' every earthly step. What a blessing He was while on earth! And now that He has ascended, we're here to represent Him.

"As he is, so are we in this world" (1 John 4:17). Like Jesus, every Christian is destined not only to be blessed but also to be a blessing to other needy mortals, believers and unbelievers. God decreed to Abraham and all his posterity sharing his faith, "Thou shalt be a blessing" (Gen. 12:2). The apostle Paul declared that Christians are recipients of this Abrahamic heritage. We "who are of faith are blessed with faithful Abraham" (Gal. 3:9)—and called to be blessings.

But, unlike Jesus, we can't command (release, initiate) God's blessing upon ourselves or others. We may request it in believing prayer, "God be merciful unto us, and bless us" (Ps. 67:1), but we're powerless to release it. Jesus clearly authorized believers to do many extraordinary things in His name—on His authority, by His orders, as His agents, and with His supernatural assistance. He explicitly told us to preach, teach, baptize, pray for the sick, expel demons, bind and loose spiritual forces, agree in prayer, and command hindering "mountains," or obstacles to God's will, to move (Mark 11:23). But never did Jesus authorize us to command God's blessing on ourselves or others. That unique privilege remains the sole prerogative of our Sovereign. Yet He didn't leave us entirely powerless.

We can help God's hand of blessing move. How? We can position ourselves to receive His blessings, be blessings, and pray effectively for Him to bless others. How? By taking three simple steps.

First, we should live in loving unity with all sincere believers. Psalms teaches that whenever we "dwell together in unity," God "commands" His blessing (Ps. 133). For confirmation, we need only review Pentecost (Acts 1:14; 2:1, 2–4). Second, we should obey God fully, not partially. God reserves His richest blessings for those who do all His commands: "If thou shalt hearken diligently…to do all his commandments" (Deut. 28:1). Third, we should please God, not ourselves or other people, in every decision, as Jesus did: "I do always those things that please him" (John 8:29). This will position us correctly.

We mortals will be firmly in place, prepared to receive the Immortal's blessings. And be blessings. And pray His blessings upon others: "If ye abide in me, and my words abide in you, ye shall ask what ye will, and it shall be done unto you" (John 15:7).

Are you positioned for His blessing?

Chapter 80

YOU WILL FIND IT

*I*N MATTHEW 10, Jesus faithfully told the Twelve—His first Word-bearers—what to expect while ministering His Word in first-century Israel. Frank and full, His prophetic briefing revealed everything—good, bad, and ugly.

Literally or symbolically, every word He uttered still applies to Word-bearers, or committed, truth-centered Christian disciples and ministers. As we go in Jesus' name, we should preach and promote only God's kingdom, not nations, ideologies, denominations, or other lesser causes (Matt. 10:7). While generously spreading Jesus' words and works, we must learn to live by faith in God's provision (vv. 8–10). Our witness and ministries will be received in some cities and rejected in others (vv. 11–15). Sheep-like in a wolfish society, we must learn to be harmless as gentle doves and wise as wily snakes (v. 16). Eventually someone near and dear will betray us (v. 21). Bitter enemies will cruelly slander us and blind judges callously condemn us (v. 17). But God will turn these hostile hearings into witnessing opportunities, as His Spirit faithfully shows us what to say (vv. 18–20). Abusive epithets and adjectives will be hurled at us, as they were our Master: "Heretic!" "Deceiver!" "Demonic!" (vv. 24–25). But we needn't fear.

In that dark hour God will draw nearer and give us much more biblical insight, and later expose our slanderers and release us to share those insights with His people (vv. 26–32). We must choose and re-choose to fear God rather than men, remembering God's constant, watchful care over the minutest details of our lives (vv. 28–30). Under no circumstances should we stop confessing Him by lip and life (vv. 32–33). We'll have distressing divisions in our families, and our fiercest foes will be in our own "households" (vv. 34–35). We'll have to endure some trials a long time, while being hated by "all [kinds of] men" (v. 22). Instead of quickly defending us, the Lord will ask us to take up our crosses, or willingly accept these injustices, and continue bearing His Word to the world "to the end" (v. 22).

When that end arrives, we'll find a sweet fulfillment awaiting us. Jesus ended His prophetic briefing with this promise:

> He that findeth his life shall lose it; and he that loseth his life for
> my sake shall find it.
>
> —MATTHEW 10:39

What did He mean? To "find" our life, must we "lose" it literally, as martyrs? Or abandon normal life for a cloistered existence, as hermits, monks, and nuns have for centuries?

No, "life" here refers to our natural or worldly life, the ordinary, unspiritual life we had in this world before receiving Jesus. This natural life consists primarily of three areas: relationships, possessions, and aspirations. If our relationships are friendly and many, life is good. If our monetary and material possessions meet our needs and wishes amply, life is comfortable. If our future looks bright, life is exciting. But if one or more of these areas is spoiled or sacrificed, our natural life is partially or wholly lost.

Besides this natural life, Christians also have a spiritual or Christian life—our personal relationship to Jesus and pursuit of spiritual growth and service. Both of these lives cannot control us simultaneously. One must rule and the other yield. One must assume first place and the other second.

Jesus promised that if we put our natural life before our spiritual, we'll eventually lose not only our spiritual but also our natural life: "He that findeth [seeks, holds, and defends] his [natural] life shall lose it [ultimately]..." (v. 39); or "If you cling to your life, you will lose it" (NLT). Lot consistently put his worldly life first, before spiritual interests. So ultimately he lost both. His spiritual life never developed, and his carefully cultivated natural life vanished in the smoke of Sodom. And God never restored it.

A much better end awaits us, because Jesus also promised if we consistently put our spiritual life first, willingly surrendering whatever natural interests interfere with His purposes, one day we shall find it. "And he that loseth his life for my sake shall find it" (v. 39). One day, when our habit of putting spiritual interests first is deeply rooted, God will restore the hopes, possessions, or relationships we've lost for faithfulness to His call.

As with Job, He will mercifully turn our captivity. Old relationships will be mended or replaced by better ones. Possessions will be restored or improved. Hopes long delayed will be fulfilled "exceedingly abundantly above" our prayers or dreams (Eph. 3:20). Christ will faithfully replace our reproaches with honors, divisions with unity, and locust-eaten years with seasons of joyful fruitfulness—and our spiritual and natural lives will thrive! Believe this! Why?

Jesus promised, "You will find it" (NLT).

Chapter 81

GO AND TELL JESUS

FTER HEROD CRUELLY executed John the Baptist, John's disciples, their hearts wounded and wondering, "went and told Jesus" what had happened (Matt. 14:12). Why?

No reason is given, so we're left to speculate. Perhaps they wanted to inform John's family and realized Jesus, his second cousin, would break the news gently. Maybe they remembered John's repeated public testimony that Jesus was the Messiah, "the Lamb of God, who taketh away the sin of the world" (John 1:29, 36) and came to transfer their full allegiance and service to Him. Possibly they came to warn Jesus, realizing that, a preacher of righteousness and protester of sin like John, He could also be in danger. Perhaps they wanted justice and hoped King Jesus would overthrow and execute Herod for murdering John. Or maybe they just needed consolation for their troubled minds and hurting hearts and saw the compassionate Nazarene as their nearest and gentlest Comforter. Whatever their reason, their reaction to this tragedy is clear: they poured out their hearts to Jesus!

Have we learned this great secret? King David did and urged us to practice it when reeling with emotional pain or turmoil:

> Trust in him at all times, ye people; *pour out your heart before him.*
>
> —PSALM 62:8

The last phrase is also translated, "Tell him all your problems" (NCV), "Tell him all your troubles" (GNT), and, "Pour out your prayers to him" (MOFFATT). Thus David calls us to "pour out," or freely tell the Lord in prayer, all our innermost thoughts, feelings, and confusion when trouble visits.

When cutting wounds—insults, unfairness, abandonments, betrayals, conspiracies, or stunning, seemingly insurmountable defeats—injure our souls, we should promptly go and tell Jesus what's happened, as John's disciples did. Just talking to the Great Psychologist is therapeutic. We should also ask Him to comfort us by His Spirit; give us biblical insight on what's happened; give us strength, grace, and wisdom to overcome; and intervene

200

to help us. This "pouring out" transfers all our burdens to His ample shoulders. Believing He hears and answers now, "when ye pray" (Mark 11:24), and thanking Him for it, enables us to enter His powerful, sustaining "rest" of faith—"we who have believed do enter into rest" (Heb. 4:3)—and His rest to enter us.

Practicing this breaks three foolish habits:

1. Stoically remaining silent and internalizing our thoughts, fears, and anger in futile self-dependency

2. Angrily complaining or arguing about what has happened, which makes us forget our diabolical trouble is divinely "given...from heaven" (John 3:27)

3. Immediately telling others—spouses, friends, counselors, even ministers—our problems before telling Jesus

Like John's wounded but wise disciples, we should always talk with Jesus first, and then tell ministers and prayer partners. This "tell Jesus first" habit is obedience to Jesus' overarching command, "Seek ye first the kingdom of God [and its King!]..." (Matt. 6:33). And it ensures we'll receive all the spiritual and natural help we need: "...and all these things [you need] shall be added unto you." It also honors the Wonderful Counselor above all counselors and increases our dependency on Him. This hastens His help, because "them who honor me I will honor" (1 Sam. 2:30). And it makes us wise.

God's wisest servants always quickly go and tell Jesus their woes. Whenever trouble visited, Moses and Aaron promptly fell on their faces before the Lord. David faithfully "cast his burden" on the Lord, who faithfully sustained him (Ps. 55:22). When persecuted, the apostles immediately went to Jesus—"Lord, behold their threatenings; and grant [us]...all boldness" (Acts 4:29). Peter instructed us, "Casting all your care upon him, for he careth for you" (1 Pet. 5:7). Paul ordered, "Be anxious for nothing, but in everything, by prayer and supplication with thanksgiving, let your request be made known unto God" (Phil. 4:6)—promising peace as our reward, "and the peace of God, which passeth all understanding, shall keep your hearts and minds" (v. 7). Are you wise?

Has something disappointing, unfair, or cruel happened and left you wounded, wondering, or overwhelmed? Go and tell Jesus about it, first, frankly, and fully! You'll feel better—relieved instead of agitated. You'll be

NOT BY *Bread* ALONE

better—no longer burdened but lifted. You'll respond better—in the Spirit, not the flesh. You'll receive better—an answer straight from Jesus, comforting your heart. You'll walk better—not wobbly but stably. You'll work better—not indifferently but "heartily, as to the Lord" (Col. 3:23). And you'll minister better—not irregularly but steadily, with Jesus helping! "They went forth…the Lord working with them" (Mark 16:20). Excuse me, please.

A problem has arisen, and I must go and tell Jesus…

Chapter 82

ARE YOU HUMBLING YOURSELF?

OINTEDLY AND PERSISTENTLY, in both Old Testament and New, the Bible calls us to humility. Moses summons us first.

Not once or twice but *three* times the lawgiver told the Israelites, who are our examples, that God led them through their wilderness tests primarily to humble them: "The LORD thy God led thee these forty years in the wilderness, to humble thee...and he humbled thee...that he might humble thee" (Deut. 8:2–3, 16). To be sure we don't forget, three colossal early church leaders repeat this call to humility. James, president of the Jerusalem church, exhorted, "Humble yourselves in the sight of the Lord" (James 4:10). The apostle Peter added, "Humble yourselves...under the mighty hand of God" (1 Pet. 5:6). The apostle Paul charged "every man...not to think of himself more highly than he ought to think, but to think soberly" (Rom. 12:3), young men to be "sober-minded" (Titus 2:6), and affluent Christians to "be not high-minded" (1 Tim. 6:17). There's a Trinity of reasons for these summons.

The Father hates pride (Prov. 6:16–17), because it reminds Him of Satan's rebellious, tragic conceit. Through James and Peter, He promises to oppose whoever manifests it: "God resisteth the proud" (James 4:6; 1 Pet. 5:5). He also served notice through David that He'll never live close to proud souls in time or eternity: "Him that hath an high look and a proud heart will not I tolerate" (Ps. 101:5).

The Son said that without the humility of repentance we won't enter God's kingdom, adding the greatest there will be the humblest here: "Whosoever...shall humble himself as this little child, the same is greatest in the kingdom of heaven" (Matt. 18:4). On three occasions in the Gospel record Jesus stated God demotes self-promoters and promotes self-effacers: "Whosoever shall exalt himself shall be abased; and he that shall humble himself shall be exalted" (Matt. 23:12; see also Luke 14:11; 18:14). This repetition reveals His calls to humility were a primary, not a passing, theme in His teaching. Jesus also set the consummate example: "As a man, he humbled himself and became obedient unto death, even the [humiliating] death of the cross" (Phil. 2:8). And He challenged us to study and emulate His humility: "Learn of me; for I am meek and lowly in heart" (Matt. 11:29).

The Spirit inspired Paul to urge us to follow Jesus' exhortation and example: "Let this mind [attitude] be in you, which was also in Christ Jesus" (Phil. 2:5). Paul urges us to do nothing in competitive pride but everything, "in lowliness of mind...esteem[ing] others better" than ourselves (v. 3). To leaders, who should lead in humility, Paul testified he served "the Lord with all humility of mind" (Acts 20:19). And he exhorted us all, "Put on [as God's elect]...humbleness of mind, meekness" (Col. 3:12). Why all this anti-pride, pro-humility rhetoric from the Trinity and teachers?

Whether we admit it or not, all human beings have pride—excessive self-esteem. The world and biblical history confirm this thesis: in our natural (fallen) state we are proud creatures, thinking too highly of ourselves, not highly enough of God, and too lowly of others. James', Peter's, and Paul's calls to Christians prove that, though saved by grace, we're still uplifted in heart—and need humbling in life.

That settled, the next question is, How? How do we humble ourselves?

While there are many ways to this end, here are some that are biblical, simple, and proven. Anytime, anywhere, any Christian who wishes to humble himself (or herself) may do so by:

- Submissively obeying God's Word, call, or guidance (Phil. 2:8)
- Thinking soberly, not too highly, about ourselves (Rom. 12:3)
- Refusing to prejudge, scorn, or condemn anyone
- Fully accepting humble circumstances, especially the "day of small things" (Zech. 4:10)
- Not despising but embracing God's "chastening," or corrective discipline (Heb. 12:5)
- Receiving godly leaders' teaching, counsel, and correction
- Deferring to others' needs and, when possible, wishes
- Handling problems by prayerfully relying on God, rather than worrying (Phil. 4:6–7)
- Freely receiving help when offered
- Confessing our sins and faults "one to another" (James 5:16) and to God
- Thanking God profusely for every blessing (1 Thess. 5:18)

- Waiting patiently for God's guidance, help, or deliverance
- Quietly accepting crosses of rejection or reproach for Jesus' sake
- Rejoicing with, rather than envying, those who are blessed or prospered (Rom. 12:15)

All these means lead to one end: Christlike humility. As we follow them, the Holy Spirit will gradually transform even the haughtiest Christian into a humble one, ready to walk and work closely forever with the King of meekness.

Today, are you humbling yourself?

Chapter 83

READY FOR MARKETPLACE EVANGELISM!

ESIDES CONTRASTING SELF-INTERESTED and selfless Christian service, the parable of the laborers also reveals how, when, and where Christ finds converts (Matt. 20:1–16).

"How" is simply by His sovereign choice, represented by the "householder" (Christ) selecting workers for his "vineyard" (present kingdom, the church). "When" is in every season of this age, even the last hour before His return. "Where" is surprising.

The "laborers" represent Christian converts, elected to salvation, endowed with spiritual gifts, and called to specific church duties and ministries. How amazing that the "householder" here finds His kingdom laborers not in the temple courts but "in the marketplace" (v. 3). Let's investigate.

In first-century Greco-Roman cities, marketplaces (Greek, *agora*) were bustling city centers with something for everyone. There was commerce there. Merchants were busily buying and selling all kinds of produce, products, and people for profit. There was religion there. Jesus observed the proud Pharisees parading and posing there, loving "greetings in the marketplaces, and to be called by men, Rabbi, Rabbi" (Matt. 23:6–7). With their strolling, shopping parents, many children were there too. Jesus portrayed it as a playground, with "children sitting in the market place, and calling one to another" (Luke 7:32).

Besides these uses, first-century marketplaces served as forums for public debate on a wide range of political, religious, or philosophical issues.[1] It was in Athens' agora that the apostle Paul, grieved over the city's gross idolatry, "disputed [discussed, debated the gospel]...daily with them that met with him" (Acts 17:16–17) and received an invitation to speak to the city's high council, the Areopagus. Public courts were also found there. In Philippi, Paul's enraged enemies dragged him and Silas "into the market place" (Acts 16:19), where the city judges summarily condemned, beat, and jailed them. Unemployed workers were found there. Christ's "householder" visited the marketplace solely "to hire laborers" (Matt. 20:1). So ancient marketplaces were multidimensional.

They were microcosms, little worlds within the larger world filled with all kinds of people—people typically interested in everything *but* Christ the "householder," His vineyard of the church (kingdom), and His harvest of redeemed souls. Yet as our text parable shows, Christ was, and still is, very interested in them. Rather than wait for the laborers to seek him, the "householder" proactively "went out…in[to] the market place," searching for them (v. 3). This represents the searching compassion of God reaching out to the spiritually lost who, from His kingdom's perspective, are "idle" (vv. 3, 6), no matter how busily they're pursuing worldly interests. We expect this proactive divine soul-seeking in gospel churches, but Jesus describes it also occurring in marketplaces. Do we catch His hint?

Christ wants us to branch out into marketplace evangelism! We know the "householder" calls men and women in evangelistic meetings and crusades, on foreign missions, and through Spirit-led witnessing and tract distribution. In our narrow religious thinking, however, we may overlook the fact that He's busily converting laborers to His service in the workplace every hour of the day. Though they have marketing, not the Messiah, on their minds, He's focused on plucking them from a meaningless existence and placing them where they can help build His meaningful kingdom: "Go ye also into the vineyard" (Matt. 20:7). So daily in this world's marketplaces He seeks merchants, salesmen, professionals, technicians, scientists, machinists, artists, craftsmen, manual laborers, bankers, government workers, and, yes, loafers, challenging them to see the utter futility of life without Him: "Why stand ye here all the day idle?" (v. 6). How does He seek these?

He doesn't use self-conscious, "pressy" Christians who awkwardly interject Jesus into every conversation whether Spirit-led or not. Their Spiritless evangelism by verbal coercion is counterproductive; instead of drawing converts to Christ, it drives them away. Rather, He saves through simple, spiritual ways and workers. His ready assistants are humble disciples who work "heartily, as to the Lord" (Col. 3:23) and pray faithfully for everyone they meet in the marketplace. Their intercessions and upright, loving daily life-witness draw spiritual idlers to the "householder." And, as God gives "door[s] of utterance" (Col. 4:3), they address their situations, souls, and Savior. Once converted, these new laborers enter covenant living with the "householder," assuming their appointed place and work in His vineyard and harvest. Will you be the "householder's" ready assistant?

If so, determine to walk closely with the "householder" and work diligently and pray faithfully in your commercial, industrial, agricultural, legal, medical, academic, technological, governmental, or other marketplace. Be prepared to witness at whatever hour He visits seeking new servants: "He went out [visited] about the sixth and ninth hour... and about the eleventh hour... and found others" (Matt. 20:5–6). The Lord needs such assistants.

Be ready for marketplace evangelism!

Chapter 84

SHOW THEM THE WAY

AFTER BRINGING CHILDREN into this world, Christian parents should help them find their way through it. How may we do so? We show them the way by directing and redirecting them to the One who said, "I am the way" (John 14:6). Such godly guidance requires three primary necessities:

1. INSTRUCTION—we should diligently teach them about God's way, His Word, and His way of life.

2. INTERCESSION—we should faithfully pray for them in the Spirit to come to, receive, walk, and persevere in God's way.

3. ILLUSTRATION—we should steadily demonstrate to them a life lived in and for the way and Word of God.

Whatever other helpful ways of parenting we discover and practice, these three are essential if we hope to help guide our innocent ones through the wicked wilderness of the world.

Naïve and vulnerable to the wily prince of this world, our children need and deserve two parents who walk with God. But with sin and stress ruining many marriages, happy nuclear families are harder to find. While two Christian parents are preferable, one, if committed, can become an inspirational parental epistle—a walking, talking Bible message, a Christian living video seen and heard in the home daily. As Christ was the Word made flesh before Israel's attentive eyes, so Christian parents can be Christianity made flesh before their children's curious and impressionable gazes. God's plan is for our parental Bible story, and our priestly intercessions, to influence our children all their lives, calling and recalling them to the way in which we walk. But our works, ways, and sayings permanently impress our children (or grandchildren) for Christ only if we are consistent "doers of the word and not hearers only" (James 1:22). So Christian parent, be consistent. Day after day, show them the way.

Demonstrate integrity, a thoroughly honest character that doesn't act deceitfully or unethically or speak falsely. Display humility, a soul that doesn't seek praises, boast on its accomplishments, deny its faults, hold prejudices, or mock anyone: "What doth the LORD require...but...to walk humbly with thy God?" (Micah 6:8). Exhibit devotion, a deeply dedicated Christian disciple who takes time first daily to fellowship with his King and strengthen His "kingdom" and "righteousness" within (Matt. 6:33). Show dutifulness, a parent who steadily pursues his vocational obligations, rain or shine, to provide his family's needs: "Not slothful in business; fervent in spirit; serving the Lord" (Rom. 12:11). Demonstrate faith, a parent who relies on God at all times, "anxious for nothing; but in everything, by prayer...with thanksgiving," asking God's help and resting in His "peace...which passeth all understanding" (Phil. 4:6–7).

Display faithfulness, a parent who always honors covenantal and contractual obligations and verbal agreements: "Timothy, who is...faithful in the Lord" (1 Cor. 4:17). Show submission, a parent who willingly yields to authorities, laws, and rules in the nation, workplace, church, and home: "Be subject to the governing authorities" (Rom. 13:1, ESV). Exhibit joy, a spirit so free in Jesus that gladness springs and flows out regularly, even during long, dark trials of faith: "Strengthened...unto all patience and long-suffering with joyfulness" (Col. 1:11). Demonstrate worship, a parent who freely lavishes adoration on the true God, not the worldly idols of money, materialism, pleasure, or self-promotion: "Then David arose...and worshiped" (2 Sam. 12:20). Display the New Testament overcomer, one who consistently rises above adversaries and adversities by persistently trusting and obeying God, regardless of what others say or do: "Be not overcome of evil, but overcome evil with good" (Rom. 12:21). Show courage, a parent who consistently obeys God and remains unmoved when the consequences are misunderstanding, criticism, slander, or betrayal: "Be strong and of a good courage...the LORD thy God is with thee" (Josh. 1:9). Exhibit mercy, a parent who doesn't rush to judge or condemn anyone and who forgives all offenders: "Be ye, therefore, merciful...judge not...condemn not...forgive" (Luke 6:36–37). And demonstrate love, a parent who is always ready to kindly listen to, counsel, or support them, whether they excel or fail: "Walk in love, as Christ also hath loved us" (Eph. 5:2). These kinds of living illustrations combined with intercession will make your instruction impressive.

Your children, and grandchildren, will remember your parental epistle and find the way and enter into, abide in, and walk in His Word and ways. And never depart: "Train up a child in the way he should go and, when he is old, he will not depart from it" (Prov. 22:6). In that day you'll rejoice, knowing you've guided through this world those you brought into it. Got kids? Grandkids?

Go show them the way.

Chapter 85

"BECAUSE OF YOUR WORDS"

*T*HE WORDS WE speak in prayer are important. God listens closely and sends angels to do as we say. Daniel says so.

Upon arrival, a dazzlingly bright heavenly messenger informed the prophet, Daniel, "Thy words were heard, and I am come *for your words*" (Dan. 10:12). Or, "God has listened to you, and I have come because of your prayers" (NCV). Or, "Your words were heard, and I have come in response to them" (NIV). Do note that Daniel's prayer, for more insight into Israel's "latter days" (v. 14), was according to God's will.

Yet it's amazing that the infinitely large God who created, named, and set in motion billions of stars actually listens to the humble, fervent prayers of His incomparably smaller prophets and people! His decisions and responses spring not only from His sovereign plans but also from our specific words. Thus our precise petitions, if aligned with His will, shape His interventions in our lives. The Exodus illustrates this.

For years the oppressed Israelites repeatedly asked God for release from Pharaoh's yoke. Compassionately attentive, God listened to every heart-wrenching word arising from their sun-parched lips. Later He revealed His undetected attentiveness to His deliverer: "I have surely…heard their cry" (Exod. 3:7). Then He sent Moses to give the Israelites the very thing they asked for, or *their words*—deliverance from Pharaoh's oppression.

Do we realize our words—the specific requests we utter in prayer regarding people, plans, and problems—make a difference? If we speak no words in prayer, no results follow; though blessed and strengthened by time in God's presence, we receive no further joy from seeing His responses. But when our words directly address issues, needs, and people, things happen in those very areas, not just because they're God's will but also because of our words, or because we've stirred our spirits to keep asking and praying in the Spirit for them with faith and determination. As Jesus promised, "Thy Father, who seeth in secret, shall reward thee openly" (Matt. 6:6).

Accordingly, Hebrews urges us, when in need, to come straight to God with plain words: "Let us…come boldly unto the throne of grace, that we may obtain mercy, and find grace to help in time of need" (Heb. 4:16). No indecision or timidity here; just decide what you need or want and ask! Jesus taught this.

When blind Bartimaeus heard Jesus was passing by, he immediately prayed, "Jesus…have mercy on me" (Mark 10:47). Though heartfelt, this petition was too general. So Jesus "stood still" and commanded that Bartimaeus come near (v. 49). "Casting away his garment" (v. 50), which symbolized the inhibiting religious pride covering him, Bartimaeus "rose" to go to Jesus—and to a new, higher level of prayer. Jesus' words revealed Bartimaeus' hadn't specified which "mercy" he wanted. "What wilt thou that I should do unto thee?" (v. 51). Alertly, the blind man saw his error and quickly got specific: "Lord, that I might receive my sight" (v. 51). Just as quickly, Jesus responded with not vague but precise action: "Immediately he received his sight" (v. 52). This vivid lesson on answered prayer transformed Bartimaeus' faith and life. Revived by this new understanding—"God hears my very words and graciously grants them!"—he entered a new, closer walk with Jesus: "and [Bartimaeus] followed Jesus [closely now] in the way" (v. 52).

Though small, this insight is immensely inspiring. Confidence that God responds to not just Daniel's, Israel's, or Bartimaeus' but also *our words*, that He sends angels because of what we say, puts fresh life and meaning into our prayers. It confirms that prayer matters! Our hidden God-talks create open life-changes. Far from mundane, our conversations with God are exalted moments! Full of stimulating hope! And explosive power!

If this seems too good to believe, maybe you're blind, like Bartimaeus. And perhaps Jesus is standing still, waiting for you to cast off your garment of religious reserve, rephrase your petitions in simple, direct words, and rise to a new level of effective prayer and a new, closer walk with Him. So rise; He's calling you.

And so is the father of lies! Satan wants you to believe your words fall on deaf ears. Yet Daniel, Exodus, and Mark's Gospel are unitedly testifying the opposite: the immeasurably large Creator is also your loving, attentive Father alertly watching over your comparatively tiny circle of activity and interest. Whenever you pray, He listens intently—"I, the LORD, will hear them" (Isa. 41:17)—and responds with surprising specificity, dispatching angels to answer your questions, grant your desires, provide your needs, and help others as you request. Why?

As the angel said, "Because of your words."

Chapter 86

ARE YOU A WAY OF LIFE—OR DEATH?

*E*VERY CHRISTIAN IS becoming a way of life or death to others. Which way we become is determined by our willingness to let God change us.

Many Christians feel they've changed sufficiently by converting to faith in Christ. Any further alteration of their soul or life ways would be too demanding and intrusive for even God to ask. Church life is pleasant for them for a season. But when God begins trying to correct them—in motives, attitudes, values, daily habits, morality, ethics, financial dealings, etc.—they quickly become disinterested, evasive, or rebellious. They may continue dutifully participating in church meetings or ministries, but they have ruled out further change. That issue is settled.

Sadly, so is their Christian growth. Godly change is the only path to spiritual development and fruitfulness. The wise Book of Proverbs says God's Word is a "lamp" and "light," adding: "Reproofs of instruction are the way of [and to more] life" (Prov. 6:23). Paraphrasing, this text teaches:

> Only by receiving the corrective criticisms of God's Word, and changing for the better, do we progress in God's way and receive more of His life.
>
> —PROVERBS 6:23, AUTHOR'S PARAPHRASE

So if we want to move forward in Christ's way and life, we must yield and change our thoughts and actions every time God's Word reproves us, either directly as we read or listen to it, or indirectly, as it is faithfully applied by one of God's messengers. God says to sinners, "You can have life through Christ alone," but to believers, "You can have more life through change alone."

I remember Costa Deir saying, "God has a one-track mind: changing you!" Truly, it's only as we change our old ways of thinking, speaking, and acting to conform to biblical ways that we delight our heavenly Father. New birth, Spirit baptism, church attendance, excellent Bible teaching, daily devotions—these things alone won't change us to be consistently like Christ. Sooner or later, God draws near to start systematically cleansing and changing us. His divine correction comes in different ways.

When read with understanding, God's Word, like an ancient oil lamp, sheds light on the areas of our inner thoughts and outward conduct we need to change. God doesn't require we change everything at once but rather deals with one issue at a time. It's very possible for us to simply read our Bibles and revise ourselves, contemplate the logos and change our living. But if we don't respond to this direct, corrective Bible light, the Spirit begins using our consciences to make us uncomfortable in stubbornness. Day by day He patiently stirs us to rise and correct ourselves according to the light we've already received: "This sin must go now, My son (daughter)…this attitude needs changing, this motive revising…start this habit, stop that one…and reconcile this relationship, break off that one." If we're still unresponsive, God begins working indirectly, prompting ministers or fellow disciples to speak to us about these issues. If still obstinate, God sends more caring counselors to try to turn us. If this also fails, He eventually leaves us to our own way—the way of pride and stubbornness. That road leads not to spiritual growth and freedom but to stagnation and bondage. And death. And that's not all.

The uncorrectable Christian always takes others to death with him (or her). Again, eternal wisdom declares, "He is in the way of life that keepeth instruction, but he that refuseth reproof erreth" (Prov. 10:17). Another translation reads:

> He who heeds instruction and correction is [not only himself] in the way of life, [but also] is a way of life for others. And he who neglects or refuses reproof [not only himself] goes astray [but also] causes to err and is a path toward ruin for others.
>
> —PROVERBS 10:17, AMP

Taught this truth years ago, I've now seen both parts of it played out many times. I've seen one meek Christian inspire humility in another, one trusting soul prompt faith in another, and one faithful believer lead another into steadfast service. And, sadly, I've seen one rebel inspire insubordination in another, one doubter snare another in disbelief, one covenant-breaker move another to infidelity, and one carnal Christian embolden another to sin. Why? The first leaders received correction; the second refused it. Then, over time, each led others into their respective ways. And ends.

The next time God tries to correct you, remember you're deciding which way you'll become—to your children, friends, and everyone around you. And their ends!

Today, are you receiving reproofs of correction or resisting them? A way of life—or death?

Chapter 87

DISCIPLESHIP—DEFINED AND DEMONSTRATED

*M*ANY PEOPLE THINK all Christians are disciples of Christ. But while all Christ's disciples are Christians, not all Christians are disciples. To clarify, let's define these terms.

Typically, we think of Christians as church-attending believers in Christ saved from hell and bound for heaven. While this is true, Christianity's founder and foremost authority, Jesus of Nazareth, defined a Christian as *one who is spiritually reborn by faith in Him*.[1] Lecturing the respected rabbi Nicodemus one evening, our Authority said, "Except a man be born again, he cannot [even] see... [much less] enter into the kingdom of God" (John 3:3, 5). He added emphatically, "Marvel not that I said unto thee, Ye must be born again" (v. 7). Thus, Jesus settled this matter forever for intellectually honest readers by using imperative language, "Ye must!" Spiritual rebirth is a necessity!

Later in His ministry Jesus described new birth, or salvation, as a conversion experience, or a distinct spiritual and personal about-face: "Except ye be converted [lit. turned around[2]]...ye shall not [even] enter into the kingdom of heaven" (Matt. 18:3). In new birth, or conversion, therefore, one is "turned around" from unbelief to faith in Christ, from sin to righteousness, by an unmerited spiritual regeneration of eternal efficacy. After this distinct new beginning, the Christian has a crucial decision.

How will he (or she) respond to God's gracious salvation? Will he fully commit to discipleship or be content to be saved? This choice marks whether he'll ultimately delight or disappoint God and be written as a mere Christian or a disciple. To facilitate this decision, we must ponder the terms of New Testament discipleship. Let's describe a disciple of Jesus.

A disciple is a self-disciplined one. The English words *disciple* and *discipline* are derived from very similar Latin words. Similarly, every disciple is a person of or under discipline. He enters into a regimen of life whereby all his spiritual, mental, and physical powers are focused on a new, ordered, biblical way of living. Why? He wants to please and serve his gracious Savior. Lazy, self-indulgent Christians, though saved, can't be disciples.

A disciple is a student of Christ. In almost every instance where the word *disciple* is used in the New Testament, it is so translated from the Greek word *mathetes*, which means "learner, pupil,"[3] or student. Christians who refuse to study the Bible in general and the sayings of Jesus in particular cannot be disciples.

A disciple is an obedient follower of Christ. In the first century, disciples were young men totally committed to learning the teachings of a particular Jewish rabbi (or Greek philosopher) and living by them. Why? They aspired to be, live, and teach like him so they could spread his words, ways, and honor worldwide. Christians who learn but refuse to live Jesus' teachings can't be disciples.

A disciple is one who continues in God's Word. Jesus said, "If ye continue in [studying, practicing] my word, then are ye my disciples indeed" (John 8:31). True disciples persevere in the Word. They are deeply serious, irrevocably committed, student-followers of the Son of God, ever seeking more of Him—more study, more obedience, more conformity to His image. Christians who start studying and obeying, but due to offenses, adversities, prosperity, or other interests stop, forfeit discipleship.

A disciple is a person of truth. Jesus added, "Ye [disciples] shall know the truth" (v. 32). Disciples love truth in all forms. They love the Bible, the sole standard of spiritual truth. They love honesty, or truthfulness of heart and speech. They love fidelity, or faithfulness in all dealings. And they love reality, preferring facing actual conditions to trusting in illusions. Christians who prefer dishonesty, unfaithfulness, unreality, or un- or extra-biblical teachings can't be disciples.

A disciple is an extraordinarily free Christian. Jesus concluded, "The truth shall make you free...free indeed" (vv. 32, 36). The further a disciple goes in loving and living truth, the more he's liberated by it. Increasingly, truth frees him from the bonds of ignorance, error, bad attitudes, fear, anger, besetting sins, deception, hypocrites, and the tyranny of selfishness. Christians who prefer living in these chains can't be free— or disciples.

Finally, a disciple is a cross-bearer. For perseverance in God's Word, ministry, call, or righteousness, every disciple must accept at least one cross of rejection, loss, humiliation, or grief daily. Christians unwilling to do so are unworthy to be disciples: "Whosoever doth not bear his cross, and come after me, cannot be my disciple" (Luke 14:27). So says our Authority.

The lost world and sleeping church still mistake Christians for disciples. You know the difference. Go show them discipleship—defined and demonstrated!

Chapter 88

THE UNREALIZED IMPLICATIONS OF PRAYER

"YE KNOW NOT what ye ask," Jesus informed His apostles, and through them, us. Why did He say this?

James, John, and their mother had just prayed without considering the implications of their prayer (Matt. 20:20–28). They had asked Him for the very highest positions of leadership in His kingdom—to sit on His right and left hand respectively—without giving any thought to the preparation process for such leadership. They had visions of sharing His power, but not qualifying for it. For that, they would have to share His "cup" of sufferings (v. 22), "baptism" of death to self-will (v. 22), and passionate commitment to serve His people's needs (vv. 25–28). Blindly ambitious, they focused only on the end and forgot the means. They knew what they wanted, but not God's way of getting there. We're just like them when we pray!

We ask the Lord to save a person, forgetting that to do so, He'll have to send a disruptive, painful plow of adversity to break open the hard ground of their proud, self-sufficient, disbelieving hearts. Without this preparation, they can't receive the seed of God's Word.

We pray we'll bear more fruit, not realizing that to prepare us, His branches, for greater fruitfulness He must periodically purge our souls: "Every branch that beareth fruit, he purgeth it, that it may bring forth more fruit" (John 15:2). Purging comes through humbling adversities that wound, reduce, or limit us.

We ask to be like Jesus, forgetting that we must then go the way Jesus went. We must willingly go down to our humble Nazareth and be subject to the human authorities God appoints in our home, work, and church. Then we can increase in "wisdom," spiritual "stature," and "favor with God and men" (Luke 2:51–52), as Jesus did. And somewhere, sometime, someone must reject us without cause, so we may be like the One "despised and rejected of men, a man of sorrows, and acquainted with grief" (Isa. 53:3).

We ask the Lord to purify us but don't realize that to remove our dross He must correct us, not occasionally but often, and test us, not rarely but repeatedly. And if we get offended with Him and grow stubbornly unresponsive,

He must lovingly but firmly chasten us until we yield and become soft and responsive again, free from pride, rebellion, or selfishness.

We ask to be made strong, courageous overcomers, forgetting that overcomers must come over some formidable object or opponent. So God must send us strong challenges and stubborn challengers, and the greater the challenger, the greater the champion. He forges heroic overcomers not in success and prosperity but on hard, painful, long-lasting anvils of adversity.

We pray for spiritual discernment, not realizing that to develop sharp spiritual vision in us the Lord must exercise our powers of perception. For this He sends hypocrites, impostors, scam artists, false prophets, and heretics to interact with us so that "by reason of use," we may have our "senses exercised to discern both good and evil" (Heb. 5:14).

We ask God for a powerful ministry, forgetting that we'll have to first seek Him, pray, study, obey, and serve Him faithfully in a "day of small things" (Zech. 4:10). Furthermore, we'll have to endure qualifying trials before we emerge, as Christ did, ready to teach and minister "in the power of the Spirit" (Luke 4:14).

We ask God to awaken His people to His End Time purposes and plans, not realizing He must first disillusion us with our false hopes and wrong goals. Then, when we're disengaged from our distracting causes, He can redirect us to "seek first" His kingdom and plans (Matt. 6:33).

We ask Jesus to prepare His bride church for His appearing by refilling it with His Spirit, truth, power, and grace. But we forget this will bring "tribulation or persecution...because of the word" (Matt. 13:21) now on earth, from religious and perhaps governmental authorities, before He takes us to heaven.

We ask God to bless our nation. But to bless it, He must first save it—and to save it, He may have to break it. If a nation won't be led to repentance by God's goodness, His only option is to humble it through judgment. It may be awash in the "wrath of the Lamb" (Rev. 6:16) before it's washed in the "blood of the Lamb" (Rev. 7:14). These are some unanticipated results of our prayers.

So when praying, ponder what you're asking. Don't just see your ends; consider God's means. When they come, don't be surprised or offended. Rejoice, God's answering your prayers! Praise Him for the unrealized implications of prayer.

Chapter 89

PURE OR IMPURE WORSHIP?

THE QUESTION BEFORE us is not are we worshiping Jesus, but *why* are we doing so? Our answer determines if our worship is pure or impure. The apostles help us understand this issue.

Matthew says James, John, and their mother came "worshiping" Jesus, adding, "and desiring a certain thing of him" (Matt. 20:20). Their worship was sincere; all three adored their Messiah. But their adoration wasn't pure, because it was laced with corrupting selfishness. They coveted a specific return on their devotional investment—no less than the top positions in Jesus' kingdom with all their authority, honor, and wealth. Their mother proposed the deal: "Grant that these, my two sons, may sit, the one on thy right hand, and the other on the left, in thy kingdom" (v. 21). Brash as they were, at least James and John were open about what they really wanted. Others were not so honest.

Many worshiped the Savior with hidden agendas. The zealots revered Him hoping that, as king, He would free Israel from Roman rule. But when "Jesus…perceived that they would come and take him by force, to make him a king," He abandoned them and their nationalistic agenda (John 6:15). The common crowds gave Him adulation hoping His bread-making miracles would free them from work. Again reading their hearts, Jesus said, "Ye seek me, not because ye saw the miracles, but because ye did eat of the loaves" (v. 26). A wealthy young ruler did obeisance to Jesus publicly, yet privately held riches nearer and dearer. Sensing this, Jesus challenged him to, "Sell what thou hast, and give to the poor, and thou shalt have treasure in heaven," and his worship immediately ceased (Matt. 19:21). Many Jewish leaders revered Jesus secretly, yet desired the approval of their religious peers more: "They loved the praise of men more than the praise of God" (John 12:43). We can't deny these people worshiped Jesus.

But neither can we claim they did so perfectly. Why? Consciously or unconsciously, their motives were mixed. Yes, they loved Jesus. How could any honest human heart behold the winsome "beauty of the Lord" (Ps. 90:17) and not love Him? But the problem was there were certain things they loved more. So to them, worshiping Jesus became a means to an end, a dutiful adulation of one deity to acquire a more-coveted idol.

Still, the vast majority came worshiping Jesus with pressing personal needs. They or their loved ones desperately needed a miracle of healing or deliverance. Their worship was purer than others, but even it wasn't the purest.

The purest worship is that offered God without any thought of getting certain things in return. We just express our full adoration for *Him*—His faithfulness, love, and power. That's all. No other ends are sought nor agendas held. Even pressing personal needs don't drive this worship. Needs or no needs, we habitually draw near Jesus daily to love and bless Him. King David practiced and described this whole worship that seeks only to give to God:

> Give unto the Lord, O ye mighty, give unto the Lord glory and strength. Give unto the Lord the glory due unto his name; worship the Lord in the beauty of holiness.
>
> —Psalm 29:1–2

Clearly, James, John, and "mom" weren't there yet.

Neither are many of us. James and John's worship represents the impure worship of immature Christians. The worst bargain with God, as Jacob did, dictating assistance God must grant to qualify as their deity of choice. The best worship the Savior with secret desires, ends, and hopes in the back of their minds. These certain things are very subtle, but very real. And very visible to Jesus.

Gracious as He is, He accepts our impure worship, as He did the apostles'. But, holy as He is, He begins steadily purifying us. He takes away a heart-idol, dashes a selfish hope, delays performing a promise, and then watches to see our reaction: will we still worship? If so, our worship is purer. Or He changes our seasons from prosperity to adversity, and then watches our response: will we still worship? If so, our worship is even purer. And more mature.

It's becoming like Job's, Habakkuk's, and Paul's worship. These pure worshipers continued blessing, thanking, and praising God when all their "certain things" failed. James and John eventually got there.

Though exiled on lonely Patmos and denied his cherished friends and ministry, John was "in the Spirit on the Lord's day" (Rev. 1:10), worshiping Jesus—*without* "desiring a certain thing of Him." If he became a pure worshiper, so can we.

Are you practicing pure or impure worship?

Chapter 90

SATISFYING HIS HUNGER?

EBSTER'S DEFINES HUNGER as "a strong, compelling desire or craving"[1] for food or other things. Our world is filled with human hunger of every kind.

Hunger for food is universal, urgent, and unrelenting. Hunger for knowledge prompts scholars and scientists to study everything under the sun and beyond it. Hunger for healing and health spawns medical studies and new equipment, procedures, and pharmaceuticals. Hunger for economic growth produces new businesses, industries, and trade agreements. Hunger for peace drives conciliatory speeches, diplomatic missions, and concessions in negotiations. Hunger for a cleaner planet produces green technologies, waste disposal systems, and environmental regulatory agencies. Hunger for travel creates more economical automobiles, trains, and planes. Hunger for companionship motivates fellowship, friendship, and dating. Hunger for communication generates e-mail, texting, and web conferences. Hunger for technology creates faster, smarter computers, cell phones, and weapons systems. Hunger for consumer goods powers product research, development, and marketing. And we could go on. There's no end to human cravings.

When Jesus visited this hungry world, "as a man" He too was hungry (Phil. 2:8). Matthew remembers, "Now in the morning…he was hungry" (Matt. 21:18). Literally, this notes Jesus' desire for an early morning breakfast of figs. Figuratively, however, Matthew implies a deeper spiritual craving. During His final week in Israel, Jesus' soul was hungry for something figs, olives, and bread couldn't satisfy, namely, for Israel to do His Father's will—repent and receive Him, their Savior-King! But this craving wasn't satisfied during Jesus' last days. To the contrary, He and His soaring teachings, miraculous healings, and temple corrections were firmly rejected by the Jewish religious leaders. When He left this world, He did so still yearning. The Bread of Life, whose words and works had satisfied the natural and spiritual hunger of thousands, was still unsatisfied, still searching, still hungry. He's still hungry today.

He longs for the lost to believe in Him and be saved. He yearns for the saved to be sanctified by "the washing of water by the word" (Eph. 5:26). He hungers for private fellowship with Christians daily—for us to visit Him in the "new and living way" (Heb. 10:20) He has opened for us, sitting in His presence, pouring out prayers, feeding on Scripture, and praising and worshiping Him. He craves the "fruit of the Spirit" in our lives, His very "love, joy, peace, long-suffering, gentleness, goodness, faith, meekness, [and] self-control" (Gal. 5:22–23). He desires for us to know His voice and follow His guidance, "led by" the Good Shepherd and His "Spirit" (Rom. 8:14). He longs for us to develop "great faith," so that, whatever impossibilities we face, we'll remain "fully persuaded" He'll perform whatever He's promised (Rom. 4:21). He hungers for churches that worship Him in Spirit and truth, not in carnality and infidelity. He yearns for abandoned disciples who, quietly bearing their crosses, persevere in sharing His Word and building His kingdom. And there's more.

He hungers for hungry believers. He wants us to crave spiritually valuable biblical goals, such as to:

- Know and rightly divide His Word (2 Tim. 2:15)
- Live by "His righteousness" (Matt. 6:33)
- Walk closely with Him (Gen. 5:22, 24)
- Know His character, ways, power, and plan ever more fully (John 17:3)

He also hungers for hungry spiritual leaders. He craves ministers and elders who, instead of feeding their worldly appetites for success, money, and fame, sense His hungers and steadily pray, work, and suffer to satisfy them.

Additionally, Jesus hungers to gather His remnant Christians, churches, and ministries to fellowship, pray, and work together in these last days. He craves the fulfillment of His prayer for the Church Age—to sanctify, unite, test, mature, and finally translate His true bride church to be "with me where I am" (John 17:24). Do you share these, His strong, compelling desires? Then take heart!

Jesus promised to satisfy everyone sharing His hunger: "Blessed are ye that hunger now; for *ye shall be filled* [satisfied]" (Luke 6:21). The psalmist agrees, "He…filleth the hungry soul" (Ps. 107:9). But there's a problem.

Few Christians today understand Jesus' hunger—and fewer still hunger to satisfy it. Unlike Christ, we're too occupied with materialistic or selfish cravings in this spiritually lukewarm, "Laodicean" era. "I am rich, and increased with goods, and have need of nothing" (Rev. 3:17) is our unofficial motto. Some Christians are spiritually hungry, but not enough. Most are ignorant or neglectful of Jesus' longings. Like the ancient Jews, we've left Him hungry, unsatisfied, searching—and figs won't satisfy Him. But repentance will.

Why not forget your hunger and focus the rest of your life on satisfying His hunger?

Chapter 91

OUR FACES, SHINING WITH JESUS!

SUSTAINED PRIVATE COMMUNION with God makes not only our hearts but also our faces radiate Jesus to others. This occurred first in Moses.

After forty consecutive days and nights alone with God on Mount Sinai, Moses' face shone with the brightness of God's glory: "The skin of his face shone" (Exod. 34:29). This occurred after not the first but the *seventh* time Moses was alone with God. (For Moses' seven ascents, see Exodus 3:4–4:17; 19:3–7; 19:8–14; 19:20–25; 20:21–24:3; 24:15–32:15; 34:4–29.) While Moses' first five visits were comparatively short, the latter two each lasted a full forty days—960 uninterrupted hours immersed in the deep, thick, permeating presence of God! No visible alteration of Moses' countenance occurred after his first six encampments in the Presence. He descended as he had ascended. But after the seventh, the people noticed a new thing: their leader was now a divinely altered man. "The children of Israel saw...behold, the skin of his face shone" (Exod. 34:30). So we conclude not a few brief encounters but *prolonged intimate fellowship with God* changed Moses' look as well as his life. Thereafter he became a kind of spiritual mirror—when people looked at him, they saw a reflection of God.

This phenomenon wasn't noted incidentally. It's God's way of telling us that spending significant amounts of time close to Him on a regular basis transfigures us, both internally and, to some extent, externally. His Spirit gradually changes us into His likeness in spirit, character, and, however subtly, visage. That Moses' transfiguration occurred the seventh time (a perfect number) suggests that our alteration occurs as we perfect our habit of spending sufficient time in deep fellowship with God daily. The shining from Moses' face was really Jesus.

Jesus is God's glory—His most majestic, beautiful, graceful, and radiant manifestation—in human flesh. The apostle John writes, "The Word was made flesh, and dwelt among us (and we beheld his glory, the glory as of the only begotten of the Father), full of grace and truth" (John 1:14). So the light beams emanating from Moses' face were really Christ-rays, the very glory of

God's Son, the living, life-giving Light of the world. The original Christians also reflected Christ's glory-light.

Because the apostles obeyed Christ's call to "be with him" (Mark 3:14) in long periods of sustained, deep fellowship, His spiritual light permeated and filled their inner beings. As they continued this "being with Him," beams of Christ's glorious character began shining out from them—His love, holiness, truth, justice, faith, faithfulness, and so forth. The longer they sustained this soaking in His presence, the more they shined with Him. This continued after Pentecost. Standing before the Sanhedrin, their faces glowed with Jesus' boldness: "When they saw the boldness of Peter and John…they marveled; and they took knowledge of them, that they had been with Jesus" (Acts 4:13). When Stephen, a deacon, stood before the Sanhedrin, his face looked angelic, reflecting Christ as the angel of the Lord: "The council, looking steadfastly…saw his face as it had been the face of an angel" (Acts 6:15).

Throughout Acts, whenever Jesus' glory-light shined through Christians' redeemed countenances, people in darkness were drawn to it—in Samaria, Paphos, Philippi, and Ephesus. When Christ's compassion radiated from Paul's trial-weary face in Malta, "others also in the island…came and were healed" (Acts 28:9). The shining fills church history.

As countless Christian confessors and martyrs suffered loss of reputation, property, liberty, and life rather than renounce Jesus and worship the "divine emperor," their faces glowed with an otherworldly love for Christ the Roman mobs couldn't understand. Yet, paradoxically, thousands were drawn to that light.

During the Reformation, the faces of brave Lollards, Hussites, Lutherans, and Puritans shone with biblical truth rightly divided. Throngs were drawn to their light from the darkness of Catholic errors, idolatry, and superstition.

More recently, Methodist, Evangelical, and Pentecostal revivalists' and missionaries' faces have radiated a penitent return to faith and devotion. Masses of sinful, worldly, or lukewarm Protestants and sinners came to their shining. This shining endures.

But to shine in the plain, we must soak in the mount. Our "mount" time in God's presence involves Bible meditation, prayer, and worship—and obedience when we come down to the public plain! It must be sustained—day after day—not sporadic. It must be deep, not as little but as long a time as we can spare. That's how the shining first appeared on Moses' face.

So follow his example. Soak regularly and shine radiantly. Let this generation see our faces, shining with Jesus!

Chapter 92

THE INSPECTOR GENERAL

AFTER ENTERING JERUSALEM triumphantly, Jesus went straight to Herod's temple complex: "Jesus entered into Jerusalem, and [also] the temple" (Mark 11:11). The Messiah was on a mission.

His assignment was to examine His Father's house. As heaven's authorized Inspector General, Jesus "looked round about upon all things" there (v. 11), carefully surveying the courts, porches, altars, priests, people, and activities. Then late in the afternoon He returned to His lodgings: "He went out unto Bethany with the twelve" (v. 11). Something was brewing.

The next morning it exploded. Suddenly Jesus moved with shocking aggressiveness to correct the sin and negligence He noted the day before. He overthrew the moneychangers' tables and merchants' seats (vv. 15). He cast out those who sold and bought doves (v. 15). And He would not allow those who wanted to misuse the temple courts as a shortcut across the city (v. 16). Thus He reproved the people's disorder.

Then He retaught them God's order. The temple was dedicated to prayer, not commerce; to God's glory, not greed; to the spiritual enrichment of all, not the monetary gain of a few: "Is it not written, My house shall be called of all nations the house of prayer?" (v. 17). Afterward the Inspector General used the reordered temple the rest of the week for healing and teaching that glorified His Father. He does the same today.

In this age, not our church buildings but our bodily lives are God's temples: "Your body is the temple of the Holy Spirit" (1 Cor. 6:19). Daily Jesus keeps a close watch on our "temple courts"—all areas of our lives, spiritual and natural.

He watches our minds. Are our thoughts, motives, attitudes, and imaginations right? Or is unacceptable thought stuff corrupting our inner courts? He observes our souls. Are our wills yielded and our emotions controlled? Or are our wills fixed pursuing shortcuts to selfish ends and our emotions unchecked, spoiling our disposition and preventing God's Word from peacefully taking root? He examines our devotional lives. Is our Bible reading, prayer, and worship regular? Or do we read His Word rarely, worship less, and pray only when forced to by trouble? He views our church life and activity. Are we helping our local fellowships and ministries? Or are we participating, giving, and laboring as little as possible? And His inspection continues.

He listens to our speech. Are our words true, loving, humble? Or are our conversations full of pride, complaining, and gossip? He searches our bodily habits. Are we keeping our temple holy? Or are we unwashed, unkempt, unchaste—and unconcerned with our uncleanness? He monitors our works. Are we laboring heartily, as unto Jesus? Or do we hardly work at all, always wishing to do something else somewhere else? He sees our giving. Is it generous, cheerful, and trusting? Or do we donate little, resent what we give, and trust our deposited reserves more than our living God? He scrutinizes our leisure. Are our hobbies and entertainments acceptable? Or are we spending too much time, energy, and money on interests that drain and dull us? He surveys our friends. Are our friends spiritually minded, fully committed disciples? Or are we unequally yoked with unbelievers or carnal Christians? He looks over our homes. Are they clean, orderly, and ready for hospitality? Or are they dirty, disorderly, and unfit to receive ministers, meetings, or the Master?

Daily the Inspector General examines these, our "courts," "porches," and activities, through His heavenly eyes, the Holy Spirit. Sometimes He also uses His earthly eyes, our pastors, teachers, and counselors. Upon detecting sins or disorder, He convicts and reproves us, showing us what to overturn or cast out. He providentially blocks us if we try to use our faith, His promises, or His people as a shortcut to selfish ends.

Then He reteaches us God's order—His biblical ways of thinking, feeling, acting, and reacting in our "courts." He also recalls us to prayer: "My house shall be…the house of prayer" (Mark 11:17). If we receive His correction, our disorder goes and His order grows, and He increasingly uses the "courts" of our lives to His honor. Some resent the Messiah's corrective mission.

How strange! We let teachers examine our tests, coaches our athletic skills, doctors our bodies, consultants our businesses, and supervisors our job performances. Why shouldn't our Messiah also "look round about upon all things" in our lives? Need more incentive?

The only way for God to increasingly use you to His glory is to cooperate with His examination. So, "whatever he saith unto you, do it" (John 2:5). Be ready daily for the Inspector General!

Chapter 93

LEARNING TO JUDGE JUSTLY?

To JUDGE OR not to judge, that is the question! Some Christians say we shouldn't judge anyone or anything at anytime. Others say we should, we must judge! Where should we stand?

Before standing, let's study. To judge is simply to render a decision. Judging, therefore, is the decision-making process. Our law courts' judgments are called "decisions." Whether we realize it or not, we all make judgments, or decisions, constantly. Jesus never commanded us to stop making decisions. That would be ridiculous and impossible. Instead He urged us to carefully make right judgments, or good decisions. The apostle John inscribed this important injunction:

> Judge not according to the appearance, but judge righteous judgment.
>
> —JOHN 7:24

Though rarely taught and little known, it is our destiny to become excellent judges.

Presently Christians are responsible to "judge righteous judgment" in various jurisdictions. We must scrutinize religious teachings, experiences, activities, and movements. We must examine and weigh our society's moral, social, and political issues. We must assess the characters of people we interact with in business: Are they trustworthy or unreliable? We must decide issues that arise in our friendships. Should we agree or disagree with our friends' suggestions? We must choose sides when quarrels arise in our churches. Will we follow or forsake our spiritual leaders' judgments? We must decide family disputes. Which sibling will we justify when one rises against another? These are just some of the judgments we must make in this life. More will follow in the next life.

In Jesus' kingdom, we'll continue rendering decisions. He promised the apostles they would "sit upon twelve thrones, judging the twelve tribes of Israel" (Matt. 19:28). He indicated that overcoming Christians will help Him judge the nations: "He that overcometh, and keepeth my works unto the end, to him will I give power over the nations; and he shall rule them with a rod of iron" (Rev. 2:26–27). At a later reckoning, "we," the redeemed, "shall judge angels" (1 Cor. 6:3). With all this adjudication ahead, we should begin learning to "judge righteous judgment" now.

Anticipating this, Jesus left us judicial training instructions in Matthew 7:1–5.

He prefaces His teaching by forbidding hypocritical judgment (examining others instead of ourselves, v. 3) and premature judgment (examining others before we've examined ourselves, v. 3), and warns violators will suffer retributive judgments: "Judge not, *that ye be not judged*" (v. 1). Then He specifies how to become skilled spiritual judges.

First, we must passionately commit ourselves to constantly examine and correct ourselves, focusing solely on our sins and faults: "First cast the beam out of thine own eye" (v. 5). With equal zeal we must refuse to consider others' sins and faults, or try to offer them counsel, leaving them entirely to spiritual leaders and God: "Why beholdest thou the mote that is in thy brother's eye…Or how wilt thou say to thy brother, Let me pull the mote out of thine eye" (vv. 3–4). Sadly, many Christians never take this first crucial step.

But persistence in this discipline transforms us. It removes the key sinful attitudes ("beams"), especially our lust to judge others, that blur our souls' vision ("eye"). This humble, determined self-examination alone sharpens our spiritual discernment until it becomes accurate: "Then shalt thou see clearly" (v. 5). In time, God will release us to begin helping other Christians recognize their sins and faults and deal with them—exactly as we've done and are still doing: "Thou shalt see clearly to cast the mote out of thy brother's eye" (v. 5). There are other requirements for just judgment.

We should judge issues only when necessary. If we're not involved or have no responsibilities in situations, we should refrain from judging. To every judge his own jurisdiction! We should decide matters slowly, "swift to hear, slow to speak [decide]" (James 1:19). Our decisions should be based on facts, not imaginations, first impressions, or rumors. We shouldn't be partial to rich or poor, friends or enemies, compatriots or foreigners, Christians or infidels. We should favor whoever is right in the issue before us, regardless of other differences or disagreements we may have. And we must be merciful, not hard or excessive, in our criticisms or disciplinary actions, mindful of our many sins and God's many mercies to us, and that, "He shall have judgment without mercy, that hath shown no mercy" (James 2:13).

That's just judgment. That's Christlike decision making. That's our duty—"Judge righteous judgment"—and our destiny: "The saints shall judge the world" (1 Cor. 6:2).

May God help us become excellent decision makers, self-examining, patient, fact-seeking, unbiased, and merciful. Then we'll be ready to judge nations and angels. Are you learning to judge justly?

Chapter 94

CONSIDER AND CHANGE YOUR MOTIVES

G OD JUDGES OUR actions by our motives—the true core thoughts and intentions from which they spring. He's concerned not merely with what we're doing or not doing, but why.

To determine this, He examines our hearts constantly: "Man looketh on the outward appearance, but the LORD looketh on [continually surveys] the heart [motives]" (1 Sam. 16:7). To Him, wrong motives render otherwise righteous acts unrighteous.

Sometimes people do noble deeds with ignoble intentions. It appeared that King Saul loved David when he offered him his daughter Michal in marriage. I'm sure young, naïve David also felt terribly flattered when the king's couriers arrived and announced, "The king hath delight in thee...now, therefore, be the king's son-in-law" (1 Sam. 18:22). But Saul's real desire was anything but affectionate. Envious of David's popularity, he hoped to eliminate his up and coming rival in the guise of elevating him. His pernicious plan was to bring David into the royal family—to get him out of his life! Specifically, Saul hoped David would be killed in battle while attempting to collect the unusual marriage fee Saul demanded—rather graphic physical proof of 100 dead Philistines! His messengers continued, "The king desireth not any dowry, but an hundred foreskins of the Philistines, to be avenged of the king's enemies" (v. 25). The king's courtiers probably rejoiced at dinner that evening. Why, the king had made such a magnanimous gesture toward the giant-killing son of Jesse! Surely Saul was lovingly grooming David to be his successor. How bright Israel's future looked. But God saw Saul's "mercy" for the malicious thing it was. The opposite is also true.

We sometimes do seemingly wrong things with right intentions. When the prophet Elijah arrived in drought-stricken Zarephath, he did something that seemed outrageous: he asked a starving widow and her son to give him their remaining food! "Make me of it [your last handful of meal] a little cake first...and, afterwards, make for thee and for thy son" (1 Kings 17:13). But this deed was not as it seemed. Elijah begged this bread in generosity, not greed; love, not selfishness. He understood and practiced Jesus' principle of giving centuries before Jesus spoke it: "Give, and it shall be given unto you" (Luke 6:38). Realizing the widow had to give to God in order for God to give to her, Elijah made the otherwise rude request. Once he received her offering as God's representative, God released to her, her son, and Elijah all the food they needed, day by day, until the drought ended: "The barrel of meal was not used up, neither did the cruse of oil fail" (1 Kings 17:16). As selfish as it appeared, Elijah's request was selfless. Though others didn't, God recognized this.

Since God examines and will ultimately judge all our motives—not the apparent but the actual reasons behind our action and inaction—shouldn't we consider, and if necessary change, our motives now? We begin by researching and studying right motives.

Jesus' chief motive was to please His Father: "I do always those things that please him" (John 8:29). His second was to glorify, or honor, Him: "Father…glorify thy Son, that thy Son may glorify thee" (John 17:1). We should adopt these. Some other worthy motives are anything done to know God better, obey God's Word, spread the gospel, bless or edify the church, fulfill our calling, obey the Spirit's guidance, walk in love, be fair or pure, help the poor, or relieve sufferers. We must also recognize impure intentions.

Everything done for pride is wrong: "Don't try to impress others" (Phil. 2:3, NLT). And anything motivated by selfishness, worldly ambition, greed, envy, lust, revenge, or deceit is sinful. Sometimes we don't recognize our wrong motives.

Prayer and the Spirit, who alone knows the deepest recesses of our hearts, are the answers for this problem. Ask the Father to reveal any wrong motives: "That which I see not, teach thou me…" (Job 34:32). And be willing to change them: "…If I have done iniquity, I will do no more." How?

Confess any sinful intentions the Spirit reveals and choose to exchange them for right ones—kingdom zeal for worldly ambition, fear of God for fear of man, spiritual hunger for material greed, thankfulness for your blessings for envy of others' blessings, honesty for deception, patience for lust, desiring God's approval for wanting people's praises, and so forth. Don't procrastinate, be proactive!

Whenever you take (or decline) a new line of action, ask, "Why am I doing or not doing this?" If your intentions are wrong, follow the simple directions above. It's that easy to consider and change your motives.

Chapter 95

COSTLY CHOICES BRING SWEET COMPENSATIONS

*I*N PSALM 91:14–16, God makes some very sweet promises to Christians meeting two conditions. The first condition appears in the psalm's opening verse.

"He who dwelleth in the secret place of the Most High" (v. 1). This describes believers who make private time with the Lord their daily, life-sustaining devotional habit. Every morning they go first to the "secret place," where only the believer and the Most High are present and privy to the loving praise and worship, meditative Bible reading, and childlike prayer they share there. (See Matthew 6:6.) Once convinced their spiritual replenishment, rest, and refuge are found only there, these Christians commit to this devotional habit, thereafter dwelling in it daily.

The more consistently we dwell in the Most High's secret place, the more we enjoy His blessings. No matter how thoroughly life drains us, we're spiritually refilled there. However frequent life's injustices or anxieties, we find rest there. No matter how suddenly or ferociously life's storms assail us, we find complete psychological and emotional refuge there—alone with Jesus, in His reviving presence, nourishing Word, and peaceful worship. Besides this replenishment, rest, and refuge, we enjoy the many benefits of His protective covering (Psalm 91:2–8). And there's more.

Our secret daily visitations cultivate love for Jesus. The more we meet with Him, the more we adore Him. This brings us to Psalm 91's second condition: our growing love for Christ in the hidden place must be tested in the open places, issues, and relationships of life. We've established our devotional time with Him; now we must prove He's our supreme love.

"Because he hath set his love upon me" (v. 14). To "set" our love on God is to fully and finally fix our dominant affection on Him above all other affections and interests. We do this by costly choices in hard tests. The Bible reveals the nature of these difficult but spiritually rewarding decisions.

Abraham set his love on God by choosing to obey Him, though that meant the death of his dearly loved son, Isaac. The apostles set their love on God by leaving everything near and dear to follow His Son: "Peter said, Lo, we have left all, and followed thee" (Luke 18:28). Esther set her affection on

God by choosing to please Him when doing so risked offending her powerful husband, King Xerxes. Ruth set her love on God by choosing to abandon her native country, culture, and gods to adopt her mother-in-law's deity, the only true God, Jehovah. David set his love on God by repeatedly choosing to loyally wait for God's deliverance during a desolate decade of painful and perilous persecution in the Judean wilderness.

Many others also set their love on God. When they couldn't please everyone, they chose to please Him rather than themselves or those they loved most. To a person their costly choices prompted God to give them His sweetest compensations.

Those remarkably rich returns on their obedience are described in Psalm 91:14–16, where God promises:

- "I will deliver him" (v. 14), or release him from every trial, faithfully making a way of escape from every kind of hindrance, injustice, or oppression.

- "I will set him on high" (v. 14), or raise him to a higher position and plain of service due to his faithful service in smaller, humbler, hidden duties.

- "I will answer him" (v. 15), or fulfill his specific prayer requests, his every intercessory petition and personal heart's desire. As David wrote, "You have given him his heart's desire; you have withheld nothing he requested" (Ps. 21:2, NLT).

- "I will be with him in trouble" (Ps. 91:15), or be manifestly near and actively supporting him—speaking, guiding, comforting, strengthening, and walking beside him—in even his most harrowing and hopeless times of trouble.

- "I will...honor him" (v. 15), or distinguish and recognize him for his faith and loyalty to Me, thus honoring My Spirit's work in him and his cooperation with My Spirit.

- "I will satisfy him" (v. 16) with gratifying rewards and fulfillments, specifically "with long life"—letting him enjoy My rich favor and blessings over an extended lifetime.

- "I will...show him my salvation" (v. 16), or reveal to him My saving power and plan for My people, his life, and his generation.

These compensations are thoroughly sweet!

Are you facing a costly choice? Instead of fretting over its bitterness, focus on the sweetness of God's rewards. You've established your devotional habit in the "secret place." So now "set"—irrevocably and gloriously fix—your supreme love on Christ. Why?

Psalm 91 promises costly choices bring sweet compensations.

Chapter 96

YOUR FRUIT OR YOUR PLACE, PLEASE!

*T*HE NEW TESTAMENT repeatedly reveals that God seeks fruit from Christians. Earnestly!

Once converted, we enter spiritual marriage—a close, covenantal union with Jesus, "that we should bring forth fruit unto God" (Rom. 7:4). As in natural marriage, in spiritual marriage fruit comes one way—by abiding close to our "husband," Jesus, daily: "He that abideth in me...the same bringeth forth much fruit" (John 15:5). As we receive biblical teaching and study the Bible, our Father, the heavenly Farmer, sows His Word in our hearts in order to grow a rich harvest of spiritual maturity, "full grain [fruit]" (Mark 4:28), "an hundredfold...[or] sixtyfold...[or] thirtyfold" (Matt. 13:8). By periodic conviction, correction, and testing, He purges us, so we'll bear "more fruit" (John 15:2). Lord of all, He wants us fruitful in every activity, natural and spiritual. His Spirit moved Paul to pray, "That ye might...[be] fruitful in every good work" (Col. 1:10). Not only does our Father desire, but He also expects every Christian to be fruitful in due season, or "the time of the fruit" (Matt. 21:34). Gracious and long-suffering, He forbears with fruitless Christians, patiently fertilizing them with more instruction, more correction, and more unmerited blessings, hoping His goodness will lead them to repentance and fruitfulness (Luke 13:6–9). Yet, ultimately, He will judge every fruitless person and thing: "Every tree that bringeth not forth good fruit is hewn down" (Matt. 7:19). Jesus demonstrated this graphically at the close of His ministry by pronouncing a curse on a fruitless fig tree—"Let no fruit grow on thee henceforward forever" (Matt. 21:19)—with shockingly sudden results, "Immediately the tree withered" (v. 19, NIV).

There are three primary fruits our Farmer-Father seeks in every Christian's life:

1. THE FRUIT OF HIS SPIRIT, or Christlikeness developed in our characters. "The fruit of the Spirit is love, joy, peace, long-suffering, gentleness, goodness, faith, meekness, self-control" (Gal. 5:22–23; see Eph. 5:9–10).

2. THE FRUIT OF HIS WILL, or God's plan fulfilled through our gifts (talents, abilities) and life work or ministry (Matt. 7:21; John 4:34; 2 Tim. 4:7).

3. THE FRUIT OF HIS HARVEST, or souls converted or discipled through us. This "precious fruit of the earth" (James 5:7) is a duel harvest of saving the lost and sanctifying the saved (John 4:35–36; 1 Cor. 3:6–7).

Besides these, He seeks "fruits worthy of repentance" (Luke 3:8), or the unmistakable evidence of truly repentant souls: changed living! He seeks the fruit of thanksgiving, or the "fruit of our lips giving thanks to his name" continually (Heb. 13:15). He also seeks the "fruits of righteousness" (Phil. 1:11), or demonstrations of Christ's morality, justice, and virtue; the fruits of charity, or generous giving and sharing (2 Cor. 9:10); and the fruits of chastening, our humble responses to God's corrective counsel or discipline (Heb. 12:11). All these fruits are delicious to God—and desired!

Jesus' parable of the householder (Matt. 21:33–46) reveals just how serious our Farmer-Father is about fruit. He planted His vineyards (Israel and the church) in the world for one purpose: to bear fruit! Jesus addressed this parable to the first-century, spiritually fruitless, Jewish religious leaders (v. 45). Indirectly, however, its principle (only the fruitful retain their place and work in God's kingdom) applies to all Christians, especially church leaders, the kingdom's "tenant farmers." Jesus somberly warns all unfruitful Christians:

> The [present] kingdom of God [the church's leadership and labors] shall be taken from you, and given to a nation [people] bringing forth the fruits of it.
>
> —MATTHEW 21:43

So to hold our place, we must bear fruit. Focused on fruitfulness, our Farmer-Father accepts nothing less!

Is the fruit of His Spirit growing in you? Is the fruit of His calling developing? Are you helping reap the fruit of His harvest? Are you growing the fruits of righteousness, thanksgiving, charity, chastening? If so, your place and service in His vineyard are secure. If not, they're in jeopardy.

At Jesus' first advent, the "time of the fruit" (v. 34) had come. When the Jewish leaders remained stubbornly fruitless, God took their place—"the kingdom...shall be taken from you" (v. 43)—and gave it to "other farmers" (the apostles) who "render[ed] him the fruits" (v. 41). Today the "time of the fruit," an appointed visitation, is again at hand. Soon the Farmer's Son will again visit His vineyard, the church, and say to us, "Give Me your fruit or your place, please!" Will we relinquish or retain our place in the emerging revived, last-day, fruitful church?

Be wise, abide close to Jesus, and bear much rich fruit. Then you'll be ready when He says, "Give Me your fruit or your place, please."

Chapter 97

CITY-QUAKE!

W HEN AT THE end of His remarkable ministry Jesus visited Jerusalem, it was a city-shaking event. Matthew tells us, "All the city was moved" (Matt. 21:10).

Moved is a translation of the Greek verb *seio*, which means "to shake, or move to and fro"[1] vigorously. *Seio* is linked to our English word *seismic*. Matthew uses *seio* again when describing the earthquake following Jesus' death: "And the earth did quake [*seio*], and the rocks were split" (Matt. 27:51). So, figuratively speaking, Jesus' visitation, with all its extraordinary occurrences, was a seismic event! Jerusalem was vigorously shaken back and forth, not geologically but spiritually, by the events of the next six days! It was not an earthquake but a "city-quake!"

Some citizens vibrated with curiosity: "All the city was moved, saying, Who is this?" (Matt. 21:10). Others swayed with joy, sure Jesus was David's Son, the long-awaited Messiah come to liberate them. In the gates, streets, and temple courts, young and old alike pulsated as they shouted, "Hosanna to the Son of David!" (v. 15). But the religious leaders shook with rage: "They were very displeased . . ." (v. 15). Agitated with envy, they longed and labored to eliminate the upstart, rival "prophet" from Nazareth: "[And] they sought to lay hands on him" (v. 46). The city also shook with the sound waves of religious debate, as all Jewish denominations "took counsel how they might entangle him in his talk" (Matt. 22:15) and sent their best debaters to stir scandal. Even Jesus' disciples were rocked, when over supper one night He announced there was a traitor among them: "One of you shall betray me. And they were exceedingly sorrowful [or 'very upset,' GNB]" (Matt. 26:21–22). Later that evening they quivered with panic as a band of Roman soldiers—led by their brother, Judas!—arrested their peaceful pastor as He prayed! Shuddering and reeling, they "all . . . forsook him, and fled" (v. 56). Instead of a peaceful week of festivities, this Passover was one tremor, quake, or aftershock after another!

The Bible describes other "city-quakes"—cities shaken with holy faith or unholy fury when Jesus visited them by His Spirit, acts, messengers, or messages.

When Jesus visited Samaria through Philip's preaching and miracles, the city's trust in Simon Magus' occultism was shaken, and "there was great joy in that city" (Acts 8:8). When Christ visited Lydda and Joppa through Peter's raising of Aeneas and Dorcas, both cities were moved to believe and obey God: "All that dwelt in Lydda...turned to the Lord" (Acts 9:35). When Christ visited Jerusalem by judging Ananias and Sapphira, many quaked with the faith-creating fear of God and converted: "Great fear [of God] came upon...as many as heard these things...and believers were the more added" (Acts 5:11, 14). These tremors were winsome.

Others were woeful. When Jesus visited Ephesus through Paul's special miracles and messages, "there arose no small stir about that way [Christianity]" (Acts 19:23). Quaking with rage, the local idol makers shook the city with a riotous rally against Christ's messenger, forcing his impromptu, inglorious exit!

Jesus' visits by His Spirit, works, servants, or words shook all these cities, moving them to reverence or rage!

He still moves cities—not their stones but their stony hearts! He sends agitating plows of adversity or calamity to disrupt trust in self-confidence, false religion, human wisdom, or national strength. He sends evangelists to shake unbelievers with conviction of sin and move them to saving faith. He sends teachers to move Christians to not just hear but also love and live His Word. He sends Spirit-empowered healers, deliverers, and prophets to shake and shift atheistic rationalists and doubting Thomases from unbelief to unlimited confidence in His compassionate power. He sends fresh outpourings of His Spirit to shake indifferent Christians from the sleep of lukewarmness and non-expectation to the joy of a reawakened faith in "Jesus Christ, the same yesterday, and today, and forever" (Heb. 13:8). These and other "city-quakes" result from Christ's visits.

His visits spring from two key prerequisites: Christians' brave obedience and steady intercession.

Are you courageously obeying God and praying for your "Jerusalem"? Do you see Jesus as a city mover or city soother? Do you want your city redeemed from judgment or reserved to it? You don't want controversy, disruption, or division, but do you love God, His kingdom, and your city enough to obey and pray in a holy "city-quake"? If so, when Jesus visits, one thing is sure: Like Jerusalem, your city will be "moved." It will "shake and move to and fro" vigorously, and settle in faith or fury, repentance or resistance. But "moved" it will be—and never again the same.

It's time to pray and prepare for your city-quake!

Chapter 98

UNDERSTANDING HEAVY TIMES

SOONER OR LATER every growing Christian runs head-on into unfairness. Sometime, somewhere, someone wrongs us—and doesn't repent! And God does nothing about it!

Instead of rushing to save His beloved from the buffeting waves, He falls asleep in the back of the boat! Or instead of quickly removing our yoke of injustice, He leaves it. This creates an atmosphere of oppression in our lives, as levity and laughter go and lethargy and listlessness set in.

To be oppressed is to be weighed down with unfair or cruel treatment without hope of relief. The adversities causing this condition are things such as indifferent or abusive authorities, judicial injustices, failures, losses, sicknesses, or delayed hopes. As we face these psychological or physical pressures, the longer God waits to help us, the heavier our burdens grow—unless we understand them.

The apostle Peter said periods of oppression are necessary: "Though now for a season, if need be, ye are in heaviness through manifold trials" (1 Pet. 1:6). These strange times of testing—also called in Scripture the "evil day," "nighttime," or "triumphing" or "prosperity of the wicked"—seem to contradict all God's good promises. Of such times David warned, "Fret not thyself because of evildoers" (Ps. 37:1), and then asked, "Why go I mourning because of the oppression of the enemy?" (Ps. 42:9). Or, "Why must I wander around in grief, oppressed by my enemies?" (NLT). Why was he, and more importantly, why are we heavy?

Again, the reason is we have no spiritual understanding, or biblical insight, as to why God allows seasons of defeat. For every low diabolical attack there are high divine purposes. Consider these.

Times of heaviness humble us, resulting in a healthier, truer self-view. This prepares us to receive promotions and honors in God's time—provided we fully accept our humble circumstances. Twice Scripture decrees, "Before honor is humility" (Prov. 15:33; 18:12). Oppressive trials drive us closer to Jesus. He's always a present help, but He's a *very* present help in trouble" (Ps. 46:1). They also build stronger faith. Every time, exhausted, we reach the end of our faith, we fall back on His faithfulness—and find He never fails us! Weighty trials increase our patience. If we occupy and wait patiently for God to release us, patience has its "perfect work" (James 1:4) in us and our characters become "mature and complete, not lacking anything" (NIV). They also increase our wisdom. Every time injustices hinder and perplex us, we're forced again to seek God's wise way where we see no way. Our burdensome situations increase our grace. When fresh waves of affliction make us cry for more of God's help, the Spirit imparts more grace—and more unmerited divine strength and ability flow through us. Our oppressions also increase our biblical insights. When deep waters threaten to overwhelm us, we're driven to prayerfully search the Word for deeper truths to keep our souls afloat. And there are more divine objectives.

By enduring heavy times, we qualify for sweet personal rewards. If our hearts "delight" in God even in distress, He delights to "give thee the desires of thine heart" (Ps. 37:4). They also qualify us for leadership. Only those who suffer for Jesus rule with Him. Weighty trials increase our capacity to minister. As "the God of all comfort" increasingly "comforteth us in all our tribulation," we become more "able to comfort them who are in any trouble" (2 Cor. 1:3–4). They also prove we're overcomers. Manifold trials provide us with formidable spiritual obstacles to rise above, or come over: "overcome evil with good" (Rom. 12:21). Seasons of heaviness are opportunities to obey Christ's most demanding teachings: "Resist not evil," and "do good to them that hate you," thus becoming "perfect," or consistently mature, in God's love (Matt. 5:39, 44, 48). They also facilitate full repentance. Our enemies have a grace period in which to repent and be saved—and we have time to repent and *want* them to be saved. Oppressive trials also enable us to glorify God. We honor His integrity and trustworthiness greatly by remaining loyal to Him, His Word, and His work when He appears to have abandoned us. Finally, our heavy trials transform us. They alone conform us to the image of Him who "endured such contradiction of sinners against himself," yet stayed true to His Father. These high goals are achieved only in our low seasons.

And don't forget, your oppression will end one day. "God is faithful" to "make a way to escape" from every trial (1 Cor. 10:13). Knowing this transforms your burdens into blessings. Why?

You're enlightened now, understanding heavy times.

Chapter 99

FOCUSED ON FULFILLMENT

$\mathcal{A}$s JESUS APPROACHED Jerusalem for His final visit, He dispatched two disciples to Bethphage to find a donkey for His triumphal entry: "Then sent Jesus two disciples, saying unto them, Go into the village opposite you..." (Matt. 21:1–2). So off they went.

But Matthew adds an explanatory note. It reads:

> All this was done, that it might be fulfilled which was spoken by the prophet, saying...thy King cometh unto thee, meek, and sitting upon an ass [donkey].
>
> —MATTHEW 21:4

Thus Matthew reveals not only what Jesus did at this moment in time but also why. Jesus' intent was to fulfill Bible prophecy, specifically Zechariah 9:9: "Rejoice greatly, O daughter of Zion...behold, thy King cometh unto thee...riding upon an ass." And He did so with great care. Note His detailed instructions to His two student-aides: "Go...find an ass [donkey] tied, and a colt...loose them...bring them...if any man say...[then you] say" (Matt. 21:2–3). Why did Jesus insist they return with a donkey?

He needed it to publicly declare His kingship. While Gentile kings rode prized Egyptian horses or ornate chariots when on parade, mules or donkeys were the preferred mounts of Jewish kings. This tradition began with David, who chose a mule for his royal mount. He extended it by later authorizing Solomon, his chosen successor, to ride his personal royal mule in his coronation parade: "The king also said...cause Solomon...to ride upon mine own mule" (1 Kings 1:33). News of this token of Solomon's kingly authority soon reached Solomon's enemies: "Verily, our lord, King David, hath made Solomon king...they have caused him to ride upon the king's mule" (vv. 43–44). Hearing this, they feared and fled. Our kings don't ride donkeys today.

In modern America, the president uses Air Force One or the heavily armored presidential limousine when flying or riding in motorcades at home or abroad. These are our traditional, universally recognized means of transporting our head of state. So anyone assuming that high office would naturally use these modern "mules" to demonstrate his or her presidential authority.

However, it was not mere tradition but Scripture that Jesus carefully pursued in Bethphage. He was focused on fulfillment—determined to perform God's inspired prediction through Zechariah. His actions here were also an extension of His teaching.

Jesus taught that the fulfillment of the whole Bible—its prophecies, promises, warnings, proverbs, principles, parables, and patterns—is imperative. He said, "The scriptures must be fulfilled" (Mark 14:49). He assured us that, ultimately, no person or force can stop the fulfillment of God's Word: "The scripture cannot be broken" (John 10:35). Does this still hold?

Absolutely! God's written and living Word remain ever "the same" (Heb. 13:8). In these perilous, frenetic, unpredictable times we may be uncertain about many things—the scholarly or calculated predictions of pundits and scientists, the disingenuous promises of politicians, and the strange prognostications of false prophets and psychics—but the Bible is not one of them. We may plant our feet firmly on this bedrock: we don't know when, where, how, or through whom God will perform His sayings, but perform them He will! Despite the world's fickleness, He's still fixed—on fulfilling His Word daily.

Every new day He performs Bible prophecies, promises, warnings, proverbs, principles, and patterns all around us. The problem is we're too blind to see it. Some common psychological "blinders" are doubt, worldly distractions, rationalism, and "herd-vision."

Excessively hesitant, doubt advises us to remain unsure God is working even when we plainly recognize His providential acts. Worldly distractions—fleshly desires, covetousness, ambition, and obsessions with entertainment, technological devices, or sports—keep us from thinking about God, much less watching for His hand. Rationalism refuses to acknowledge God's presence and work behind natural events, admitting only human causes and effects. "Herd-vision" limits us to seeing only what others acknowledge—and nothing else!

Jesus can remove these "blinders" and, by His Spirit's illumination, open our eyes to see His hand fulfilling God's Word all around us. For this, we need only stay full of His Word and prayer, ask Him to open our eyes, and start watching for His hand daily. Why do so?

As the chaotic uncertainty of these last days grows, you need to rest peacefully assured that, "The scriptures must be fulfilled!" Some Christians may prefer to keep their "blinders," but you don't have to. Dare to be different! Fling off your "blinders" and, like your Master, focus on fulfillment. Expect to see Him perform His Word in your personal life, family, church, ministry, and nation as carefully as He did at Bethphage! He won't disappoint: "Unto them that look for him shall he appear" (Heb. 9:28).

Stay focused on fulfillment.

Chapter 100

GOD'S GOLDEN INHERITANCE

OST CHRISTIANS CONSIDER our eternal inheritance, but not God's. Yet the Bible reveals His inheritance as clearly as ours.

Paul prayed for the Ephesians, and all believers, to receive a revelation of God's inheritance: "That ye may know…the glory of his inheritance in the saints" (Eph. 1:18). Paul's prayer reveals God's inheritance is not a new earth, city, temple, river, garden, or mansion, though all these will be present in God's glorious new creation. Rather, God's inheritance is His overcoming people, "His inheritance *in the saints.*" So ultimately, we—our company, fellowship, worship, and work with and for Him—will be God's perpetual prize.

Mindful of this, Jesus called the Laodiceans, and us, to "buy of me gold tried in the fire" (Rev. 3:18). "Gold tried in the fire" is not a literal but a figurative expression. Jesus isn't talking about earth's precious metals but our most precious spiritual possession—faith in God and knowledge of Him proven in "fiery," or hot, intense, and purifying, trials. How do we "buy" this?

We trust and obey God in the fire. Every time we do so, we surrender our wills to His; this surrender or yielding is the price (cost) God requires. Every time we yield and obey God's Word or guidance in hard tests, we "buy" more faith in God and knowledge of Him. Afterward we emerge more confident in His faithfulness and promises and more well rounded in our understanding of His character and ways. Nothing is more valuable to us that these precious commodities. And, incredibly, the more we "buy" this "gold," the more we become it!

Job, God's greatest overcomer, said that not only his faith and knowledge but also his soul became "as gold" in his fiery trials: "When he hath tested me, I shall come forth as gold" (Job 23:10). Scripture confirms that God's overcomers, or tested, refined people, are His "gold"—or heaven's most valuable commodity. He speaks of purifying us in fiery trials as refiners do gold and silver in blazing furnaces (Mal. 3:3; Zech. 13:8–9). By calling us His "gold," God hints we're His inheritance. (Is there any more valuable worldly inheritance than gold?) Consider these parallels between gold and overcomers.

Gold is one of earth's most precious and noble metals. Overcomers are God's most valuable and honorable servants. Gold is found throughout the creation, in earth's crust and seas. Overcomers are found all over the world, in the dust of every continent and sea of humanity. Gold is a mark of worldly wealth. Overcomers are spiritually wealthy, or rich in truth, spiritual insight, intimacy with God, and confidence in Him. Gold is exquisitely beautiful, rare, and useful. Overcomers exhibit the "beauty of the LORD" (Ps. 90:17), are comparatively few in number, and are very useful to God. Pure gold is malleable, soft enough to be impressed and molded by hand. Purified overcomers are impressionable in God's hands, and He shapes them to His Son's image and their predestined work. Gold is stable, unchanging in its appearance, density, and value. Proven overcomers are unchanging in their beliefs, values, and life purpose. Indestructible, gold endures the afflictions of time, neglect, and weather. Overcomers "endure all things" (2 Tim. 2:10), whatever season, treatment, or "weather" God sends.

Gold also conducts electrical power. Overcomers' prayers and words convey God's life-giving power to spiritually dead people—and they live! Gold is refined in blazing furnaces. Overcomers are refined in trials blazing with fears and pressures. Gold overlaid the ark of the covenant, where God's presence dwelt. Overcomers visit God's presence daily and "they shall see his face" eternally (Rev. 22:4). God's earthly throne, the mercy seat, was covered with gold. God's heavenly throne will be covered or surrounded by overcomers enthroned with Him. Gold's chemical symbol (Au) springs from the Latin *aurum*, "shining dawn." Wherever overcomers live and work, their lives are a dawning (first light) of God's coming earthly kingdom. Gold inspired dreams of the mythical El Dorado, where gold was as plentiful as sand. Overcomers inspire visions of the true Utopia, New Jerusalem, where "pure gold, like clear glass" (Rev. 21:18) will be so plentiful it will fill its streets, walls, and buildings.

We dream of our inheritance in this golden city, with its beautiful gates, mansions, river, and trees—sometimes forgetting the glorious One in its midst. But He dreams of the unending rapturous fellowship He will enjoy there with His golden inheritance, overcomers! Are you golden?

Behold God's gold—the precious, enduring faith and truth of God in His Word. Buy it—by trusting and obeying Him in tests. Become it—a part of God's golden inheritance!

Chapter 101

HE SENDS SOME AWAY

NOT ONCE BUT twice Matthew says just before the disciples' second stormy crossing of Lake Galilee Jesus "sent the multitudes away" (Matt. 14:22–23). Normally inclusive, why didn't Jesus invite everybody to come along?

He wanted the multitude out of the way. Like the surly infiltrators who troubled Israel in the wilderness, this crowd was a "mixed multitude" (Num. 11:4). They weren't fully committed to Jesus, as were the Twelve, the women, and the other faithful disciples who followed Him throughout His ministry. John illuminates Matthew's story.

John's Gospel reveals that this multitude Jesus sent away followed Him not for truth or love but for politics and provisions.

When the nationalists, who saw Him as a means to their end of restoring Israel's autonomy and honor, moved to "make him a king," Jesus "departed" (John 6:15). Thus instead of sending them away, He walked away. When some of them later pursued Him for nothing more than a free meal, He rebuked them: "Ye seek me…because ye did eat of the loaves, and were filled" (v. 26). Thus these too were sent away. Why?

At core, these king and bread seekers were self-serving, not God-serving. Their hearts were stirred by the Savior's benefits, not His truth or will. Such unbroken, disloyal followers would never endure the thorough testing soon to befall Jesus' sold-out disciples on Galilee's stormy waters— or, later, in the early church's deadly persecutions. Like Israel's "mixed" companions, their presence would only foster troublesome sins, such as murmuring, unbelief, and rebellion, among His devout ones. "Bad company" always "corrupts good character," (1 Cor. 15:33, NIV). The power and food seekers would have only weakened the faith of the Christ seekers. To prevent this hindrance, Jesus sent them away.

It wasn't the first time. Before the disciples' earlier Galilee crossing, Jesus "sent away the multitude" (Mark 4:36). How? When His wondrous miracles drew "great multitudes," He quietly announced the high costs His true followers must pay, knowing this would repel those who were delighted with His miracles but disinterested in His message (Luke 14:25–33). Also, before raising Jairus' daughter, He "put them all out" who laughed when He foretold her miraculous resuscitation (Mark 5:40). Though patient, Jesus had no time for mockers or miracle mongers.

He's the same today. To bring churches and ministries to spiritual maturity, strong faith, full fruitfulness, and the fulfillment of His predestined plans, Jesus puts them through periods of special testing. But before these storms, He arranges circumstances that separate committed and uncommitted believers. Once the unholy mixed multitude leaves, He gets down to holy business: thoroughly examining, purifying, and proving His "disciples indeed" (John 8:31) so their churches, ministries, and personal lives will fully please, serve, and honor Him. Few understand this today.

Our obsessive, illicit love affair with mega churches has prompted many unspiritual congregations to use any means to attract more members. And even spiritually minded leaders and disciples justifiably seek more fruit on their ecclesiastical branches. But we must also accept that our Head—the Jesus of the Gospels—both draws and drives followers. He permits, and so ordains, every unexpected distressful situation that causes inward doubters, secret sinners, self-serving spiritual parasites, power or fame seekers, or contentious troublemakers to leave churches without cause. Some ask, "Aren't these betrayals and persecutions Satan's work?" Certainly! Satan has deceived these dropouts, as he did Judas and Demas, but there's another side to the story.

In sovereign foreknowledge, Jesus has used their sinful attitudes and decisions to send them away. With these unfaithful multitudes gone, He may then more perfectly test His faithful remnant's trust, obedience, loyalty, and endurance. When the Corinthian church was boiling with divisions caused by carnally minded Christians, the apostle Paul wrote: "Of course, there must be divisions among you so that you who have God's approval will be recognized!" (1 Cor. 11:19, NLT). Translation? Jesus had sent away the troublemakers to develop and distinguish the remaining overcomers.

Have some of your mixed multitude left? King or bread seekers? Miracle mongers or mockers? Others deceived by sin, selfishness, or heresy? Christ, not chance, has done this: "*He* sent the multitude away." They're gone, but He's still present, so don't be shaken: "It is I; be not afraid" (Matt. 14:27). Instead of striving to resist, refute, or recover your abandoners, release them. Then refocus on Jesus, His Word, and His call on your church or ministry until the powers of the air subside: "The wind ceased" (v. 32). So look up!

And look ahead! On the other side, you'll fulfill Jesus' kingdom purposes—"many" will be made "whole" (v. 36, KJV). Ultimately, that's why He sends some away.

Chapter 102

HIS HIDDEN ONES

EAUTIFULLY IMPARTIAL, JESUS loves and uses not only high-profile Christians but also hidden ones. Scripture establishes this.

Psalms speak of "thy hidden ones" (Ps 83:3), who "dwell in the secret place of the Most High" (Ps. 91:1). And Jesus urged us to seek our heavenly Father "in secret" (Matt. 6:6). *Hidden* (Ps. 83:3) means literally *a favorable hiding or covering of something or someone highly valued.*[1] So "hidden ones" are "precious ones" (NLT), "treasured ones" (NAS), "those you cherish" (NIV), "those you protect" (NRSV). God's hidden ones are His treasure, not His trash; adored, not abandoned; watched over, not overlooked! Constantly they "abide under the shadow [hovering, watchful, protecting presence] of the Almighty" (Ps. 91:1). People forget them, but God focuses on them. The apostle Paul appreciated and actively recruited hidden ones.

While hidden from public view in a Roman prison for Christ's sake, Paul called others to the veiled life. He challenged us to no longer seek worldly ends and notoriety but rather heavenly purposes: "Set your affection on things above, not on things on the earth" (Col. 3:2). He then reminded us that, in Christ, we're "dead" to this world and called to the humble yet spiritually high life of God's hidden ones: "...your life is hidden with Christ in God" (v. 3). He's not recruiting monks or nuns.

He's summoning all believers, whether of high or low public profile, to a new double life—not a criminal one, working by day and burglarizing by night; nor a vocational one, plowing fields weekdays and drilling soldiers weekends; nor an avocational one, splitting time between our profession and our hobby. Instead He's calling us to the holy double life of God's hidden ones. They're ordinary people with ordinary interests and lifestyles who foster an extraordinarily close walk with Jesus in this world that walks afar from Him.

Unlike others, this dual life is Christlike. Jesus lived it for thirty years in the sleepy little village of Nazareth in the dull, uneducated, religiously prospectless region of Galilee. Outwardly He looked like any other young, unremarkable Jewish craftsman. Inwardly, however, He was remarkably full of God's Spirit, Word, and zeal, and walking in constant union, communication, cooperation, and worshipful fellowship with His heavenly Father. Thus the Father highly valued and protectively hid His Messianic treasure in the rolling hills of Galilee until the time came to uncover and distribute His priceless wisdom, compassion, and power to Israel's spiritually impoverished masses.

To some degree, God's hidden ones relive the Nazarene's dual life. They seem like everyone else waiting in line to purchase groceries, but they're meditating inwardly on God's Word, not the tabloid headlines. They look like other motorists on the interstate highways, but they're worshiping God in song and Spirit as they go. Publicly they're ordinary housewives, but privately they're helping their husbands and children study, love, and serve God. Openly they seem like regular businessmen, but secretly they trust God for sales, not marketing gurus, methods, or tricks. They look like typical college students, but while pursuing academic studies they're also learning biblical disciplines. On the job they're everyday merchants, mechanics, and craftsmen, but at home they're prayerful Bible students. Publicly they're professional teachers, coaches, or counselors, but privately they're committed intercessors. To many they look like quiet congregants of little value, but their gifts, prayers, and labors are the priceless, invisible drivers that make churches and ministries thrive. These are God's hidden ones.

They continue the heavenly tradition of Moses, David, Mordecai, and others highly valued but long covered by God. God hasn't hidden these from society but in it. They haven't shut themselves away in monasteries; God has purposely scattered them throughout municipalities and nations. There their quiet but effective lives, witnesses, and ministries assistance please God and build His kingdom daily. When He wills, He brings them out for open service.

He raised Moses, David, and Mordecai from low- to high-profile ministry. More recently, young Oswald Chambers felt he would be hidden in obscurity, flame out and do his work, and then be taken.[2] And he was. God summoned these to the light because it was His sovereign plan (He leaves many hidden), and they lived the hidden life well, as we may.

It's a simple, sweet life, just Jesus and you—meditating in His Word, learning and listening for His voice, following His guidance, loving His people, seeking His presence, looking for His hand, longing for His appearing. The humble love it.

It's our pride that agitates to be recognized—and displeases and drives us from the Prince of Peace. Don't worry about your profile. Be one of His hidden ones.

Chapter 103

WHOSE IMAGE ARE YOU WORSHIPING?

*T*HE POLITICALLY MINDED Herodians asked the popular but apolitical teacher Jesus, "Is it lawful [biblical] to give tribute [tax] unto Caesar?" (Matt. 22:17). His response was illuminating and liberating—and timely for us.

Returning question for question, Jesus inquired of His inquisitive adversaries whose image and inscription was on the Roman coins they held: "Whose is this image and superscription?" (v. 20). When they conceded, "Caesar's," He commanded, "Give Caesar what belongs to Caesar, give God what belongs to God" (v. 21, MOFFATT). His use of the word "image" is key.

The image struck on the Roman denarius was a profile of Tiberius Caesar, and its inscription blasphemously proclaimed his purported deity: "Tiberius Caesar Augustus, Son of the Divine Augustus."[1] In other words, the coin claimed Tiberius was a son of the Greco-Roman gods, or even worse to Jewish thinking, Jehovah's Son. This is why the Jewish priests refused to accept Roman and other idolatrous coins as temple offerings, requiring instead that foreign Jews attending the festivals exchange their Gentile coins for Hebrew before buying sacrificial animals or making donations to the temple. Jesus' carefully worded question directed the Herodians to the denarius' idolatrous likeness and language and implied, "Whose image are you worshiping when you use this coin?" His allusion goes further.

From the viewpoint of biblical symbolism, Caesar's image may be linked to the impressive image of Gentilism Nebuchadnezzar envisioned and erected (Dan. 2–3), and to its final form, Antichrist's image (Rev. 13). Why? The spirit of antichrist inspired all these idols and their one essence: the worship of man usurping the worship of God. So by using the term *image*, Jesus was also trying to redirect His opponents to the first and second commandments, which forbid other gods and their images respectively (Exod. 20:2–5). They certainly needed correction.

The Herodians were a Jewish political party that supported the dynasty of the Herod family, which then ruled Israel by Rome's permission, and promoted Roman culture to the detriment of Jewish values, ways, and worship. By condoning Rome's emperor, the "Herod party" supported the worship of his image that pervaded the Roman world. Thus they violated God's first two commandments and offended His Son! Jesus instructed them to repent and thereafter give Caesar their taxes but God their worship! We need the same correction today.

The public images of our "Caesars," or heads of state, are always over-inflated by public relations propaganda. We should therefore respect our leaders' authority and obey their laws (including paying taxes), but never give them our "worship"—unrestrained adoration, profuse praise, and full trust. We must not see them sensationally but soberly. They are temporary heads of temporary nations in a temporary, fallen world order. We should reserve our worship for another.

His image is struck not on silver coins but in human flesh. It profiles the Son not of Augustus but of the Almighty. He's no ordinary prince or king but the Prince of life and King of kings. He'll rule not temporarily but eternally—after Armageddon! Our approved, worthy image is Jesus, "the image of God" (2 Cor. 4:4), "the express image of his person" (Heb. 1:3), and "the visible image of the invisible God" (Col. 1:15, NLT). Not understanding this, mankind has historically longed for a man-image.

In Samuel's day Israel cried, "Give us a king," and their kings disappointed them. In medieval times Christians cried, "Give us a Holy Roman emperor or pope," and they disappointed them. In modern times Christians are crying, "Give us a president or prime minister," and they too can only disappoint.

It's time we grow up spiritually and stop being "Herodians"—blindly committed loyalists to political parties or popular politicians. Why? Jesus said the Herodians worshiped the wrong image. Let's stop being swept off our feet by the overly optimistic visions of new political leaders and stand firm hoping in the infallible visions of New Testament prophecy. Let's never again blindly trust the wisdom or integrity of rising politicians but only in that of our risen Prince. "It is better to trust in the LORD than to put confidence in princes" (Ps. 118:9). Let's pause and remember our dual citizenships, in this passing nation and God's perpetual kingdom, but emphasize the latter. That's where we'll find the Leader who never disappoints: "Our citizenship is in heaven, from which also we look for the Savior" (Phil. 3:20).

He commanded us to give government leaders our revenue, but not our reverence; our obedience, but not our obeisance; our votes, but not our veneration. Be illuminated and liberated by His correction. Today He's asking you...

Whose image are you worshiping?

Chapter 104

THE SURPRISING BOLDNESS OF JESUS

W HEN THE SADDUCEES challenged Jesus with a hypothetical test question, He responded: "Ye do err, not knowing the scriptures, nor the power of God" (Matt. 22:29). Let's review this response.

First, consider exactly what Jesus said:

- You're teaching religious error.
- Your knowledge of the Scriptures is deficient.
- You're ignorant of God's power.

Second, consider whom He addressed. The Sadducees were a powerful religious party with significant influence in the Jewish priesthood and temple. Third, let's consider who Jesus was. From a natural perspective, He was an uneducated religious teacher from a lightly regarded, heavily Gentile, rural district not known for producing prophets or rabbis, much less Messiahs! This leads us to one inescapable conclusion: Jesus' retort was surprisingly bold! He had other options.

He could have abstained from answering His enemies. He had wisely used silence, or a postponed response, before (John 8:6–7). He could have been vague: "You may possibly need to review, restate, or even revise your beliefs." He could have veiled His correction with a parable, as He often did. For instance, "Once there was a group of older, distinguished Bible teachers who didn't fully understand the human spirit, resurrection, or divine miracles. So one day God sent a humble, young rabbi to help them see the light." He could have softened His terse reprimand with carefully chosen euphemisms: "Reverends, your teaching needs a few minor adjustments." But this day He chose none of these. For three years He had responded gently to His adversaries' rough words. Now it was time for the full, frank facts.

So out they came, straight and blunt—the naked truth, unvarnished, unwanted, but undeniable! "Take or leave it, this is the way it is! You're spiritually deceived, biblically ignorant, and in disbelief of God's power!" This sudden change in Christ's manner of address left the Passover-week bystanders stunned: "When the multitude heard this, *they were astonished* at his doctrine" (Matt. 22:33). And no wonder! Jesus didn't just ruffle these powerful and respected religious leaders' feathers. He plucked them! Clean!

Usually the crowds were astonished at Jesus' graciousness. He spoke so winsomely to the woman by the well, so mercifully to the woman caught in adultery, so hopefully to Jairus, and so tenderly to the formerly blind man excommunicated by the Jews! But here He spoke boldly, because it was necessary. He had done so before.

When the ruler of a synagogue indirectly rebuked Him for healing on the Sabbath, Jesus directly rebuked His host pastor: "Thou hypocrite..." (Luke 13:15). When His Pharisaic dinner host secretly judged Jesus for receiving a penitent sinful woman, Jesus openly judged His host, contrasting his callousness with her caring: "Thou gavest me no water for my feet. But she...Thou gavest me no kiss. But this woman...My head with oil thou didst not anoint. But this woman..." (Luke 7:36–50). And, as stated, in His last week on earth, Jesus openly charged His repeatedly false accusers—the scribes, Pharisees, Sadducees, and Herodians—with multiple true allegations. His indictment's language was intrepid, full of piercing adjectives and metaphors: "Hypocrites," "blind," "fools," "whited sepulchers," and "serpents" (Matt. 23:13–36). He knew these last bold words would bring sudden crucifixion, which they did. But let's clarify.

On these occasions when Jesus was boldly blunt, He was never hateful, contemptuous, self-righteous, or arrogant. He just made piercingly straight, precisely true statements when they needed to be stated. After observing Him and receiving His nature and Spirit, His disciples learned to do the same.

When the Sanhedrin asked the apostles how they healed a crippled beggar, they responded, "By the name of Jesus Christ of Nazareth, *whom ye crucified*," asserting further, "there is no other name under heaven...whereby we must be saved" (Acts 4:10–12). Their rebuke of Israel's high and mighty jurists—who only days earlier had disposed of Jesus—was noted: "When they saw the boldness of Peter and John..." (v. 13). They concluded Jesus' surprising boldness had surprisingly filled His followers. "...they marveled; and...took knowledge of them that they had been with Jesus."

To be like them, and Him, we must learn how and when to speak boldly—to shoot arrows of vital, timely truth straight at sin-, error-, or self-deceived hearts—like Nathan and Mordecai. The life of a David or Esther, or destiny of a church or nation, may depend on it. Be willing and ready to be bold, but never eager! Temerity is as bad as timidity!

So wisely pray to recognize the "time" (Eccles. 3:1). When it's time for quietness, tact, or stories, respond accordingly. When it's time for frankness, speak with the surprising boldness of Jesus.

Chapter 105

GO FOR THE GOAL!

APTIZED BY MANY fiery ordeals, Peter warned us to expect our own hot trials for Christ's sake: "Think it not strange concerning the fiery trial which is to test you" (1 Pet. 4:12). Do we understand the nature and goal of fiery trials?

An earlier veteran of fiery conflicts, Daniel, gave us the clearest illustration of trial by fire. He describes how his three godliest friends, Shadrach, Meshach, and Abednego, were tossed into King Nebuchadnezzar's fiery furnace for refusing to compromise their loyalty to God's Word (Dan. 3). Let's focus on the turning point in their terrible tribulation.

Everything changed when Nebuchadnezzar, stunned, looked into the blazing inferno and testified:

> I see [not three but] four men loose, walking in the midst of the fire, and they have no hurt; and…the fourth is like the Son of God.
>
> —DANIEL 3:25, KJV

Immediately he released the three from his cruel inferno: "Ye servants of the Most High God, come forth" (v. 26). Thus, just as suddenly as their fiery trial began, it ended—and they emerged forever changed. When will our heated tests end?

We'll come forth when we reach the condition the three were in when released: loose, walking, with no hurt, near God's Son, and yet still in the fire! This is God's goal. Let's examine it and what it means to us.

Just before release, the three were:

- "LOOSE"—or liberated from all their former bonds. This depicts us becoming free from everything that has formerly hindered our fellowship with Jesus and ministry to others. Surprisingly, the fiery pressures that should ruin us release us. They spur us to examine our besetting sins and faults—fear of man, envy, anger, gossip, laziness, impatience, imaginations, and so forth—with new clarity and dispatch them with new urgency. If we continue this humble self-examination, though still in the fire, we'll become deeply free, or as Jesus promised, "free indeed" (John 8:36).

- "WALKING"—or stable, upright, and steadily moving forward. This portrays us established in an excellent spiritual walk that's steady, righteous, and advancing. The severe difficulties we face in the fire press us to obey God with greater consistency—or collapse! Thus we become more upright, practicing "his righteousness" (Matt. 6:33) more closely and abandoning all remnants of unrighteousness and hypocrisy. The pressure of the fire forces us to keep advancing—or be consumed! So we keep moving on to the next step of obedience, seeking and serving God. Soon a new steadiness is evident. Happy or hurting, triumphant or troubled, we now "walk, and [do] not faint" every day (Isa. 40:31).

- "NO HURT"—or uninjured by the lethal assault. This represents us as being amazingly unoffended and unaffected by our terrible troubles. Why? We've learned to think spiritually (scripturally), practice forgiveness quickly, see that we obey God's Word, and rest in His all-sufficient, protective grace. Thus we endure the worst conditions in the best condition, our souls unhurt by the poison of anger at God, self-pity, or bitterness toward adversaries, and our bodies free from psychosomatic illnesses. Wondrously, our injurious treatment fails to injure us spiritually, mentally, or physically.

- NEAR "THE SON OF GOD"—or closer to Jesus than before. This speaks of us in a new closeness to Jesus. Inexplicably, injustices that should drive us from the Lord drive us to Him! Why? We've learned to refuse to get offended with Jesus—"Blessed is he who does not take offense at me" (Luke 7:23, NAS)—choosing instead to draw near Him daily whatever happens! This steadier reliance establishes us in a much closer walk with "the Son of God" (Dan. 3:25, KJV). Every morning we drink in long drafts of sweet fellowship with Him while still in the "fire"—the bitterest, hottest, seemingly inescapable conflicts.

Nebuchadnezzar's testimony was really Satan's concession speech—his acknowledgment that his diabolical campaign to destroy God's servants had failed miserably: "All I've done has had no effect on these three Jews. They're free from my bonds. They're not hurt with an offended or self-pitying spirit. They've not fallen into unbelief, sin, or indolence. Instead of abandoning God, they're walking closer to Him! All the suffering I inflicted has failed to stop their service, hinder their growth, or discourage them!" Thus he conceded God's goal was reached after all.

We reach God's goal when we're "loose," "walking," close to the "Son," without "hurt," and yet still in the fire! Sometime after we reach this condition, Satan will concede defeat and God will release us into a new, higher, more fruitful walk and work with Him: "Come forth..."

So whatever your fiery trial, go for the goal!

Chapter 106

GOD'S STARS IN THE NIGHT

HE BOOK OF Daniel opens by describing the darkest hour in Israel's history to date: the Babylonian captivity. Not since the Israelites' bitter Egyptian slavery had they been subjected to the tyranny of a faithless, merciless Gentile monarch.

Yet it was in this pitch dark, seemingly hopeless, spiritual nighttime, when haughty Bel worshipers were ruling over David's humbled posterity, that God shaped and flung one of His brightest stars into ministerial orbit, Daniel!

Unchanging, God still reserves His brightest witnesses for His people's darkest times—periods of idolatry and apostasy, the puzzling triumphing of the wicked, or other seasons of extraordinary trouble, confusion, or oppression. As spiritual darkness falls increasingly upon our nation and the world in these last days of the Church Age, we'll see God again shaping and flinging bright, new stars into the ministry.

Their brilliant appearances and ministries will demonstrate anew for our generation the unfailing faithfulness of God and the inexhaustible sufficiency of His grace. No matter how low His people get, no matter how sinful our times or how apparently complete our adversaries' victories, God is still present, faithfully sending spiritual light-bearers—tested believers filled with timely, biblical truth-light and spreading it by example, teaching, and testimony—to give us sustaining hope and strength. Prophets have foreseen, and wise scholars noted, God's habit of helping His helpless ones in hopeless times.

Alluding to Psalm 20:1–2, the insightful twentieth-century writer A.W. Tozer wrote:

> Invariably where daring faith is struggling to advance against hopeless odds, there is God sending "help from the [heavenly] sanctuary."[1]

Indeed, Daniel's loyal obedience to God, persistence in prayer, professional prominence, public profession, and prophetic messages were a mighty "help from the sanctuary," a bright guiding lodestar to the downtrodden, disillusioned, confused Jews. And not briefly; his light endured.

Daniel's bright witness shone throughout the long darkness of the seventy-year captivity. He began rising and radiating knowledge of the true God at the start of that long nighttime. While only a teenager Daniel obeyed God's Word uncompromisingly, received remarkable gifts of intelligence and interpretation, and by his meteoric success brought great honor to Jehovah (Dan. 1). Daniel's character, courage, competence, and devotional commitment kept shining, decade after decade, until Judah's long night of trouble ended and its day of restoration dawned (Dan. 5:30–31). God's stars still shine all night.

Today His stars are Christian overcomers. They are born-again "disciples indeed" (John 8:31) who passionately and patiently persist in seeking, studying, and serving God until they rise above every obstacle and opponent—their old nature, sins, and selfishness, and every person and thing that hinder their calling in Christ. Their witness to God's gospel, goodness, and greatness will not stop shining until Christ removes His true body and bride to end this age. In the following Tribulation period, new Jewish stars will rise. During the first half, 144,000 divinely selected Jewish evangelists will shine the Light throughout Israel and the world, drawing masses of Jews and Gentiles to Him from every nation (Rev. 7:1–8). During the second half, God's unnamed "two witnesses," His only remaining public truth-beacons, will shine until earth's darkest nighttime ends (Rev. 11:3–12).

So from beginning to end, God's faithful light-bearers will illuminate the growing gross darkness of these last days. All night long they'll radiate the Word of God's hope—biblical portions, principles, parables, practices, and prophecies that sustain believers with timely, uplifting, guiding truth— against a backdrop of increasing unbelief and wickedness worldwide. Like Daniel, these stars will endure until the new day dawns: the day of Christ's millennial kingdom! But now night is falling.

"And it was night" (John 13:30). The Light of this world wants every Christian to become a light-bearing overcomer, a beaming star of hope in this present darkness. Are we preparing ourselves for this? Prayerfully studying, obeying, and sharing His illuminating Word? Even as the midnight hour draws near? Daniel endured the long seventy-year night of Judah's captivity. Will we follow his example in our night?

Will we keep loving biblical truth-light and walking in it while the church increasingly compromises controversial biblical truths? Our nation grows increasingly secular? Biblical faith is mocked? Atheism fills the world? Opposition or injustice envelops us or other faithful Christians in our nations, cities, or personal lives to test our faith, patience, and loyalty to God? Or will our star—the godly influence of our Christian walk, words, and work—grow weaker and dimmer? Don't be a falling star!

In this night, rise and overcome the growing darkness! Like Daniel, grow brighter and endure! Watch for the rising of, and be among, God's stars in the night.

Chapter 107

THOU SHALT LOVE!

W HEN ASKED WHICH Old Testament precept was great-est, Jesus gave a surprisingly simple answer: "Thou shalt love…" (Matt. 22:37). He immediately divided this chief duty into two parts.

First, we must love God with our whole being, "with all thy heart, and with all thy soul, and with all thy mind" (v. 37), and, Mark adds, "with all thy strength" (Mark 12:30). Second, we must extend our loving thoughts and acts to those around us: "Thou shalt love thy neighbor as thyself" (Matt. 22:39). The order here is important. We must keep the first command to keep the second. Why?

Our love for people comes from our love for God. If we love God, we'll believe and obey His Word: "He that hath my commandments, and keepeth them, he it is that loveth me" (John 14:21). And, as His Word urges, we'll receive the fullness of His Spirit: "Be filled with the Spirit" (Eph. 5:18). This is key, because only the Holy Spirit gives us God's own affection: "The love of God is shed abroad in our hearts by the Holy Spirit who is given unto us" (Rom. 5:5). The Spirit enables us to love people in general and Christians in particular: "Everyone who loves the Father loves whoever has been born of him" (1 John 5:1, ESV). As we continue loving God and others and maintain-ing a Spirit-filled lifestyle, God's love in us grows and matures: "Whosoever keepeth his word, in him verily is the love of God perfected" (1 John 2:5). It's established when we continue loving others even while suffering: "I will very gladly spend and be spent for you; though the more abundantly I love you, the less I be loved" (2 Cor. 12:15). This grace-given, Christlike compas-sion "beareth all things, believeth all things, hopeth all things, endureth all things," and "never faileth" (1 Cor. 13:7–8). But if we stop loving God, this love for others, especially unlovable ones, withers. Jesus' love commands are of utmost importance.

He said they're the very pillars of the Old Testament: "All the Law and the Prophets hang on these two commandments" (Matt. 22:40, NIV). Indeed, the Ten Commandments demonstrate this. The first four reveal ways God wants us to love Him (Exod. 20:2–11); the last six, ways He wants us to love others (vv. 12–17). Still effective, "Thou shalt love" is the basis of every New Testament directive. And Christ's ministry.

All four Gospels testify that Jesus' ministry and messages were motivated by His "compassion." Matthew, Mark, and Luke reveal it prompted Jesus' healings (Matt. 14:14), feedings (Matt. 15:32), deliverances (Mark 5:19), teachings (Mark 6:34), and resurrections (Luke 7:13–14). John implies love moved Him to order ministers to lovingly care for His followers after His departure: "Lovest thou me?...Feed my sheep" (John 21:15–17). He recalls Jesus' high priestly prayer climaxed with His request for God to manifest His love in us: "That the love with which thou hast loved me may be in them" (John 17:26). Jesus' "new commandment" states we should "love one another, as I have loved you" (John 13:34), adding that this love—not our doctrine, piety, gifts, or power—is *the* distinctive sign that we're authentic: "By this shall all men know that ye are my disciples, if ye have love one to another" (v. 35). And there's more evidence.

In His loftiest lecture, the Sermon on the Mount, Jesus taught that when we consistently walk in love toward everyone, even our enemies, we're "perfect"—spiritually mature or Godlike (Matt. 5:38–48). The apostle Paul lists "love" as the first "fruit of the Spirit" (Gal. 5:22–23). In his epistles, he prayed for us to understand God's love (Eph. 3:19) and "walk in love" (Eph. 4:30–5:2). He also chose love as the theme of his loftiest inspired essay: "Love suffereth long, and is kind..." (1 Cor. 13:4; see vv. 1–8). The epistles of John, the apostle of love, repeatedly refer to and recommend God's love (1 John 3:1, 14–19, 23; 2 John 5–6; 3 John 5–6). Thus all Scripture speaks of and serves to foster growing God's love in and among us.

It's time we realize every demand our heavenly Father makes is motivated by love for Him or others—and every act of obedience we render should be also. The Bible isn't just the Word of faith, the Word of life, and the Word of truth. It's the Word of love. But not everyone follows it.

Offended with God, many Christians are loathing and leaving the Word of love: "Because iniquity shall abound, the love of many shall grow cold" (Matt. 24:12). Don't follow them. Follow Jesus' teaching.

"Thou shalt love!"

Chapter 108

WHEN JESUS GOES ON THE OFFENSIVE!

ATTHEW 22:41–46 MARKS a key turning point in Jesus' three-year dialogue with the Jewish leaders. Previously He was always on the defensive and they the offensive.

For three years the Pharisees, Sadducees, and Herodians watched Jesus' rising ministry. Envious, they periodically approached and questioned Him, hoping to use His responses against Him. Initially, Jesus' final week among them seemed to be no different. During Passover, they again repeatedly assaulted the wise Nazarene with perplexing, potentially ruinous test questions, still longing to "entangle him in his talk," end His ministry, and execute Him (v. 15). But this conversation took an unexpected turn.

After Jesus fielded their malicious verbal challenges (vv. 15–33), He went on the offensive: "Jesus asked them...What think ye of Christ? Whose son is he?" (vv. 41–42). Suddenly the tables were turned: the Interrogee was now the Interrogator!

Unprepared for His probing, His new interrogees were confounded and silenced: "And no man was able to answer him a word" (v. 46). This must have been very satisfying for Jesus' disciples. Finally, after years of relentless, rude badgering, Jesus stood victorious and vindicated and His vicious critics vanquished. Jesus' brief verbal blitzkrieg didn't end His trials, but it terminated His enemies' vexing questions: "Neither dared any man from that day forth ask him any more questions" (v. 46). So for three long years God permitted Jesus' enemies to go after Him, but in the end, He went after them—and won!

Here's a pattern of divine action: Sometimes God seems strangely passive, deliberately letting His enemies have the upper hand over His people. Then, when they're finished and convinced they've won the conflict, God suddenly goes on the offensive, confusing and defeating them. Scripture repeatedly confirms this.

God let Judas and the Jewish leaders move first, plotting, arresting, and crucifying Jesus. When they finished, He fought back, raising Jesus, restoring the apostles' faith, pouring out His Spirit, and raising the church in power to spread Jesus' message and ministry all over Jerusalem—and the world!

He let the corrupt Benjamites win initially in Israel's civil war. For two days their soldiers felled those of Israel's godly tribes. But on the third day God intervened, and His servants soundly defeated Benjamin's armies.

God let Baal's prophets prevail first on Mount Carmel. All day they commanded center stage, calling on Baal to act while God and His prophet sat silent! But when Baal's servants finished, Elijah prayed and God "fell" on the scene, suddenly and decisively, by fire and rain.

Goliath won initially on the battlefield. For forty days he challenged and intimidated Israel's petrified soldiers. But when he finished, God attacked through a young shepherd boy, a sling, a few stones—and down came the giant!

At first God let King Saul cruelly persecute David. For years Saul falsely accused and relentlessly assaulted Jesse's son, forcing him to flee, scavenge, hide, and pray for protection. Then, just when David looked hopelessly defeated, God arose, sending the Philistines to attack Israel, slay Saul, end David's oppression, and begin his reign.

Antichrist will triumph first in the Tribulation. Through satanic miracles and speeches, the arch deceiver will rise and reign over all nations. Then God will go on the march, sending plagues to destroy his realm and Christ to decimate his armies.

The insightful writer F. B. Meyer encapsulated this, God's way:

> When men have done their worst and finished, it is the time for
> God to begin. And when God begins He is likely, with one blow,
> to reverse all that has been done without Him.[1]

Have your enemies been on the offensive? Three years? Or more? Has God done little to help? Or nothing? Take heart! He's just waiting His time, and yours: "To every thing there is a season, and a time to every purpose…" (Eccles. 3:1). When it comes, He'll go on the offensive for you—with superior wisdom: "There is no wisdom, nor understanding [insight], nor counsel [that can stand] against the LORD['s wisdom] " (Prov. 21:30). Or, if necessary, He'll move in superior power. One way or another, He'll turn the tables on your adversaries. How?

He'll send the "fire" of guilt on their consciences. Or "rain" His Spirit's gifts and blessings on you as they watch. Or sling "stones" of adversity to slow or stumble them. Or send contentious "Philistines" to oppose them. Or send "plagues" exposing and withering their deceptive, harmful works. Or, if necessary, send "Armageddon"—one blow to reverse everything they've done and raise you to higher service. Like Christ, you'll stand victorious and vindicated, and your critics vanquished. When?

When Jesus goes on the offensive!

Chapter 109

WHAT'S YOUR CHURCH WORTH?

*E*VER WONDERED WHAT your church is worth in God's sight? If you could, how would you assess its true, lasting value?

Some Christians would appraise their church's material assets. How much property does it own? Others would weigh its reputation. What do other Christians, pastors or the public think of it? Many would number its congregation. How many attend its meetings? Some would examine its programs. How numerous and helpful are they? Others would scrutinize its social impact. How much has it improved its neighborhood, ward, or city? Many would analyze its leadership. How well educated, godly, and effective are its ministers, elders, and deacons? Some would measure its stewardship. How well does it support its ministers and assist its needy members?

Others would calculate its charity. How much does it give to the poor and victims of disasters? Some would assess its fruitfulness. How many saved souls, trained disciples, ordained ministers, or church plants has it produced? Many would evaluate its mission work. How many missions has it sponsored or missionaries has it sent and supported? Some would gauge its intercession. How frequent and fervent are its prayer meetings? Others would measure its worship. How enthusiastic is its praise, spiritual its worship, and diverse its music? All these factors hint at a church's real worth.

Yet one supersedes them all: testing! A church's true value cannot be known in peace and prosperity, but only in its trials and troubles. To evaluate churches, God must test them. For that, He uses neither fun nor fluff but *fire*—and the hotter and longer the better!

Paul declared, "Every man's [minister's] work shall be made manifest; for the day [of testing] shall declare it...it shall be revealed by fire; and the fire shall test every man's work of what sort [quality] it is" (1 Cor. 3:13). Interpreted narrowly, this says the quality of a pastor's ministry—whether his (or her) teaching and counsel is biblical, strong, and spiritual, or erroneous, weak, and worldly—is revealed by how well his obedient students endure fiery testing. Viewed broadly, it speaks of assessing any minister's works, and more broadly, of assessing every believer's works, since every Christian is a minister, or believer-priest, of Christ. But there's more.

This fire test also declares every church's true value. If a pastor's instruction enables his congregation to abide the fire, or endure long, intense challenges to its faith, obedience, patience, and loyalty, he'll be rewarded: "If any man's work abide...he shall receive a reward" (v. 14). And his church will be assessed as valuable. But if because it's shallow or erroneous his instruction causes his people's devotion and faithfulness to fail or "burn" in fiery trials, he'll lose his rewards—but not his salvation: "If any man's work shall be burned, he shall suffer loss [of rewards]; but he himself [his soul] shall be saved" (v. 15). And however valuable his church seemed, God will declare it worthless.

Many churches look very valuable before strong testing: meetings are packed, faith is growing, zeal is strong, worship is heavenly, brotherly love abounds, donations flow in, missionaries flow out, and ministers are sent forth. But when "tribulation or persecution ariseth because of the word" (Matt. 13:21), they're soon offended. Then faith and zeal wane. Their works wither. Their Christlikeness turns to corruption. Their numbers decline. Their worship withers. Why? Their teaching and training were worthless. They prepared them for good times, but not hard; for success, but not opposition; for God's blessing, but not His testing.

Other churches prove just as valuable as they appear. They receive excellent teaching and respond to it. When fiery trials visit, they only refine them and confirm that, like pure gold or silver, they're of highest value: "I will bring the third part through the fire, and will refine them as silver...and will test them as gold" (Zech. 13:9).

So, "think it not strange concerning the fiery trial which is to test you, as though some strange thing happened unto you, but rejoice" (1 Pet. 4:12–13). When, suddenly, unwanted "fiery trials"—controversy, slander, financial troubles, moral failures, lawsuits, unjust judgments, heresy, betrayals, church splits, public rejection, violent opposition—descend upon your church and strongly test its character for weeks, months, or years, rejoice! You're about to discover the true worth of your church and its teaching. The fire will "manifest," "declare," and "reveal" it with perfect accuracy (1 Cor. 3:13).

Will your congregation be gold tried in the fire or tin melted in the heat? Silver purified by fire or stubble consumed by flames? Not sure?

Be sure of this: whatever remains *after* the fire, that's what your church is worth.

Chapter 110

MARRIAGE GOD'S WAY

ITH DIVORCE AND remarriage rising, and the very definition of "marriage" being debated, it's time we review matrimony's biblical origins. Scripture reveals marriage two ways: God's and man's.

Genesis unveils marriage God's way. Perceiving man's need of a loving companion, God decreed, "It is not good that the man should be alone" (Gen. 2:18). So He pronounced His plan: "I will make him an help fit for him" (v. 18). God first prepared the man for his wife, creating a deficiency only she could fill: "The LORD God caused a deep sleep to fall upon Adam, and...took one of his ribs, and closed up the flesh" (v. 21). Then He prepared the wife for her man, carefully forming her to be "fit" (v. 18), or "suitable" (NIV) and "just right" (NLT), for him in every way: "The rib...made he a woman" (v. 22). Afterward He presented the wife to her man: "And brought her unto the man" (v. 22). Delighted, man proclaimed God's provision perfect: "This is now ['At last!', NLT] bone of my bones, and flesh of my flesh" (v. 23). The first couple then adapted to their new living arrangement: "They were both naked...and were not ashamed" (v. 25). Satisfaction and children followed. This was marriage God's way.

It was heterosexual, not homosexual; monogamous, not polygamous; lifelong, not temporary. It was pure, without adultery; faithful, without abandonment; loving, without abuse. It was also fruitful, not futile, fulfilling God's primary purpose: "Be fruitful, and multiply" (Gen. 1:28). Delighted, God proclaimed Adam's union His prototype: "Therefore shall a man [henceforth] leave his father and his mother, and shall cleave unto his wife; and they shall be one flesh [like Adam and Eve]" (Gen. 2:24). The Bible then describes marriage man's way.

Before the Flood, men preferred polygamy (harems or unlimited successive marriages) to monogamy: "They took them wives of all whom they chose" (Gen. 6:2). This demonically inspired indulgence hastened society's moral decay and divine judgment (v. 3). The indiscriminate intermarriage of the godly and ungodly lines corrupted families and children. Soon the world's social fabric fell apart. Maliciousness, murder, and chaos ruled (vv.

5, 11–13). Why? "All flesh had corrupted his way…" (v. 12). This reckless, ruinous "marrying and giving in marriage" continued till the Flood (Matt. 24:38). Stunning as it was, God's judgment didn't change fallen man's way.

In Jesus' day, many Jewish men divorced their wives "for every cause" (Matt. 19:3), or frivolously, to take new wives "of all whom they chose." Christians today are tragically similar. Despite God's grace, gifts, and goodness, Christians divorce spouses invalidly (without biblical cause) and take new ones "of all whom we choose." This has dishonored marriage, split families, confused children, and weakened our witness. Consequently, our culture's dizzying freefall into immorality has reached a new, dark low. We now take same-sex life partners "of all whom we choose!" Bizarre, confusing, corrupting, and fruitless, this is marriage modern man's way. But God remains unchanged.

He still follows His way when joining Christians in marriage as He did Adam and Eve: "What…God hath joined together" (Matt. 19:6). We marvel at the Matchmaker.

Seeing single Christians' needs, He quietly gives them hope He will meet them His way. He then prepares a man for his wife by making him willing to seek God's wisdom, accept responsibility, and lovingly and faithfully provide for his soul mate. He prepares a wife for her man by reshaping her thinking until she's willing to graciously submit to a husband's leadership, competently add whatever he lacks, and willingly work alongside him in their family and church. One fine day, when they least expect it, He arranges for them to meet. Soon they acknowledge His hand in their meeting, join their hands in marriage, and adapt to their new life together. And bear fruit!

They produce natural fruit—children born into families. Or spiritual fruit—sinners reborn into church families. Or both! If they abide near their Matchmaker, they yield Him the Christlike "fruit of the Spirit" daily (Gal. 5:22–23). Also, their joint prayers, obedience, and labors help churches and ministries plant, grow, and mature "the precious fruit of the earth" (James 5:7)—a priceless End Time crop of fully taught, trained, and tested Christians ready to be harvested to heaven, married to Christ, and prepared to return with Him to reign for a thousand years! In these and other ways the divinely appointed joining of Christian couples will achieve God's primary purpose in marriage: natural and spiritual fruit! This fruit will help save, not destroy families; redeem, not ruin society; bless, not curse nations. That's marriage God's way.

Anything less or other is marriage man's way. Learn, live, and labor for marriage God's way.

Chapter 111

OUR NEW TITLES

*J*N MATTHEW 23:1–12, Christ critiqued His critics, the scribes and Pharisees. Among these religious leaders' many faults, Jesus cited the following.

They preached but didn't practice God's Word. They "say, and [or but] do not" (v. 3). Their excessively strict teachings oppressed people. They "bind heavy burdens and grievous…on men's shoulders" (v. 4). They were unmerciful. They did nothing to remove others' burdens: "They…will not move them with one of their fingers" (v. 4). Their prime motivation was not to please God but to impress men. They did all their works "to be seen of men" (v. 5). They were ostentatious. "They make broad their phylacteries, and enlarge the borders of their garments [to draw attention]" (v. 5). They sought honors for themselves. They "love[d]" the "chief seats" in synagogues and reverential "greetings" in marketplaces (vv. 6–7). All these sins sprang from pride! Jesus warned them, "Whosoever shall exalt himself shall be abased" (v. 12). Thus they were unworthy officeholders. They sat "in Moses' seat" (v. 2) yet lacked his character. Let's examine their "love" for special seatings and greetings.

"Love" implies they were fond of, hoped for, and craved these honors.[1] Indeed, the Pharisees felt they deserved honorable chairs and greetings—and were offended when they didn't receive them. So the Jews were careful to not only seat them properly but also address them correctly, as "Rabbi" (my great one[2] or teacher), "father," or "master" (my guide or leader[3]). All these terms imply superiority. Jesus flatly rejected these titles of superiority.

He calls us to abandon them and adopt humbler designations. In this context, He suggests two: "brother" and "servant." "Be not ye called Rabbi; for…all ye are *brethren*…[and the] greatest among you shall be your *servant*" (vv. 8, 11). Are we embracing these new titles or craving more prestigious ones?

My fellow minister, must we always be addressed as Reverend, Doctor, Pastor, Evangelist, Bishop, Apostle, Prophet, Deacon, Elder, and so forth? If our titles are overlooked, are we offended or oblivious? Furious or fine?

The ultimate egalitarian, Jesus defined the new viewpoint by decreeing, "All ye are brethren" (v. 8). No Christian is above or beneath others, regardless of office or ministry. We're all peers and equally adopted children in God's house. Just as there's no "respect of persons" (James 2:1–9) due to material wealth, social standing, or worldly success, so there's none due to ministry or office. Cleric or laymen, "apostle, prophet, evangelist, pastor, and teacher" (Eph. 4:11), or merely Christian, *All ye are brethren.*" Jesus' decree fosters spiritual greatness.

To a person, the "greatest" Christians see themselves as other Christians' "servants." "He that is greatest among you shall be your servant" (Matt. 23:11). Paul, who held the highest office—apostle!—wrote of himself in the humblest terms, "Ourselves your servants for Jesus' sake" (2 Cor. 4:5). He shows us that the higher God lifts us in church office or ministry, the more we must see ourselves not as sovereigns but as servants of God's people; not entitled to "be ministered unto" by reverential titles, but all the more obligated to selflessly "minister and to give" to the needs of God's children, as Jesus did (Matt. 20:28).

Following Christ's teaching, some churches refer to every member, ministers and congregants, as simply "brother" or "sister." What if we all started doing this? Or using the other new title Jesus recommended, "servant"? It might start a new fad, and a refreshingly biblical one for a change! I can hear it now: "Brothers and sisters, this morning servant Bob has come to speak to us. Please welcome our servant."

We may or may not renounce our titles—Scripture itself calls ministers (or their labors) "teachers," "leaders," "guide(s)," and spiritual "father(s)" (Acts 13:1; Matt. 15:14; Acts 8:31; 1 Cor. 4:15)—but we must reject the Pharisaic attitude that "loves" and demands them! And if we call our ministers "teachers," "leaders," or spiritual "fathers," we must do so with the understanding that they are our peers and merely agents of our only superior Teacher, Guide, and Leader—Christ—and our only heavenly Father!

With the Spirit's help, we can strike this balance. We can "esteem" our ministers "very highly in love for their work's sake" (1 Thess. 5:12–13), yet neither think nor speak of them as superiors. And they can receive salutations without imagining they're special and sit on platforms without mistaking them for pedestals! We can greet or introduce them as our "pastor" or "teacher," yet remember they're just undershepherds serving our "great One" and "chief Shepherd," Christ (1 Pet. 5:4).

Better yet, we can call them, and every Christian, "brother," "sister," or fellow "servant"—according to our new titles.

Chapter 112

TIME TO MOVE ON

As MANY AS are led by the Spirit of God, they are [walking as] the sons of God," declared the consistently Spirit-led apostle Paul (Rom. 8:14). To be "led by the Spirit," we must recognize our heavenly Father's directions.

The Director of heaven and earth, He controls all people and events that touch our lives. He faithfully starts, manages, and turns all our circumstances, coordinating them with others, for good—His good will and our good blessing—provided we continue obeying His Word and following His guidance. We may be sure of this! "We know that God causes all things to work together for good to those who love God...[and are] called according to His purpose" (Rom. 8:28, NAS). But how does our Director direct us?

Typically, He leads us by Bible portions quickened in reading or study, speaking to our hearts during prayer or worship, counsel from pastors or elders, or more rarely, by repeated dreams addressing our situation, or prophecy. But He often leads us through circumstances, by simply giving or withdrawing our favor (approval, acceptance) with people.

If He wants us in a particular place of labor, worship, or service, He favors us there. By turning hearts to accept us, He draws us to people for new relationships; churches, for new teaching and fellowship; employers, for new jobs; cities, for new residence and friendships; and so forth. God used favor to place Joseph in Pharaoh's court: "God...gave him favor...in the sight of Pharaoh" (Acts 7:9–10). But the Director also removes favor.

When He does so, we've either wronged someone or been wronged. If we've given offense to the people involved, our loss of favor is God's way of calling us to repent. We should quickly ask their, and His, forgiveness. Jesus taught that if when drawing near to worship we remember we've wronged our brother, we should break off the worship and do our best to reconcile: "Leave there thy gift before the altar, and go...first be reconciled to thy brother" (Matt. 5:23–24). Then we may resume worship: "Then come and offer thy gift." Usually God will restore our favor with the offended party, but we mustn't presume He'll always do so! If, however, we've lost favor without cause, and our prayerful, humble attempts to reconcile fail, something else may be afoot. The Lord may be leading us elsewhere.

When Jacob arrived in Haran, God gave him enthusiastic favor with Laban, who "ran...and embraced him, and kissed him, and brought him to his house" (Gen. 29:13). For years Jacob's family and flocks grew in the sunshine of Laban's favor. But one day Laban's sentiments, and Jacob's favor, changed. Jacob's brothers-in-law began falsely accusing him. Soon Jacob noticed, "The countenance of Laban...was not toward him as before" (Gen. 31:2). While Jacob pondered these unwanted changes, God spoke: "Return unto the land of thy fathers...and I will be with thee" (v. 3). Laban's disfavor and God's dispatch made it clear: it was time to move on! So Jacob gathered his family and returned home. Expert at reading divine directions, Paul had a similar experience.

After Paul ministered three years in Ephesus with extraordinary success, the local idol makers led the whole city in a riotous protest against Paul's pro-Jesus, anti-idolatry gospel that was seriously disturbing their city's economy. Paul quickly saw the handwriting on the wall—the Ephesians' and His Father's—and quietly moved on: "After the uproar...Paul...departed to go into Macedonia" (Acts 20:1). But most Christians aren't experts in recognizing the Director's signs.

We fail to get the message when He removes our favor. We stay, strive, and defend ourselves when God wants us to quietly go and look for the next person, place, job, church, or door of ministry He has for us. Jesus taught, "Whosoever shall not receive you, nor hear your words...depart out of that house or city," and, "when they persecute you in this city, flee into another" (Matt. 10:14, 23). To where, or whom, shall we depart? If we first ask God's guidance and then seek open doors while watching for His checks or confirmations, we'll find our Director never fails.

Like a good shepherd, "when he putteth forth his own sheep, he goeth before them" (John 10:4). Whatever comes next in His plan and path—whether green pastures and still waters or valleys of the shadow—is only leading us to more good. So follow your Director.

When He gives you favor, thank Him and remain. When He takes it, thank Him and respond. If it's your fault, be reconciled. If not, ask His direction and patiently watch for it. It may be time to move on.

Chapter 113

Is Your Eye Evil?

J ESUS' PARABLE OF the laborers (Matt. 20:1–16) closes with this searching question: "Is thine eye evil, because I am good?" (v. 15). What's an "evil eye"?

Our physical eyes are dedicated to vision. So, figuratively speaking, our eye represents our personal viewpoint or attitudes. It speaks of how we see, think of, and feel toward people, events, and issues. Furthermore, we use our eyes to focus on the purpose at hand, whether it's working, reading, or other activities. Wherever our eyes are fixed, our mind is focused. The machinist's eyes are kept on his gauges, the carpenter's on his nail, and the artist's on his canvas. So our eye also represents our soul's focus, or purpose, intention, or goal. Though redeemed, we may still have "evil eyes," or *consistently wrong attitudes or focuses*. What does Scripture say about the evil eye?

The Bible usually associates it with two root sins, envy and greed:

- ENVY. In Jesus' parable of the laborers, the early laborers clearly envied their late coming, less burdened yet equally paid brethren, "Are you envious because I am generous?" (Matt. 20:15, NIV). Also, in Jesus' list of the defiling sins of our hearts, "evil eye" (Mark 7:22) is translated "envy" by several excellent modern translations (NIV, NAS, NLT, ESV). This suggests we tend to "eye," or competitively watch out of the corner of our eyes, those we envy.

- GREED. Various Bible references identify an evil eye with three forms of covetousness: greedy selfishness—"Take care lest…your eye look grudgingly on your poor brother, and you give him nothing" (Deut. 15:9, ESV); love of money, or a longing for wealth—"A man with an evil eye hastens after wealth" (Prov. 28:22, NAS); stinginess—"Eat thou not the bread of him that hath an evil eye ['a man who is stingy,' ESV]" (Prov. 23:6).

When our attitude becomes envious or our focus greedy, it's often reflected in our physical eyes. They look evil—narrow, cold, and hostile—instead of open, warm, and friendly. Once envy took hold, King Saul "eyed

David, from that day and forward" (1 Sam. 18:9, KJV), or "kept a jealous eye on David" (NIV), or "looked at David with suspicion" (NAS). Once envious of Abel, Cain's facial expression was "fallen" (Gen. 4:6). But there's more.

Evil eyes also look with unchecked sexual lust (Matt. 5:28). They constantly examine others yet never themselves (Matt. 7:1–5). They are pitiless toward pitiable sinners (Jonah 3–4). They give arrogant looks springing from haughty thoughts: "An high look and a proud heart will not I tolerate" (Ps. 101:5). They hide mixed motives. Jesus said if while worshiping Him we secretly long to accumulate earthly treasures, "your eyes are evil" (Matt. 6:23, NCV; see vv. 19–24). It's time we confess and cleanse all these "evil eyes." Why?

Our place in God's kingdom, now and later, depends on it! Jesus' parable of the laborers reveals this.

In it the estate owner (Christ) gave all those initially serving him (Christians) the same wage. When others came and served him later in the day, he generously gave them the same benefit. Some who were envious and stingy resented this. He rebuked them for their evil eye and sent them away: "Go thy way" (Matt. 20:14). This story suggests that some Christians who were last to convert will be first in kingdom position, or nearness to and ministry for Christ, while others saved earlier, who served first and longer, will sit last.

Primarily, this reckoning will occur at the judgment seat of Christ. But it also has a near application. Every time Christ visits His church to renew or revive it, He assesses and awards His people anew for their previous season of service. Those who stubbornly hold to their evil eyes, of whatever kind, are here informed they may lose the privilege of having Jesus' full approval and fellowship if they don't repent. And its future application implies this same standard will be applied to our position and service in Christ's millennial kingdom. How's your eye?

Is your viewpoint twisted by envy—anger at others receiving Jesus' generous blessings when you feel you're more deserving? Or distorted with pride—thinking that, due to other Christians' poverty, race, ignorance, past sins, or recent conversion and brief service, they're beneath you? Or twisted with judging—relentlessly examining others' sins and shortcomings? Or selfishly focused on money—always longing or planning for more wealth or material things? Or obsessed with sexual lust? Or harboring mixed motives? If so, deal with your eye now! Why?

Your place in Christ's kingdom depends on this question: Is your eye evil?

Chapter 114

WHEN THE BONES COME TOGETHER

*E*ZEKIEL 37:1–14 REVEALS how God brings revival and restoration when His people are spiritually divided, defeated, dead, dry, and discouraged. The Jews were in this condition at the time.

They were divided. The northern and southern kingdoms had long been separated. They were defeated. Their division hastened their decline and defeat—by unified enemies! Nationally, they were dead. Both kingdoms were militarily defeated and their people dispersed among the nations. They were dry. The Spirit hadn't rained on them for years. They were discouraged. With hope gone, despair was their daily companion. But hope was returning now through Ezekiel's vision (Ezek. 37).

It revealed God's sovereign plan to revive them (vv. 1–14), reunify them (vv. 15–19), and restore their national holiness, leadership, land, growth, communion, and glory (vv. 20–28). God further promised to renew their protection, through their restored "exceedingly great army" (v. 10), ready now to overcome all enemies. But this vision wasn't automatic. Cooperation was required: the people had to believe the vision and prepare to come together with other "bones," and Ezekiel had to preach this Word by blind faith. Let's review the prerequisites to this vision's fulfillment.

The mighty, creative Word led the way. When it was fully heard, a remarkable re-creation began: "O ye dry bones, hear [deeply ponder, believe, and practice] the word of the LORD" (v. 4). To have the "times of refreshing...from the presence of the Lord" that God promises (Acts 3:19), ministers must proclaim His promises to revive us. Ezekiel did so: "So I prophesied as I was commanded" (Ezek. 37:7). Sure of God when others doubt, leaders must persistently believe and proclaim His Word despite persistently disheartening evidence—when God's people seem as uninterested as dry bones and unstable as the wind: "Prophesy upon these bones...prophesy unto the wind" (vv. 4, 9). Once released into our hearts, the Word-seed begins creating a new genesis, or beginning. Soon something previously not present appears.

The first sign of life Ezekiel received was the joining of the bones.

"Behold…the bones came together" (v. 7). In his vision, full revival followed in due course.

Figuratively, these bones, or key structural body parts, speak of *leaders*, in the body of Israel then and in the body of Christ today. Like physical bones, these spiritual bones minister vital strength and order (structure) to Christ's body and join it together. God has always "fitly joined together" (Eph. 4:16) these bones, or key leaders, just before every spiritual awakening.

Before launching the Exodus, God linked Aaron and Moses, and together they gave strength and order to the weak, confused Hebrew slaves. Forty years later He linked Joshua and Caleb to revive His people's faith and lead them into Canaan. After the Exile, God linked Nehemiah and Ezra to restore, revive, and reunite their disappointed, divided brethren.

In the first century, He linked Jesus and His apostles—the "spine" of His ministry—before launching their revival in Israel. After Jesus' death, the briefly scattered apostles reconnected with other disciples to form the 120-bone "skeleton" of the initial body of Christ, which revived the Mediterranean world with the faith. A decade later He linked Paul and Barnabas as the primary bones of His new work among the Greeks in Antioch. He has continued this down the centuries.

William Tyndale visited Luther just as Tyndale began his biblical translations that later revived England. John Wesley connected with the Moravian leader, Zinzendorf, before leading the Methodist revival that swept England and America. More recently, God joined Billy Graham with Grady Wilson, Bev Shea, and Cliff Barrows before using their evangelism to revive millions. Bones aren't always ordained ministers.

Many are committed laymen. Aquila and Priscilla were two key bones Jesus connected to Paul to build His body in Corinth and Ephesus. And the Third Great Awakening (1857–1859) was led mostly by laymen whose prayer meetings brought new life to a million souls. More awakenings await us in this Laodicean era. Like Israel, the church today is divided, defeated, dead, dry, and discouraged. But don't despair!

Prepare! Become a bone ready for the coming revival. Believe the figurative application of Ezekiel's vision and cooperate with it. Dig into God's Word and obey it. When tested, don't faint. Persist! Bones must be strong to hold Christ's body together! Like Ezekiel, believe and minister the creative Word faithfully. It can revive anyone, even Christians who seem as unresponsive as dry bones and unstable as wind: "Preach the word…in season, out of season" (2 Tim. 4:2). And ask God to link you to other bones—fully committed remnant pastors, disciples, churches, and ministries. Then watch for His hand.

You'll rejoice when you see the bones come together!

Chapter 115

EVERY END IS A NEW BEGINNING

W HEN PLEASANT CIRCUMSTANCES, relationships, employments, or pursuits come to an end, we sometimes become anxious or depressed. Thoughts race through our inquisitive minds.

Who will replace this person, provide that service, or fill this job? Who will replace this leader, minister, or ministry? Or, personalizing, where will I find another job, friend, house, church, ministry, customer, or assistant? But Christians need never fear when things draw to a close. Why? With God, every end is a new beginning. The prophet Samuel learned this early in life.

While just a child, Samuel perceived God saying, "When I begin, I will also make an end" (1 Sam. 3:12). God was foretelling what He would do in Samuel's life. Samuel's priestly and prophetic training under Eli would continue until his ministry to God's people began. Once it was fully begun, or established, God would terminate the ministry of His weak and compromised priest Eli and his corrupt sons, Hophni, and Phinehas (1 Sam. 2:12–25). This is exactly what followed.

After God tested Samuel's faithfulness—by requiring him to deliver a message of judgment to his own mentor, Eli!—God began growing Samuel's ministry. "Samuel grew, and the LORD was [obviously] with him, and did let none of his words fall to the ground [unheeded or unfulfilled]" (1 Sam. 3:19). Word spread of Eli's gifted prophetic understudy and the inspiration and accuracy of his messages. Soon everyone recognized God had called Samuel to succeed Eli as Israel's spiritual leader: "All Israel…knew that Samuel was established to be a prophet of the LORD" (v. 20). Therefore, the whole nation eagerly awaited Samuel's new messages: "And the word of Samuel came to all Israel" (1 Sam. 4:1). This was what God had foretold Samuel. His ministry had begun.

So God immediately acted to "make an end" of Eli and sons. He moved the Philistines to attack Israel, and during the ensuing battle Hophni and Phinehas fell. This news prompted Eli's death. Thus God performed His promise, "When I begin, I will also make an end." He also taught us every end is a new beginning. The Old Testament displays this truth frequently.

When Abel's life ended, Seth's began. When Moses passed, Joshua arose. When Joshua expired, the judges appeared. When the judges left, the prophet Samuel arrived. When Samuel passed, God promoted David to lead Israel. When David retired, Solomon rose and reigned. The New Testament confirms this pattern.

When John the Baptist's ministry abruptly halted, Jesus' ministry burst onto the scene. When Jesus' ministry ceased, the apostles' work commenced. The biblical ages demonstrate the same pattern.

The end of Israel's period of law was the beginning of the church's age of grace. The end of the Church Age will initiate the Tribulation. The end of the Tribulation will launch the Kingdom Age. The end of the Kingdom Age will mark the beginning of our eternal life on the new earth. This world's times and seasons further illustrate this truth.

The seasons testify to us four times annually. Winter's death is spring's birth; spring's end is summer's beginning; summer's departure is autumn's arrival; and as autumn fades, winter flourishes again. The centuries add their testimony every hundred years. The termination of one century is the turn of the next. Generations add their amen. The death of one generation's dominance marks the birth of the next generation's prominence. Rulers display this pattern. The ouster of one head of state marks the entrance of the next. The international community also demonstrates this. While one leading nation is declining, a new dominant nation is rising.

Has something recently ended—a friendship, employment, marriage, ministry, church, career, or mission? Or is your dwindling brook of provision declaring an end is near? Is this change unexpected? Unwanted? Unfair? Your viewpoint is vital. If you focus on the termination, it will trouble you—and terminate your faith, hope, and joy! But if you see it spiritually, through the eyes of faith in God's ways, your spirit will soar through the transition.

Here's a sure "flight plan." Acknowledge God, not chance, has made this end: "I will make an end." "In everything give thanks; for this is God's will for you" (1 Thess. 5:18, NAS). Believe the Good Shepherd has gone before and lovingly prepared your new "pasture." While Elijah's brook was dwindling, God was preparing Zarephath: "I have commanded a widow there to sustain thee" (1 Kings 17:9). He's working "all things" for your "good" too (Rom. 8:28). Don't resist His goodness by nostalgically looking back. Courageously look and move forward, confident something new and wonderful awaits. Why?

Every end is a new beginning!

Chapter 116

CALLING STANDARD BEARERS!

HEN PREPARING TO visit Jerusalem with His disciples, "Jesus sent two disciples on ahead" (Matt. 21:1, AMP). He still sends chosen servants ahead of His visitations.

These divinely prepared and sent forerunners are Christ's standard bearers. To understand exactly who they are and what they do, let's revisit history.

A thousand years before Christ, King David wrote, "Thou hast given a banner [standard] to them that fear thee, that it may be displayed" (Ps. 60:4). In David's day, a "banner" was not a banner or flag as we know them today but rather a battle standard—a pole with national, tribal, or military symbols affixed to its top used to unify and inspire soldiers in battle or citizens during parades. Military commanders selected standard bearers to carry these battle standards. Later nations developed cloth flags or banners carried by color bearers. It was an honor to carry the standard or flag into battle and a disgrace for it to fall to the ground, or worse, into enemy hands. When battles were going badly, morale was low, and desertion growing, the standard or flag was raised high to rally the troops. Reinspired, regathered, and reunified, they surged forward to victory. God does the same with His oft-embattled people.

Whenever His spiritual armies, whether in Israel or the church, struggle, weaken, and waver to the point of confused capitulation, God raises a standard to rally them. He began this by raising a literal standard in Moses' day.

When thousands of Israelites fell in sin and judgment in the wilderness, God commanded Moses to raise a standard—a brass serpent on a pole representing Christ on the cross (Num. 21:5–9). When they looked to it in faith and obedience, their sins were forgiven and wounds healed. God's next standards were men. Isaiah called for them: "Prepare the way of the people...lift up a standard for the peoples" (Isa. 62:10). They still are.

Today God's standard bearers are *spiritual role models*, believers who set before us examples of excellence in various areas of Christian life or work. God raises them to prominence among us so we will consider and follow their excellent ways in God. They hold high before us the virtues, truths, or methods God wants us to emulate in our living and labor. Whenever we look to their examples, we're reinspired to walk closely with God in this god-less world. Rallying to them in spirit, we abandon lukewarmness and selfishness and reunite with believers around us to faithfully prepare for God's next visitation. God lifts up many standard bearers in the Bible.

Abraham set a standard for faith and Joseph for prophetic insight. Joshua raised one for bold leadership and Ruth for humble loyalty. David raised one for worship and Hezekiah for trust in God. Daniel lifted one for uncompromising obedience and Esther for courage. Jeremiah and other prophets raised a standard of suffering patiently for faithfully speaking God's Word: "Take...the prophets who have spoken in the name of the Lord, for an example of suffering affliction, and of patience" (James 5:10). Standard bearers are also prominent in church history.

The martyrs and reformers raised a standard for cross-bearing (accepting rejection). John Wycliffe raised one for scholarship and protesting against error. Matthew Henry lifted up one for Bible study. John Wesley raised one for diligent ministry and teaching self-examination. George Mueller lifted one for funding ministries by faith. Charles Spurgeon raised one for expository preaching. Hudson Taylor lifted one for wise missionary methods. And recently Billy Graham set one for evangelism. Military history adds something else.

When standard bearers fell in battle, others rushed to raise the standard again to prevent disunity, discouragement, and defeat.

In this spiritually and morally lukewarm Laodicean era, the enemy's doctrines and deceptions have flooded Christianity. Many of our former standards—uncompromising obedience, holiness, faithfulness, courage, cross-bearing, the Spirit's wisdom, biblical ways—have fallen, and the specter of defeat looms. Christ's righteous remnant is scattered and its morale low. But the battle isn't lost.

God will lift up His standards again. "When the enemy shall come in like a flood, the Spirit of the LORD shall lift up a standard against him" (Isa. 59:19). He will send new standard bearers in faith, patience, purity, love, humility, wisdom, boldness, divine guidance, testing, cross-bearing, biblical scholarship, preaching, teaching, spiritual gifts, prophetic insight, and kingdom focus. These highly visible, spiritually excellent men and women will reinspire, reunify, and redirect Christ's army of believers to victory—the full accomplishment of God's will in the coming visitation. Here's more good news: you can be one!

Today God is calling standard bearers!

Chapter 117

THE NAME CALLER

GOD'S GRACE INCARNATE, Jesus was no hasty, ill-tempered name caller. Yet He repeatedly assigned specific nicknames to people He met or addressed.

For instance, when King Herod Antipas threatened to kill Him, Jesus called the crafty monarch a fox: "Go, and tell that fox" (Luke 13:32). When He called Peter and Andrew to ministry, He prophesied they'd become "fishers of men" (Matt. 4:19). When He called James and John, two young zealots a little too eager to invoke judgments, He dubbed them "Boanerges," meaning "sons of thunder" (Mark 3:17). While praying, He referred to His disciple-turned-traitor, Judas, as a "son of perdition" (John 17:12). His use of epithets climaxed when addressing the Jewish religious leaders at the close of His ministry. For three years He had been silent while they released upon Him a river of false names: "Beelzebub," "deceiver," "winebibber," "glutton," and so forth. Now it was His time to respond. Thus He loosed upon them a flashflood of nefarious names: "hypocrites," "blind guides," "fools," "whited sepulchers," "serpents," "sons" of prophet-killers, and "child[ren] of hell" (Matt. 23:13–33). Why did Jesus pin these derogatory name tags on these highly religious men? Here are three reasons.

First, all these uncomplimentary labels were true. Every one described perfectly the character traits of typical first-century Jewish scribes, Pharisees, and chief priests. Second, this kind of name-calling was biblical. The Bible repeatedly associates peoples' names with their characters: the faithful exhorter, Joseph, is nicknamed Barnabas, or "son of consolation" (Acts 4:36). Third, Jesus had authority to do this. He can justly assess characters and assign names because the Father has appointed Him Judge of all: "The Lord Jesus...who shall judge the living and the dead at his appearing and his kingdom" (2 Tim. 4:1). Believers should pause and ponder this.

One day we will stand before "the judgment seat of Christ," while He evaluates our earthly lives (2 Cor. 5:10). He may well judge or sentence us as He did others during His earthly life. If so, He will encapsulate His assessment of our character in a name. Whether nice or nefarious, complementary

290

or caustic, smooth or shocking, the name He gives us will perfectly summarize our lifelong walk and work with Him.

For example, He may pronounce us unfaithful or faithful: "Thou hast been faithful" (Luke 19:17). Or He may declare us wise or foolish: "A foolish man, who built his house upon the sand" (Matt. 7:26). He may call us self-serving or His servant: "Well done, thou good…servant" (Matt. 25:21). Or He may decree us diligent or slothful: "Thou…slothful servant" (v. 26). He may label us upright or wicked: "Thou wicked…servant" (v. 26). Or He may call us unclean or holy: "A righteous man, and holy" (Mark 6:20). He may proclaim us upright or a thief: "He was a thief" (John 12:6). Or He may assess us as true or a liar. "He is a liar" (John 8:44). He may proclaim us impatient or patient: "I know…thy patience" (Rev. 2:2). Or He may reckon us a failure or overcomer: "Ye have overcome" (1 John 2:13).

Furthermore, He may call us a stranger or friend: "Friend, go up higher" (Luke 14:10). Or He may pronounce us barren or fruitful: "So shall ye bear much fruit" (John 15:8). He may proclaim us proud or humble: "Thou didst humble thyself before God" (2 Chron. 34:27). Or He may call us fervent or lukewarm: "Thou are lukewarm" (Rev. 3:16). He may judge us as having little faith or great faith: "Great is thy faith" (Matt. 15:28). Or He may rule we're callous or compassionate: "Ye had compassion" (Heb. 10:34). He may conclude we're discerning or blind: "Thou art…blind" (Rev. 3:17). Or He may decree us joyful or miserable: "Thou art…miserable" (v. 17). He may evaluate our soul (spiritual life) as poor or rich: "Thou art rich…thou art…poor" (Rev. 2:9; 3:17). What will Jesus call us?

Presently, we don't know. But we know this: Whatever name He assigns will describe us perfectly! And permanently! We can't change our name in the next life! "It is appointed unto men once to die…after this the judgment" (Heb. 9:27). But we can change it now. It's time to reassess ourselves.

What kind of character are you forging by your consistent decisions and actions day by day? Test by test? Decision by decision? That's determining what the Name Caller will say when you stand before Him. Don't be troubled by this prospect and sink. Rise and, with God's help, go make a name for yourself! "To him that overcometh will I give…*a new name*" (Rev. 2:17).

That's a sure promise from the Name Caller.

Chapter 118

THE PRODIGAL IN US

ESUS' PARABLE OF the "lost" or prodigal son describes the foolishness of wastefulness (Luke 15:11–32). It starts with spiritual immaturity.

The "younger," or less mature, son was not content to dwell near his father and brother and serve faithfully on the family farm (v. 12). Too focused on money and material things, and hasting to have them, he requested his inheritance early: "Father, give me the portion of goods that falleth to me" (v. 12). Insensitive and unthankful, he had no desire to be near his father. Soon after receiving his inheritance, he went as far away as possible, journeying to not a neighboring or near but "far" country (v. 13). There he served himself instead of his father and the family farm. There he forgot his father's virtues and indulged his vices. And there he evaded his faithful but uncongenial brother, whose dislike (and verbal abuse) he disliked (vv. 28–30). These symptoms betray his spiritual immaturity.

They also caused his tragic backsliding. Powerful spiritual forces, they drove him from his father's loving presence, purpose, provision, and protection into a howling wilderness of wastefulness. This younger son's ways and woes represent spiritually immature, self-serving Christians. They have no interest in getting to know God, fellowship with Him and other Christians, or serve God's kingdom, yet they are eager to enjoy the benefits of their heavenly Father's salvation. Invariably these become squanderers. What did the younger son waste?

Primarily, he "wasted his substance with riotous living" (v. 13). Rather than wisely use or invest his precious inheritance, he flung it away. *Wasted* means literally "to scatter abroad"; or figuratively, "squandering property."[1] Thus we call this young man "prodigal," or wasteful. An immature, undisciplined rich brat, he had no concept of financial responsibility, liked wild parties, and frequented prostitutes. Spending recklessly, he soon "devoured" his father's estate funds (v. 30). Most Christians feel we have nothing in common with this undertrained, oversexed, hyper-sinful wastrel. But prayerful reflection may change our minds.

There's a "prodigal" in us all—not a crude, rude dude, but a refined, religious ruiner of redemptive blessings. Though most Christians aren't party animals, insatiable whoremongers, or compulsive spendthrifts, we may still waste things far more valuable than money. Thus we too may be prodigals. While we typically don't care, Christ is distressed when we squander the spiritual assets of our heavenly inheritance. Let's consider our oft-overlooked wastefulness.

Every born-again Christian has Christ's nature in his (or her) heart. Are we feeding and growing His life by prayer, devotional reading, and worship—or starving it?

When baptized with the Spirit, the Holy Spirit invades us to purify, empower, teach, and guide us. When He convicts, do we confess our sins so He can purify us? When the Teacher gives biblical insight, do we note and share what He reveals? When He calls us to wait on God and renew our strength, do we draw near or walk away? When He offers wise guidance, do we follow or abandon it?

Bible teachings are valuable disbursements from our Father's estate. Do we wisely invest these priceless truth-deposits—the "sound words" and "that good thing which was committed to thee" (2 Tim. 1:13–14)—or ignore them? Are we careful doers of the word or careless hearers only?

The natural and spiritual gifts God gives us can be squandered or developed. Are we working hard to develop and perfect our talents or hardly working?

Every ministry is a service inheritance or spiritual mantle granted us. Are we forgetting or "fulfilling" the ministry given us: "Take heed to the ministry which thou hast received…that thou fulfill it" (Col. 4:17). We may use or misuse other inheritances.

Do we use well the time allotted us daily, nightly? Do we fully develop our mind by reading, studying, and thinking on biblical, historical, current, and other worthy subjects? Do we nurture our Christian friendships or neglect them through faultfinding or apathy? Do we nourish our bodily health or ruin it by substance abuse, indulgence, or overwork? Do we use our income well, giving first to God and prioritizing responsibilities? Do we use our tests to show God we're trusting, obedient, and fit for His use, or do we waste our opportunities for approval? It's time we answered our Father.

Your answer reveals whether you're tragically spiritually immature or triumphantly mature; discontent or content serving your Father; seeking more of Him or only His benefits; near or far from Him; prudent or prodigal. If immature, take heart! You can still change. Even the prodigal son repented!

God had to send a mighty famine to deal with him. Famine or no famine, let's deal with the prodigal in us.

Chapter 119

THE SIGNS OF REAL REPENTANCE

W HEN SINNERS OR backsliders, especially those for whom we've long prayed, suddenly profess repentance, we may wonder if their profession is real. But we needn't wonder.

We can be sure. Very sure. The prodigal son's famously sudden turnabout showcases biblical evidence of real repentance (Luke 15:11–32). The signs of godly sorrow he displayed proved that, indeed, this prodigal was penitent. Let's examine them.

This wayward young man first experienced the realization of repentance. In deepest distress among pigpens, pods, and prostitutes, he "came to himself" (v. 17), or "came to his senses" (NIV). Suddenly, probably due to his father's prayers, his former right feeling and thinking returned. God gave him "repentance to the acknowledging of the truth" (2 Tim. 2:25). Awakened from the sleep of sin, he saw life very differently. He began feeling softly and thinking humbly again.

The refocusing of repentance followed. His heart changed, he now stopped focusing his thoughts on the things the "far country" held most important—materialism, lust, pride, man-reliance, and self-serving—and refocused on the one thing he hadn't considered for a long while: returning to and pleasing his father: "I will...go to my father, and will say unto him..." (Luke 15:18).

He also felt the regret of repentance. He was deeply sorry that he had hurt his kindly old father. And he was angry with himself for forfeiting not only the loving fellowship and joys of sonship but also its generous privileges and provisions. In want, he bemoaned all he had wantonly wasted: "My father's hired servants have bread enough [provision] and to spare [abundance], and I perish with hunger!" (v. 17).

Furthermore, his words now rang with the rhetoric of repentance. He frankly acknowledged his sins without excusing himself, misrepresenting his former home life, accusing his father, or blaming even his unloving elder brother (vv. 28, 30). With unmistakable biblical terminology, he described his demise as not a mistake or misunderstanding or unintentional

NOT BY *Bread* ALONE

slip but as deliberate, willful sin: "I have sinned against heaven, and before thee" (15:18; or, "in thy sight," v. 21).

Moreover, he displayed the distinctively humble reasoning of repentance. His conscience was greatly exercised over his formerly proud heart that felt he was above serving his father, as his brother was doing (v. 25). Broken, contrite, and sober minded now, he openly confessed his unworthiness for sonship: "I...am no more worthy to be called thy son" (v. 21). And the miracle is, he meant it.

Most importantly, he exhibited the reality of repentance: a steady reversal of action! Fine as his penitent thoughts and words were, his recovery wasn't real until he acted. Not until "he arose, and came to his father" (v. 20) did his father, and God, know definitively that, yes, his penitence was not flimsy but firm. This was no jailhouse religion. This contrite con was walking the walk he talked—and not turning back.

Finally, he demonstrated the remarkable relinquishing of repentance. Overjoyed to be back in his father's loving favor, care, and protection, he abandoned all former claims to his father's estate—the very benefits, rights, and privileges he had idolized and selfishly grasped! He also gave up his status as a son-servant, or family member who served the family farm, and happily accepted the distinctly lower rank and duties of a hired servant: "Make me as one of thy hired servants" (v. 19). Purged of worldly ambition, he desired only to live near his loving father and serve his will.

These penitent practices brought the results and restoration of repentance. Real repentance always revives the fruit of the Spirit—"love, joy, peace, patience, kindness, goodness, faithfulness, gentleness, and self-control" (Gal. 5:22–23, NIV). The prodigal manifested all these while returning home. There he experienced the amazing restoration of repentance. Everything he ruined by waste—provisions, prosperity, authority, sonship, usefulness, family, friends, fellowship, joy—his father restored by grace (Luke 15:22–24)! Why? He knew his son's change was real.

It might have been a religious sham. If he had not shown respect and interest for his father, had no regrets, blamed others or excused himself for his backsliding, still demanded privileges or honors, scorned to serve his father, and idolized money and materialism, his professed repentance would have been false, not famous. His father, and God, knew this.

So should we. Let's start evaluating people by their walk, not their talk: "By him actions are weighed" (1 Sam. 2:3). When sinners profess salvation and backsliders repentance, let's quietly look for the prodigal's penitence and Spirit's fruit in them. If we see them, we'll know the change is real. The Son, not the serpent, is now ruling. The Spirit, not sin, is guiding.

Lacking these proofs, let's keep praying and watching for the signs of real repentance.

Chapter 120

FATHER IS WATCHING

W HEN THE RETURNING prodigal son was still "a great way off," his father first "saw him" (Luke 15:20) and then "ran" to shower his broken son with affection and blessings. The penitent youth was probably as surprised to see his father watching for him as his father was to see him returning. But he shouldn't have been.

His earthly father, who symbolizes our heavenly Father, was driven by unfailing love to constantly watch over all his children, near and far off. Like him, our heavenly Father keeps a perpetual affectionate vigil over us, even when we're "a great way off" from Him struggling with the stressful issues of this hectic, unspiritual world. No place on earth is excluded from His view: "The eyes of the LORD are in every place, beholding the evil and the good" (Prov. 15:3). His eyes search not slowly with apathy but rapidly with intense desire: "The eyes of the LORD run…" (2 Chron. 16:9). Rather than focus on one place, they maintain a ceaseless circuit of surveillance: "…run to and fro" (v. 9). God wants to powerfully assist all who submissively trust Him: "to show himself strong in the behalf of them whose heart is perfect [in trust] toward Him" (v. 9). Let's observe how He observes us.

He beholds us when we pray. Jesus taught us to get alone with, and pray to, "thy Father, who seeth in secret" (Matt. 6:6). He watches approvingly to enlighten us with insight when we study His Word: "Study to show thyself [observed and] approved unto God…" (2 Tim. 2:15). He watches and listens when we humbly confess our sins. The moment Job turned and confessed his prideful self-defense, God "turned" his captivity (Job 42:6, 10). He observes when we win small battles and appoints us to lead others through larger conflicts. He saw Othniel take one small city and later summoned him to lead Israel's national defense. He sees us when we're laboring. He watched as Rebekah worked long and hard to draw water for Abraham's ten thirsty camels in the heat of the day. He watches when we suffer. As the Hebrews endured Pharaoh's relentless and pitiless oppression, God "looked upon" their plight, "heard" their cries, and sent Moses to deliver them (Exod. 2:23–25).

When we give, He watches us by His Spirit—or Son: "Jesus sat opposite the treasury, and beheld how [grudgingly or willingly] the people cast money into the treasury" (Mark 12:41). He observes when we need further instruction. He sent Paul's students, Priscilla and Aquila, to teach Apollos the Christian faith "more perfectly" (Acts 18:26). He watches over us to correct us. He sent Nathan to reprove David for ignoring his sin. He sees us when, as Jesus taught, we "do good" to our "enemies" (Matt. 5:44). When Isaac graciously received his Philistine adversaries, that very day his herdsman discovered a valuable new well—a sign of God's delight in His obedient servant. He sees when we trust Him during fearful crises. After seeing King Hezekiah rely wholly on Him during a terrifying Assyrian invasion, He memorialized Hezekiah's exceptional trust in Scripture (2 Kings 18:5–6). And He perceives more.

He sees us waiting for His guidance. After observing Elijah patiently awaiting His direction by the brook Cherith, He spoke, revealing the prophet's next parish and provider: "Arise, get thee to Zarephath...I have commanded a widow there to sustain thee" (1 Kings 17:9). He sees our fasting. When Daniel fasted and prayed for insight three weeks, God noted his self-discipline and granted his petitions "from the first day" (Dan. 10:12). He sees our perseverance in adversity. When Joseph suffered a second major injustice, yet continued faithfully trusting and serving God in prison, the Lord saw his rare submission and prompted Pharaoh's butler to call for Joseph's release. And He sees us still worshiping in persecution. Hurting, hungry, and helplessly bound in stocks in Philippi's dark, filthy jail, Paul and Silas bravely "prayed, and sang praises unto God" (Acts 16:25)—and seeing their sacrificial praise, God sent an earthquake to suddenly release them. Unchanging, our Father's observations continue to this day.

Today, are you working, studying, praying, fasting? Giving, laboring, suffering, waiting for guidance? Doing good to your enemies, persevering in adversity, or worshiping in persecution? Yet are you worried weak because God's help seems "a great way off"? Don't be a doubtful prodigal! Your heavenly Father is maintaining an affectionate vigil over you—in every place, running to and fro, ready to show Himself strong for you.

So get ready for Him to shower His love and blessings upon you, confident that Father is watching.

Chapter 121

PRAY THE WORD!

*I*F WE ASK anything according to his will…we know that we have the petitions that we desired of him" (1 John 5:14–15). With these words the apostle John describes the prayer of faith, or the way to petition God with complete confidence.

But to pray "according to his will," we must know His will. How can we?

The Holy Spirit reveals God's will generally[1] in the Bible, which He inspired: "All scripture is given by the inspiration [breath or Spirit] of God" (2 Tim. 3:16). Thus the Word of God is the general will of God for everyone, where applicable. It conveys His thoughts, decisions, values, and plan perfectly—as revealed by the Spirit of truth.

The Holy Spirit also prays according to God's will. The apostle Paul informs us that when the Spirit prays in our bodily temples for us or others (and when we pray "in the Spirit"), "He maketh intercession for the saints according to the will of God" (Rom. 8:27). If the Holy Spirit, who has revealed God's will in Scripture, also prays according to God's will, shouldn't we follow His example? Since God's will is revealed in His Word, shouldn't we pray according to God's Word? Then we'll be certain our petitions are "according to his will." And ours will be prayers of faith. Every time we pray, we'll be confident God has granted our petitions, and we'll be energized by the joyful expectation that we will see His answers openly. We'll practice daily what Jesus taught about the prayer of faith: "Whatever you ask in prayer, believe that you have received it, and it will be yours" (Mark 11:24, ESV). But we won't be the first to do so.

The Old Testament tells of reformers, kings, and prophets who prayed the Word long before us. When seeking favor with King Artaxerxes, Nehemiah pleaded God's promise from Deuteronomy 30, asking God to, "Remember…the word that thou commandest thy servant, Moses…" (Neh. 1:8). When pleading for God's help against a huge army of invaders, King Jehoshaphat prayed God's Word promising deliverance (2 Chron. 20:7–9). When Elijah confidently summoned God to send rain, he did so based on God's promise, "I will send rain" (1 Kings 18:1, 42–45). The New Testament records additional biblical prayers.

The greatest is Jesus' high priestly prayer, in which He asks that all believers be sanctified, unified, perfected in unity, filled with God's love, and indwelt by Himself (John 17:17–26). In his epistles Paul asked that the Ephesians, and us, may receive the "spirit of wisdom and revelation" in the knowledge of Jesus, have the "eyes of your [our] understanding" enlightened to know our hope, God's inheritance, God's power, and be "filled with all the fullness of God" (Eph. 1:15–21; 3:13–19). He asked also that we "walk worthy of the Lord" and be "filled with the knowledge of His will" and "strengthened with all might...unto all patience and long suffering with joyfulness; giving thanks" (Col. 1:9–12). He asked further that God would "fulfill all the good pleasure of his goodness, and the work of faith with power" and that "the name of our Lord Jesus...may be glorified in you" (2 Thess. 1:11–12). He also noted an apparently constant prayer of the devoted intercessor, Epaphras, "That ye may stand perfect and complete in all the will of God" (Col. 4:12). By inscribing these pleas in the Bible, God has assured us that they are indeed inspired and His will—so we too should pray them.

Elsewhere He openly challenges us to pray His written plan and promises: "Put me in remembrance [of my Word]..." (Isa. 43:26). Then we pray not "amiss" (James 4:3), or apart from or against God's will, but in agreement with Him: "...let us plead together" (Isa. 43:26). And we use our prayer time wisely.

Sadly but truly, the demands of work, ministry, and family limit the time most Christians devote to the vital task of intercession. Often our "priest time" is our least time. So we mustn't waste it with petitions that deviate from God's will. This is equally true as we learn to devote more time to prayer.

So from now on, pray confidently. Pray God's will by praying His Word—its phrases, petitions, promises, and objectives—for your family, church, friends, and others. You will be rewarded. As John promises, you'll know you have your petitions the moment you ask. And you'll have the satisfaction of knowing God is using your prayers to help accomplish His primary will—enlarging His glorious kingdom in this inglorious world: "Thy kingdom come. Thy will be done in earth" (Matt. 6:10).

So today, pray the Word!

Chapter 122

TREATED AS OUR LORD

O NE OF THE greatest honors God bestows on Christians is to let us be treated as Jesus was treated. John the Baptist is a case in point.

The Baptist received vastly different treatment from his disciples than he did from King Herod Antipas! Herod rendered John the greatest indignity by decapitating him and displaying his head on a platter to amuse his guests. Only hours later John's disciples, deeply grieved by Herod's villainy, highly honored their prophetic teacher by preparing and burying his body with loving dignity: "His disciples came, and took up the body, and buried it" (Matt. 14:12). Stephen received similarly bipolar treatment.

Enraged by Stephen's convicting sermon, the Sanhedrin cruelly disgraced him by shoving him out of their chamber, dragging him through Jerusalem's streets, and pelting him to death with stones outside the city walls like a common criminal. But afterward the local Christians, as broken in spirit as he was in body, "carried Stephen to his burial" with "great lamentation" over the loss of his Christlike life and ministry (Acts 8:2). Why were these godly, anointed men treated this way?

They stirred the same feelings and received the same reactions from people as their Lord. Note the similarities between their and Jesus' sufferings.

King Herod's men, Pilate's torturers, the Roman soldiers, and the scribes and Pharisees all heaped cruel and humiliating physical and psychological abuse on Jesus during His crucifixion. But later that day, Joseph of Arimathea and Nicodemus begged Pilate's permission to remove Jesus' exposed, bloodied body from the cross so they could wash and wrap it for honorable burial. Thus the foes and friends of Jesus, John the Baptist, and Stephen all treated them alike. In their time and way, John the Baptist and Stephen got what Jesus got, hatred from those who hated Jesus and love from those who loved Him. Why? They were identified with Jesus.

So are all faithful Christians. Only Jesus knows how many millions of times this same contrast of brutal loathing and brotherly love has been shown Jesus' true followers during the Jewish-, Roman-, Catholic-, and

Protestant-driven persecutions in church history—and is still being shown today. Why? This truth is timeless.

If we stay true and close to Jesus, we too will find people treating us as they would Him. They'll warm up to us or cool off, draw near or back away, according to their attitude toward Him—provided we neither callously offend them nor cravenly seek their favor. If we deal justly and lovingly with them, their reaction to us will reflect their true sentiments toward our Lord. There are several reasons for this.

First, Jesus lives in us: "Christ in you, the hope of glory" (Col. 1:27). Second, His character is being increasingly revealed in us. Every day we're learning to think, speak, act, and react more like Him: "It is enough for the disciple that he be like his teacher . . . like his lord" (Matt. 10:25). Third, we represent His authority. We delight to submit to His lordship—but many despise it! Fourth, He works through us. Daily He draws, saves, and transforms people through our prayers, labors, and witness. Fifth, He works for us. Because He graciously answers all our prayers and faithfully meets our every need, some will envy us! For these reasons, Christ-rejecting people reject us and Christ-accepting people accept us. Why? As Christ prayed, the Spirit has made us "one" with Him (John 17:21). The same holds true for the body of Christ.

Christ's spiritual body of born-again ones worldwide is abhorred and abused by those who, if they could, would gladly crucify Him again. Conversely, all who laud, love, and long for Jesus joyfully salute, support, and serve His people. Every local church or ministry will also experience this.

If a congregation is obeying Christ's Word, Spirit, and call, it's identifying itself with Him. Therefore its treatment by the public will reflect how they feel about the Head of that local body. Disciples will respect it, hypocrites despise it, and sinners denounce it. As Jesus said, "He that heareth you, heareth me; and he that despiseth you, despiseth me" (Luke 10:16).

So whenever people eagerly accept you, your church, or your ministry, remember they're honoring Jesus—and humbly thank Him. When rejected without cause, remember Jesus is honoring you by letting you be treated as He was—and forgive your offenders. Then you'll also share His authority, in His church now and kingdom later, because, "If we suffer [with him], we shall also reign with him" (2 Tim. 2:12). So rejoice!

Loathed or loved, it's a great honor to be treated as our Lord.

Notes

1: The Wonder of Righteous Exhilaration!

1. The "first ways" of David were his exemplary godly ways of living before his infamous affair with Bathsheba.

4: Ready for Spiritual Construction Testing?

1. By "Laodicean era," we mean the final period of church history in which Christians generally are like the ancient Laodiceans Jesus addressed in Revelation 3:14–19. They were: materialistic, self-satisfied, proud, morally and spiritually compromised (or "lukewarm"), spiritually blind, dominated by their fleshly nature (or "naked"), and without true spiritual riches (or "gold tried in the fire").

5: Swift as Eagles!

1. These are conservative figures. Rebecca L. Grambo, editor, *Eagles: Masters of the Sky* (Minneapolis, MN: Voyageur Press, 1997).
2. This is the meaning of the Latin and English words *raptor*.

8: Do You Have This Compassion?

1. W. E. Vine, *Vine's Complete Expository Dictionary of Old and New Testament Words* (Nashville: Thomas Nelson Publishers, 1996), s.v. "*splanchnizomai*."

13: Comforted or Chafed by His Rod?

1. W. Phillip Keller, *A Shepherd Looks at Psalm 23* (Grand Rapids, MI: Zondervan Publishing House, 1970).

15: The Forge of Extraordinary Leaders

1. S. Smith and J. Cornwall, *The Exhaustive Dictionary of Bible Names* (North Brunswick, NJ: Bridge-Logos, 1998), s.v. "Manasseh."

24: Great Help for Great Hearts!

1. F. Brown, S. R. Driver, and C. A. Briggs, *Enhanced Brown-Driver-Briggs Hebrew and English Lexicon*, electronic ed. (Oak Harbor, WA: Logos Research Systems, 2000), s.v. "*salem*."

29: The Mighty Mustard Seed

1. J. F. Walvoord, R. B. Zuck, and Dallas Theological Seminary, *The Bible Knowledge Commentary: An Exposition of the Scriptures* (Wheaton, IL: Victor Books, 1983).
2. Charles F. Pfeiffer, Howard F. Vos, and John Rea, *The Wycliffe Bible Encyclopedia* (Chicago, IL: Moody Press, 1975).

31: Are You Considering the Poor?

1. Vine, *Vine's Complete Expository Dictionary of Old and New Testament Words*, 180–182, s.v. "poor."

33: God's Enablers

1. A. Kenneth Curtis, J. Stephen Lang, and Randy Peterson, *The 100 Most Important Events in Christian History* (Grand Rapids, MI; Fleming H. Revell, 1991).

37: If Peter Walked on Water…

1. James Strong, *A Concise Dictionary of the Words in the Greek Testament and the Hebrew Bible* (Bellingham, WA: Logos Research Systems, Inc., 2009), s.v. "doubt."

40: Come, Holy Spirit!

1. I've paraphrased Edwards' outdated prose for clearer understanding by modern readers. These points are taken from William DeArteaga, *Quenching the Spirit* (Lake Mary, FL: Charisma House, 1996), 43.

41: The Overriding Good News!

1. Matthew Henry, *Matthew Henry's Commentary in One Volume* (Grand Rapids, MI: Zondervan Publishing House, 1961), 1276.

42: About Those Stormy Tests

1. Since only men were counted in this numbering, and their wives and children were surely with them, the actual crowd present and fed was much larger, perhaps as large as 15,000 to 20,000. See Walvoord, Zuck, and Dallas Theological Seminary, *The Bible Knowledge Commentary: An Exposition of the Scriptures.*
2. W. W. Wiersbe, *The Bible Exposition Commentary* (Wheaton, IL: Victor Books, 1996).

43: At Trial's End

1. Mrs. Charles E. Cowman, *Streams in the Desert* (Grand Rapids, MI: Zondervan Publishing House, 1965), 143.

44: He's Never Outdone!

1. Oswald Chambers, *Run Today's Race* (Fort Washington, PA: Christian Literature Crusade, 1976).

47: Not Every Crossing Is Stormy

1. W. A. Elwell and P. W. Comfort, *Tyndale Bible Dictionary* (Wheaton, IL: Tyndale House Publishers, 2001).

53: Will You Be Enlarged?

1. J. Swanson, *Dictionary of Biblical Languages With Semantic Domains:*

Hebrew (Old Testament), electronic ed. (Oak Harbor, WA: Logos Research Systems, Inc., 1997).

2. The New Scofield Study Bible states, "David was in trouble and helpless. The Lord gave him strength and courage. David was 'enlarged'; he became a greater man for the tasks ahead of him." [C. I. Scofield, *The New Scofield Study Bible* (New York: Oxford University Press, 1967)].

57: How Soon We Forget!

1. See note 1, 42: About Those Stormy Tests.

58: Have You Received This Power?

1. R. L. Thomas, (1998). *New American Standard Hebrew-Aramaic and Greek Dictionaries: Updated Edition* (Anaheim, CA: Foundation Publications, Inc., 1998), s.v. *"dunamis."*

2. See in order: "power," Matthew 22:29; "mighty works," Matthew 11:20; "a miracle," Mark 9:39; "strength," Hebrews 11:11; "virtue," Luke 6:19.

3. Thirteen hundred feet below the Mediterranean Sea level. [Merrill C. Tenny, *Zondervan Encyclopedia of the Bible,* vol. 2. (Grand Rapids, MI: The Zondervan Corporation, 2009).]

60: Worse Than Abortion!

1. National Right to Life, "Report: Abortion Numbers Essentially Unchanged," January 11, 2011, http://www.nrlc.org/press_releases_new/Release011111.html (accessed August 20, 2011).

79: Positioned for His Blessing?

1. See Luke 18:15–17, note, in W. W. Wiersbe, *The Bible Exposition Commentary* (Wheaton, IL: Victor Books, 1996).

83: Ready for Marketplace Evangelism!

1. Comparable to London's Hyde Park, where in Speakers' Corner orators address whatever topics they wish to whoever wishes to hear.

87: Discipleship—Defined and Demonstrated

1. This is a practical, scriptural definition of the term. Literally, the name *Christian*, first used of Christ's followers in Antioch (Acts 11:26), means "Christ's men" or "Christ's loyalists."

2. Swanson, *Dictionary of Biblical Languages With Semantic Domains: Greek (New Testament).*

3. Strong, *A Concise Dictionary of the Words in the Greek Testament and The Hebrew Bible,* s.v. *"mathetes."*

90: Satisfying His Hunger?

1. *Webster's Encyclopedic Unabridged Dictionary of the English Language*

(New York: Gramercy Books, 1996), s.v. "hunger."

97: City-Quake!

1. G. Kittel, G. W. Bromiley, and G. Friedrich, eds., *Theological Dictionary of the New Testament*, electronic ed. (Grand Rapids, MI: Eerdmans, 1964), s.v. "*seio*."

102: His Hidden Ones

1. Swanson, *Dictionary of Biblical Languages With Semantic Domains: Hebrew (Old Testament)*, s.v. "*tsaphan*."
2. Mark Galli and Ted Olsen, *131 Christians Everyone Should Know* (Nashville: Holman Reference, 2000), 278.

103: Whose Image Are You Worshiping?

1. Walvoord, Zuck, and Dallas Theological Seminary, *The Bible Knowledge Commentary: An Exposition of the Scriptures*.

106: God's Stars in the Night

1. A. W. Tozer, *The Best of A. W. Tozer*, compiled by Warren W. Wiersbe (Harrisonburg, PA: Christian Publications, 1978), 242. Bracketed word is the author's insertion.

108: When Jesus Goes on the Offensive!

1. F. B. Meyer, *Elijah and the Secret of His Power* (Chicago: Moody Press, 1976).

111: Our New Titles

1. J. Strong, *Enhanced Strong's Lexicon* (Bellingham, WA: Logos Bible Software, 1996).
2. Ibid.
3. Ibid.

118: The Prodigal in Us

1. Vine, *Vine's Complete Expository Dictionary of Old and New Testament Words*, s.v. "*diaskorpizō*."

121: Pray the Word!

1. God's general will is what He wants or desires for every human being and applies universally. By contrast, the particular will of God is His personal plan for us and includes specifics not stated in Scripture: our individual calling, gifts, graces, duties, blessings; where we should attend school; whom we should marry, etc. We discover this will as we walk with God, obey His Word, ask His will, and observe His providential responses.

Notes